Forged under the Sun / Forjada bajo el sol

Women and Culture Series

The Women and Culture Series is dedicated to books that illuminate the lives, roles, achievements, and status of women, past or present.

Forged under the Sun / Forjada bajo el sol

The Life of María Elena Lucas

Edited and with an introduction by
Fran Leeper Buss

Ann Arbor
THE UNIVERSITY OF MICHIGAN PRESS

Copyright © by the University of Michigan 1993
All rights reserved
Published in the United States of America by
The University of Michigan Press
Manufactured in the United States of America

1996   1995   1994   1993   4   3   2   1

A CIP catalogue record for this book is available from the British Library.

Library of Congress Cataloging-in-Publication Data

Lucas, María Elena, 1941–
    Forged under the sun : the life of María Elena Lucas = Forjada
bajo el sol / edited and with an introduction by Fran Leeper Buss.
        p.   cm. — (Women and culture series)
    Includes bibliographical references.
    ISBN 0-472-09432-7 (alk. paper). — ISBN 0-472-06432-0 (pbk. :
alk. paper)
    1. Lucas, María Elena, 1941–   . 2. Labor leaders—United States—
Biography. 3. Mexican American agricultural laborers—Biography.
4. Mexican American women—Biography. 5. Farm Labor Organizing
Committee (Ohio)—Officials and employees—Biography.   I. Buss,
Fran Leeper, 1942–   . II. Title.   III. Title: Forjada bajo el sol.
IV. Series.
HD6509.L83A3   1993
331.88'13'092—dc20
[B]   92-46311
                                                        CIP

To Olgha Sierra Sandman,
the brave farmworking women of Onarga,
Mary R., David F., and Joanne C.

Acknowledgments

María Elena Lucas and I have been aided by many who have believed in the work that follows, but we especially wish to thank Olgha Sierra Sandman, from the Illinois Migrant Ministry, and Professor Karen Anderson, chair of Women's Studies and the Southwest Institute for Research on Women at the University of Arizona. Both women read several drafts of the work and engaged us in an interpretive effort that was profoundly important to our joint project.

Within the text that follows, María Elena thanks many others who are important to her work, but I also wish to express personal gratitude to those who helped me in this long project. María Elena, her adult children, and vulnerable women and their families took me into their homes and treated me with kindness as María Elena and I cemented our friendship and then began this work. Many others also helped me. Susan Geiger listened with empathy as I struggled with the ambiguity of my dual role as historian and friend; Michelle Groseclose and Stacy Hinetz-Holdcraft helped me transcribe tapes; the Emery and Ann Johnson Scholarship Fund at the University of Arizona gave me a small travel grant; Janice Faust shared her library and valuable insights with me; Penny Waterstone helped me grapple with editorial decisions; Michael Matejka, Karen Sandhass, and other organizers commented upon early drafts of our work; Raquel Rubio-Goldsmith and Yolanda Leyva helped me think through several issues; and my editor LeAnn Fields believed in the importance of María Elena's vision and my skills as an oral historian. After María Elena and I had finished our tapes, Jan Monk, Karen Anderson, Pat Seavy, and the Southwest Institute for Research on Women, with the assistance of a grant from the Ford Foundation, prepared my oral histories and placed them at the Arthur and Elizabeth Schlesinger Library of the History of Women in America at Radcliffe College, Harvard University.

People also helped María Elena and me in many personal ways. Mary Robinson, a labor organizer from Alabama, responded with exuberance and enthusiasm to each new segment of the work; history graduate students, a generation younger than me, welcomed me and made my work a part of their political and intellectual journey; and Drs. Margaret Díaz and John Misiaszek helped María Elena and me survive physical disabilities that might otherwise have ended our productive lives.

The love of my friends and family, especially my husband David Buss and our adult children, Kimberly, Lisa, and Jim, has helped me achieve the sense of direction, centeredness, and serenity necessary for the years of sometimes isolated labor needed for our project. David and the others have assisted me immensely, and for their daily wisdom, caring, and humor, I thank them deeply.

Finally, I live in the Arizona desert, surrounded by a beauty that wakes me every morning and in some way echoes María Elena's mind and vision. That beauty energized me for this work and reinforced externally the deepening awe I experienced within, as María Elena, in a gift to us all, shared the poetry of her work and words.

Contents

Introduction

Possibilities for Which We Had No Name

María Elena Lucas, a forty-seven-year-old Chicana farm worker and organizer,[1] sat in the late afternoon light coming through the trailer's window. Chickens squawked as they searched beneath her kitchen table for
any forgotten crumbs of food, and the summer breeze blew through the
many holes of the old recreational vehicle in which she lived just north of
the Texas-Mexico border.

The manuscript for the union organizing play María Elena had written in 1983, *Flor Campesina* (Farm Worker Flower), lay on her lap, but
she rarely glanced down as she translated it from Spanish into English.
She had loaned out her drugstore glasses again and could barely see the
written words, so she spoke mostly from memory. Much of the time she
talked with her normal enthusiasm, but occasionally she stopped speaking,
her eyes becoming blank and confused, as they had been at times since her
poisoning, then she seemed to remember again and recited her lines with
animation.

Later, when I looked at the play at home, I realized I had two somewhat different versions. María Elena's play, like her poetry, was something
still living to her, a work still being created. In the written version of the
play, the migrant farm workers were tomato pickers and the Virgin of
Guadalupe appeared and spoke to the heroine Rosamaría, telling her to
go "where the eagle flies in my name." In the spoken version, the migrants
worked in grape fields, the Virgin was silent when she appeared to Rosa-

maría, and she gave the grieving woman a red handkerchief containing a political message. María Elena had designed her union organizing play to be adaptable to the settings and situations of her particular audience.[2]

Months before, on March 3, 1988, a crop-dusting airplane had swept down over an open car María Elena was driving, blanketing her with pesticides. María Elena notified the Department of Agriculture before losing consciousness, and for the next three days she fought to live. By the time I arrived in Texas a few weeks later, she still struggled with breathing difficulties and chest pain, loss of memory, and sudden periods of intense confusion. Although frightened and bewildered by her disorientation, she described to me her love for the diaries, poems, songs, drawings, and plays she had been driven to create since childhood.

When I asked if any of the works still existed, she said she thought some were buried in a trunk among the rubble in the back of an old truck which was itself sunk in the mud of a field. However, she felt too sick and overwhelmed even to help me begin to locate the trunk's contents.

Not until many months later, and now seven years into our friendship, was she finally strong enough to direct the search for the trunk that we hoped would contain her writings. With the help of two *indocumentados*,[3] with whom María Elena and her common-law husband Pablo shared their tiny trailer, we located the trunk and carried it inside.

This document, our book, was born during the days that María Elena and I spent sifting through the layers of papers inside her trunk. But our common work may have in fact begun when we were both children. Although far removed from each other geographically and growing up in different ethnic and language systems, both of us struggled with violence, beauty, and a confusing legacy of poverty and promise. María Elena and I both hid, created, and looked up past the shrubs and trees of our individual hideouts to the Catholic world and religious mythologies that surrounded us like overlapping arches. And each of us, in our own little worlds of clay and sticks and leaves and words, tried to envision possibilities for which we had no images, no names, no descriptions.

I, however, was born Anglo-American, into a racial/ethnic group given the promise of mobility almost as a birthright. Although I did face hardships as a working-class girl, much of the world was not closed to me: my teachers read me poems, I was expected to read and write, and when I wandered into a small store and found folders of maps, I could look at those maps and dream and not be sent out the door because I had dark skin or wore no shoes or smelled of chilies, wood stoves, and crowded housing.

One afternoon I explained to María Elena that in my background reading for our book, I had found evidence that during her childhood it was public policy in South Texas to make sure that so-called Mexican children did not attend school past the age of ten or twelve. In fact, school systems exchanged suggestions for circumventing attendance laws. They worked out techniques to ensure they received tax credits for the Mexican children in their districts while guaranteeing that none of those children would achieve a sufficient education to equip them for work beyond the fields. Public humiliation and separate seating were common tactics.[4]

María Elena looked incredulous as I told her what I had read. "You mean it wasn't just because of my parents or an accident or because I was poor that I didn't get school? You mean they actually planned it that way?" I nodded, and she cried. To read no poetry, to teach no history, to give no books to such a child: This is cruelty; this is a crime.

One of the primary goals of this work for both of us has been to bear witness to that crime and the other degradations of body and spirit suffered by María Elena and her people. To do so María Elena stretched deep into the recesses of her memory, and I traveled and searched through primary and secondary sources and field notes, preparing pages of new questions to ask her each time we met. The result is primarily the product of memory, with all the personal slants and perspectives memory brings, but we have also sought to set those memories within a social context.

It was not until our work was nearly completed, however, that either María Elena or I truly grasped the profundity of what had taken place in the schools, neighborhoods, and fields of María Elena's childhood. It was not chance that such a brilliant child was repeatedly crushed until she bore her load in near silence.

The whole social, political, symbolic, and, above all, economic structure of the Valley was predicated upon a complex interaction of racial, class, and sexual or gender[5] oppression. This oppression ultimately guaranteed that, at the very bottom of the social hierarchy, a young, poor Mexican American woman would submit to yearly pregnancies, eke out a bare subsistence, and awaken her young children each morning to work another long, hungry day in the white man's fields. It was her reproductive and subsistence labor that ensured the Valley and its white commercial farm owners their great profits.

"Texas Friendly Spoken Here": The Tragic World of the Valley

Extending along the United States–Mexico border from about Rio Grande City in the west to Brownsville in the east, the Valley resembles the northern segment of a separate country, a nation arbitrarily severed by the Rio Grande River, or the Rio Bravo, as it is known to Mexicans.

The river itself originates as a lovely, life-giving stream in the mountains of Colorado, then winds down New Mexico, past indigenous pueblos, old Hispano villages, and modern Anglo developments, bestowing life along the arid landscape with green cottonwoods, tall grasses, water birds, and irrigated crops. (I usually use the term *indigenous* to refer to those Americans usually labeled American Indians or Native Americans.) When the river enters Texas near El Paso, its life-giving nature metamorphoses into one of death and separation, and, picking up raw sewage and an occasional body along the way, it continues its long journey eastward to the sea. By the time it reaches Brownsville, right before it enters the Gulf of Mexico, the Rio Grande River resembles an open sewer, whose brown waters are estimated to have bacteria levels exceeding accepted safety margins by several thousand percent.[6]

No other national boundary on earth separates two such unequal nations for such a long distance, and each day thousands of desperate *indocumentados,* most of them barefoot, swim or wade through its polluted water. If these men, women, and children avoid bandits and rapists on each side and reach the U.S. shore alive, they scramble up the muddy banks through broken glass, barbed wire, and thorns and begin the dangerous game of eluding *la migra,* the United States Border Patrol, in order to make it farther north.

Above the river, on the bridge linking Brownsville and its Mexican sister city Matamoros, tens of thousands of additional Latin Americans, both with and without documents, also pass each day. The sidewalks lining the bridge are filled with crossing pedestrians. Young women with day passes put a quarter into the turnstile on the Mexican side of the bridge, then slide themselves and their small children through with one turn of the lever and begin their slow walk to the United States side. Many will sell plasma ("five dollars extra for new donors"), buy a few items, and return home.

The worn, crowded bridge is crammed with lines of old vehicles inching their way across from Mexico. Some of the cars and trucks stall in the process, and men tinker with engines as they wait in line. The air is heavy with exhaust, pollution, and the panic of those who are attempting to smuggle drugs, contraband, themselves, their children, and others into the United States.

Many of the undocumented people leaving northern Mexico, or *la frontera,* as it is known, come as political refugees, especially to escape the wars and executions in Central America. Ironically, they seek safety in the same country that has armed and trained the militias from whom they flee.[7] But the majority of *indocumentados* are poor Mexicans who repeatedly risk their lives at the river itself in the simple goal of trying to help their families by making a little money from the voracious desire for cheap labor of the *norteamericanos.* The lucky ones, often with the help of *coyotes,* expensive smugglers of human cargo, survive the river crossing, make it up past the Sarita checkpoint about sixty miles north of the border, then disperse throughout the United States, where they find menial jobs in agriculture, manufacturing, and the service industry and send home money orders to their hungry families. Many continue their migration, following crop cycles around the country. Some migrating families, both citizen and undocumented, eventually try to "settle out" of the life-style; they choose a community and attempt to live there permanently.

María Elena became especially close to such a community of undocumented Mexicans, people living year round in the attics, garages, and small trailers of Onarga, Illinois. The nurseries that were the economic base of this small town south of Chicago had welcomed this new class of workers, who were desperate enough to do stoop labor outdoors, even in the winter.

The first time I met with María Elena was in Onarga during the summer of 1981. I rode with her and a young undocumented father to a nearby hospital where they picked up his newborn baby and her mother, then took the family back to their house. Six men were living in an unconverted one-car garage next to the house, and another six men and the young woman and her husband lived upstairs in a semiconverted attic. All of these people shared one small kitchen and toilet, located in the attic, and each one paid $10.50 a week in 1981 dollars for that right. The young woman, too weak to climb to the attic, was placed on a lawn chair and hoisted up the steep stairs.

María Elena had great affection for the women in that community, and over the years I came to love them too. And, throughout our years together, in old cars, tiny kitchens, hospitals, and the fields, they told us stories of their multiple trips across the border in an effort to bring their children north with them; they spoke of drugging their babies to quiet them during the crossing; they told of raids and attempted rape; of horror and near death.

Most Mexicans caught by Border Patrol or INS, the Immigration and Naturalization Service, accept immediate "voluntary return." They then are returned to the United States side of the bridge, where they are dropped off and instructed to walk back into Mexico, and there they begin the whole process all over again.

However, undocumented Central Americans or other political refugees face a much more serious situation. Convinced they will be killed if they return home, they either try to pass as Mexicans or apply for political asylum. Before 1988, the application for asylum was a fairly easy procedure. The Central Americans registered in the Valley with INS were generally released without bond on their "own recognizance," then dispersed to other parts of the country where they were supposed to appear for their asylum hearings. However, thousands went underground, knowing their chances for receiving legal asylum were negligible.[8]

In late 1988, as conditions worsened in Central America and the stream of refugees became a flood, INS abruptly changed its policy. Refugees were no longer allowed to disperse to the rest of the country, and within days thousands became trapped in the Valley. The Valley already contained two of the three poorest counties in the country, and the raw need quickly swamped its meager social services. Thousands of men, women, and children, many of them ill from their journeys, were forced to camp outdoors without food, water, or toilets. Within a few weeks, hate groups coalesced against these refugees, and Brownsville became a near police state as helicopters hunted aliens and unsympathetic community spokespeople accused the refugees of importing communism.

Eventually, the Red Cross set up a shelter, primarily for families, and hundreds, then thousands, of refugees were imprisoned in the INS detention center, or prison, called the Port Isabel Service Processing Center. There the inmates were surrounded by double barbed-wire fences and watched by armed guards and television monitors.

Many people speculated that the new INS policy was a deliberate attempt to make life in the United States so miserable that other Central Americans would be discouraged from coming.[9] But it did not work. The suffering in Central America was so intense that sick, desperate families continued to arrive.

They came into a strange world that those not familiar with the Valley have difficulty grasping. The Valley, as a region, is overwhelmingly Latino and wretchedly poor. As Robert Maril, in his book *The Poorest of Americans,* states, "By almost every quantifiable measure which describes poverty or correlates of poverty, Valley Mexican Americans are much poorer than those who live in other cities or regions in this country."[10]

The situation is actually far worse than the numbers indicate. No one knows how many undocumented are not included in the statistics and how far down they would bring the income figures, yet all sources agree that many more people make it in than are arrested.[11] Given that more than two hundred thousand residents of the Valley, many of them women, are already defined as poor, the potential number of extraordinarily poor people becomes staggering.[12]

Quality-of-life statistics also paint a bleak picture. Unemployment and subemployment rates rank the area at the bottom of the nation. Other statistics, such as level of education, age of death, age of first birth, number of deaths from parasitic and infectious illness, incidence of conditions indicating malnutrition, and disability rates create a devastating picture. Ironically, although these immigrants leave Mexico to improve their bleak economic prospects, their "quality of life" actually deteriorates in the Valley.[13]

While, nationally, people of Mexican or Mexican American backgrounds are much more likely than Anglo-Americans to live beneath poverty levels, millions of people of Mexican heritage have made it into the mainstream of North American life. However, the people in María Elena's life, who tend to have rural, near-peasant backgrounds, are the poorest of Mexican Americans. For example, María Elena's income for 1989 probably did not exceed $2,500, and almost none of her close relatives or neighbors had incomes above the poverty line.[14]

The impoverished masses in the Valley live in a bewildering state of extra-legality that contributes to stress and a high incidence of emotional disability and family problems.[15] So many aspects of daily existence are illegal that penalties and arrests are often random and chaotic, and frequent enough to cause continual anxiety. Nobody knows when and for what they will be arrested. The very actions of waking up, eating, drinking, and going to sleep may be technically illegal.

In the Valley poor people drink water from illegal hookups or illegally transport it from irrigation ditches in barrels which they set outside their doors and cover with plastic. People go to the bathroom in outhouses and holes in the ground that do not meet safety codes, and when the frequent heavy rains flood out the outhouses and holes and spread raw sewage throughout the yard, barefoot adults and children squat on boards laid across the mud in order to relieve themselves.

In this largely rural region, much of daily existence centers around attempts to obtain transportation in whatever vehicles happen to be running. Because people must often share rides with family, friends, and also strangers, a person on a simple trip to the grocery store may unwittingly engage in the illegal transportation of aliens or the smuggling of drugs.

Extended families also share food stamps with members considered outsiders by Anglo-American welfare standards, and families double, triple, and quadruple up in welfare housing designed for the Anglo model of a single nuclear family. When people get sick, older women travel across the border, where they enter *boticas* to buy herbs, vitamins, and potent medications to give as injections to the person at home. Women sometimes exchange babies to make a sick child eligible for medical care, and poor people do their shopping and selling in large, informal flea markets where licensing and the use of sales tax are at best erratic.

Compassionate families who find undocumented boys and girls attempting to sell their bodies for food will sometimes take those children home and will search through the extended family for legal documents that might resemble the child. Then, illegally using these documents as a cover, they will attempt to ship the child north to someone who will give the child shelter.

It is a world in which having the right documents can determine whether one lives or dies. Even a citizen must be ready to prove his or her legitimacy. Yet keeping track of such important papers is difficult in the chaos of extreme poverty, especially in a region of frequent tropical storms that break through fragile roofing and drench both papers and people. Also, for a myriad of reasons, a family might lose the shelter they had that morning and be forced to sleep outside in an abandoned car or a chicken coop. In such settings, precious documents can easily be lost, destroyed, or stolen.

The harshness of such a world seems almost surreal to the outsider. After all, this is the United States; luxury condominiums and vacationing Anglo-Americans line the beaches of South Padres Island just outside Brownsville. Other Anglos, mostly retired people from the Midwest, live in tidy walled-off resorts for recreational vehicles where signs proclaim "Welcome Home" and "Texas Friendly Spoken Here" to their selected guests.

In contrast, an estimated seventy thousand Valley residents, most of them the poorest of the poor, live in unincorporated rural neighborhoods called *colonias*. Without plumbing or water, housing consists of cardboard shacks or little homes built in segments from found materials. Fields of crops bordering the *colonias* expose the residents to regular pesticide spraying, and children are in danger of drowning in the deep irrigation ditches.

María Elena's father lives in a *colonia* right outside of Brownsville, and her mother, who currently lives in a public project in town, works as a licensed *partera*, a midwife, in a room of María Elena's father's modest blue house. The house is marked by a small sign saying "Partera" and by an image of the Virgin of Guadalupe. Women, most of them undocumented, come to the door when they begin labor; then, if all appears normal, María Elena's mother assists the birth, makes sure the infant is registered as a citizen, and makes arrangements for it to be examined by a clinic. Her skills are thought to be a gift from God, and midwifery is considered an almost religious profession.[16] A fruit stand, gas station, fireworks shop, and store announcing "Gonzales Tortilla Factory" are the only indications on the highway that mark the existence of the *colonia* in which María Elena's mother practices, and tourists traveling to the beach are usually unaware of its presence or of the existence of hundreds of destitute residents.

Hidden from outsiders, these barefoot families of the *colonias*, and the Mexican laborers in migrant communities scattered throughout the United States, lead lives shaped by a four hundred fifty year history of exploitation and resistance.

The Subjugation of a People

The history of María Elena and her people in the New World begins with the indigenous Native American cultures and the bloody sixteenth-century Spanish conquest that looted and eventually destroyed the Aztec Empire. The Roman Catholic colonizers, from a hierarchical and patriarchal society, spread disease and death among the indigenous peoples, attempted to destroy the native religions or graft them onto Catholicism, and coerced indigenous people into labor in order to extract gold and other riches from the New World.[17]

The Spanish colonists,[18] who originally brought no women with them, raped, took as concubines and later sometimes married the native women. These connections became symbolized in the union of the *conquistador* Hernán Cortés and an Aztec woman, probably called Malinal and known to the Spaniards as Doña Marina, who later appears in legend as La Malinche.[19] The children born from these unequal relationships were known as mestizos, meaning people of mixed indigenous, Spanish, and, to a lesser degree, African background. From this intermingling evolved a dynamic mestizo culture, a culture whose religion, symbols, traditions, ideals, and art still provide María Elena and her contemporaries with the tools for struggling against oppression.[20] The people known as mestizos eventually formed the majority group of Mexicans, a population sandwiched between a ruling elite of light-skinned people of primarily Spanish descent and the surviving indigenous who continued a bare subsistence. The agrarian economy was controlled by elite families who, primarily through systems of land grants, acquired vast rural estates to which poor mestizo and indigenous peasants gradually became bound. These feudal *haciendas*, usually governed by the oldest male of the land-owning family, kept their workers in a state of destitution.[21]

The lower Rio Grande Valley, María Elena's homeland, like virtually all of the southwestern United States, was part of Mexico through much of its history, and its culture and economic structure are one of the legacies of the Spanish conquest. Following Mexico's independence from Spain in 1821, the area became a sparsely populated province of Mexico. However, when the new government in Mexico City opened its northern frontier to foreign settlement, thousands of Anglo-American land speculators and settlers poured into Texas, carrying with them a vision of empire, racial superiority, and economic progress.

"Texas fever" spread; fighting broke out in 1835, and in 1844 the United States formally annexed Texas, triggering the war with Mexico which ended with the Treaty of Guadalupe Hidalgo in 1848. Mexico lost nearly half of its territory to the United States, and the lower Rio Grande River was declared the new boundary between the conflicting nations.[22] The Chicanos of the Southwest are thus the products of two bloody conquests, first by Spain and then by the United States; and in today's barrios, *colonias,* and remote farming communities, "the social, economic and political patterns of a defeated people persist."[23]

Following the war, Anglo-American colonization of much of the Southwest increased, displacing Mexicans from their lands, turning them into an indigent working class, and extracting natural resources to be used in the industrialized Midwest and Northeast.[24] However, southern Texas remained isolated, with a population primarily of Mexican heritage, until the simultaneous invention of the refrigerated railroad car and improved irrigation techniques made large-scale commercial farming and exportation possible in the fertile valley.

Quick to recognize the potential, Anglo-American land speculators used violence, intimidation, and legal maneuvers to wrestle the land from Mexican owners. Then they advertised their new treasure in the North and East and sold the land at inflated prices to Anglos lured by the promise of a life as gentlemen-farmers.

These gentlemen-farmers were faced with labor problems, however. Large-scale commercial farming required cycles of intense, rapidly mobilized labor, especially during peak periods of planting and harvest, but labor costs needed to be kept low so the farmers could make their steep land payments. The new Anglo farmers believed that the Mexican residents of the Valley presented an ideal solution to this dilemma. Not only were they destitute from the loss of their lands and the breakdown of the ranch economy, but the farmers also assumed that Mexicans were content with low wages and endowed with a unique physiology that made them especially adapted to do stoop labor.[25]

In 1929, Paul Schuster Taylor recorded a farmer's explanation of his work force.

The Mexicans are the only class of labor we can handle. The others won't do this work; the white pickers want screens and ice-water. . . . You know how God created the Negro race to labor, and marked them so you'd know them. If He hadn't intended it, he'd have made them white, and the Mexicans too. The more you pay them, the less they do . . . [26]

The new farm order[27] maintained itself through racism and violence. Supervisors with shotguns kept workers in the fields, and reinforced their authority with beatings and lynchings; families were required to buy supplies from farmers, who kept them working in a state of perpetual debt; rules were written to keep Mexicans from owning automobiles and to prevent them from leaving Texas in search of better work; immigration authorities were tipped off when workers became restless; vagrancy laws were devised so that any Mexican who was unemployed could be arrested and required to work on a farm.[28]

According to David Montejano, the most striking feature of the new order was the almost total segregation of Mexican workers from Anglo owners.[29] Separate and inferior schools, or programs within schools, encouraged Mexican children to drop out before they became "too educated" to work in the fields, and separate living quarters and "colored only" facilities kept Mexicans isolated.

Existing prejudice against "inferior" Mexicans became more virulent with the advent of the new farm order. Popular Anglo nativism,[30] Texas history and folklore, Southerners' previous experiences with African Americans, and the various "scientific" theories of race and medicine popular during the early part of the twentieth century offered the emotional and intellectual mechanisms for such systems of control.[31] Mexicans were considered dirty, overly physical, and a conduit for disease. Consequently, to the Anglos of South Texas, their newly segregated world, so necessary to their continued class status, reflected goodness and a natural social order.[32] And this new class order was reinforced by the great northern migration of desperate Mexican peasants fleeing the violence and disruption of the Mexican Revolution.

Inadequate wages and restrictions on Mexican American mobility forced farm workers to supplement their meager resources in various ways. The most common was the massive use of child labor. Poor families relied on women giving birth each year, and by the time a child was five or six, she or he would be working in the fields. Many Anglo farm owners required a family to have at least eight sets of hands and a wife who could work in the fields "like a man," and some believed that "a woman who can't have a child a year isn't worth her salt."[33]

A careful hierarchy of discipline ensured the obedient labor of entire families. To keep a large family of hungry young children working for twelve to fourteen hours each day, farmers insisted on the father's control of the children's labor, at any cost. That control at times included physical violence, compounding the already extreme hardships suffered by children in the fields. The widespread use of this system ensured that grower profit was based on various types of violence against children.[34]

Other means were used by families to generate income. Some men drew extra wages through such activities as pecan shelling, working in the fishing industry, on the railroads, or as mechanics, gathering edible plants, and, later, as the enforced labor system of south Texas broke down, some men left home to search for wage work elsewhere.

Women brought additional resources into the family through both wage and nonwage labor. They supplemented their farm income by wage work as waitresses, chambermaids, dance girls, dressmakers, domestics, laundry workers, and as piecework laborers in canneries and fisheries. They also scavenged through garbage, selling or eating what they could; they traded; they did laundry and housework for others; they begged; they delivered babies and faked documents; and some sold their bodies.[35] Finally, through their reproductive abilities and years of pregnancy, child care, and unpaid household labor, they added more workers to the family unit. Without such work the labor force would have starved, not reproduced, and the commercial farming enterprise could not have been sustained.

Many of the poorest women also faced sexual exploitation in this society where Anglo farmers joked with Mexican men about the importance of fertility and sexual activity of Mexican women. Anglo men widely held the view that Mexican women were immoral, highly sexed, and suitable prostitutes, so much so that for Anglo males, the term *señorita* often became synonymous with "prostitute." This happened despite Mexican families' attempts to keep young women in semi-seclusion.[36] Caught between desperate financial need, a demand for prostitution, and strong family injunctions against sex outside of marriage, young, poor women were extremely vulnerable, and that vulnerability itself may have been experienced by Anglo men as a source of sexual stimulation.[37]

As the years passed, the commercial farm system never lost its exploitative underpinning. When migrant farm laborers began to try to organize and eventually even to leave the farms for work in factories, agribusiness enterprises evolving throughout the United States organized themselves politically in order to ensure a steady supply of workers.

The National Labor Relations Act (Wagner Act), passed in 1935, guaranteed United States workers the right to organize and bargain collectively. However, alarmed by the possibility of migrant labor unions, agribusiness lobbied Congress and excluded farm laborers from the act. Farm workers were also excluded from the Fair Labor Standards Act, which governed minimum wages and child labor, and from the Occupational Safety and Health Act, set up to maintain health and safety in the workplace.[38]

Growers also pressured the government into establishing the bracero program which admitted Mexican farm and railroad workers for a limited time only, allowing them to work the fields at subminimum wages, then returning them to Mexico. The program, beginning in 1942 and ending in 1964,[39] had two major results. First, it repeatedly undermined attempts to organize farm workers, where protesters could easily be replaced by nonorganized workers.

Second, the growers were able to obtain labor at costs beneath the level necessary both to support that person in the United States and to reproduce another worker who eventually would take his or her place. Continuing the tradition in which the Mexican American farm worker woman's additional nonwage labor made it possible for Anglo farmers to reap high profits, the bracero program now required families actually living in Mexico to invest in the costs of raising and training future workers who would earn profits for U.S. companies.[40]

The migrant labor system eventually spread nationally. Families or groups of families who had originally migrated back and forth between Texas and Mexico began to travel across state lines, moving north to the Colorado beet fields and further.[41] Many of the features of Mexican origin migrant work in Texas were retained, including a strict separation of workers and owners that encouraged racism and exploitation. Today, some 80 to 90 percent of migrant workers are still Latino, primarily of Mexican heritage; the next largest group is African American, followed by a mixture of workers of various minority backgrounds.[42]

The life expectancy for migrant workers today is about forty-eight years, the lowest in the nation.[43] This early mortality reflects such continuing conditions as inadequate nutrition and medical care, frequent bouts with food poisoning, heat stress, animal bites, travel in unsafe vehicles, lack of clean water and toilets, inadequate heat and clothes for warmth in winter, exhaustion, farm accidents, and self-medication, especially with alcohol, for the resulting emotional problems.[44] Also, since the late 1940s, the vast majority of commercial crops have been sprayed with pesticides, which are presently available in about thirty-five thousand different commercial products or formulations. Among these is the herbicide Sonalan, with which María Elena was poisoned.[45] Agricultural workers are repeatedly exposed to these toxins, resulting in such immediate effects and long-term consequences as damage to the nervous system, disorders of the skin, severe allergies, cancer, birth defects, neurobehavioral deficits, neuropsychological changes, and reproductive and fertility problems.[46]

As difficult as the migrant lifestyle has been for farm workers throughout the decades, in recent years even these jobs have been disappearing. Crops such as corn, wheat, soybeans, and the staple of María Elena's childhood, cotton, have now been almost completely mechanized, leading to the loss of thousands of jobs. Today only labor-intensive fruits and vegetables still require some hand cultivation and harvest.

In response to these changes and in an attempt to build a better life for their children, many migrant families have tried to "settle out" of the life-style. These families pick a location and attempt to live permanently in the community, hoping their children will obtain an education and begin experiencing some upward mobility. The Latino community in Onarga, Illinois is the result of such a process as extended family members followed each other to it. Recently, with the passage of the 1986 Immigration Reform and Reform Act, sponsored by Simpson, Mazzoli, and Rodino, many of these people became eligible for legal status. Their legalization was joyfully celebrated in September, 1990, with a community fiesta and pig roast.

However, the situation in Brownsville and along the Rio Grande border has become increasingly serious. Countless agricultural jobs have been lost to a major freeze and mechanization,[47] and hundreds of Brownsville businesses have failed as the result of Mexican economic problems. Also, manufacturing in the Valley has been dominated by clothing and electronic assembly, work customarily offered to minimum-wage female employees.[48] Some of these plants are "sister operations" of much larger manufacturing plants on the other side of the border. These factories are part of the Border Industrial Program, an arrangement that gave U.S. and multinational corporations economic incentives to establish low-overhead plants along the United States–Mexico border. In this program, products are first processed in United States plants, then they are shipped across the border to be assembled by low-paid workers in Mexico and then returned briefly to sister plants in the United States, where the manufacturing process is completed.[49]

The number of *maquiladoras,* as the Mexican plants are known, has increased greatly,[50] and hundreds of thousands of young Mexican women and men have left interior rural areas, coming north to border cities where they search for work in these factories and live in squatters' camps built of cardboard and other found materials. The largely female work force labors long hours for low wages under health and safety conditions not acceptable within the United States.[51]

This system repeats the earlier patterns underlying grower profits. The constant nonwage labor of Mexican American women allowed Anglo farmers to pay lower wages than were necessary to maintain subsistence for Mexican farm workers and their children. Borrowing from this tradition, U.S. companies pay Mexican workers an inadequate wage, and the costs of reproducing new workers for American companies are met by the nonstop labor of impoverished Mexican families and by meager Mexican social resources.

In the United States, the new immigrants and poor citizens share and barter goods and services among each other in order to function without cash. Some also become part of what Maril calls an "alternative economy."[52] North Americans, primarily Anglos, present them with a voracious and insatiable demand for such services as prostitution and the smuggling of drugs, goods, and people. A percentage of the Valley residents undertake such work, performing as stigmatized service workers laboring under profoundly dangerous conditions. Stress, violence, and the threat of AIDS and other diseases accompany these people on a daily basis.[53]

This is the modern world of the Valley: children and teenagers selling their bodies on the streets; young families caught in drug transportation systems; parents terrified for their children. This is the culmination of the sad history of María Elena's birthplace.

To survive under such conditions, and to begin to challenge the inexorable forces of impoverishment and exploitation that have imprisoned them, the people of the border, and those of the barrios, farms, and other Chicano communities of the United States, have employed a variety of tactics; for solace and a transforming vision, many of them, including María Elena, have drawn upon their rich mestizo heritage.[54]

Saints and Heroes

Remnants of indigenous traditions and of the new mestizo culture that had been forged from Spanish and native backgrounds appear in the religious beliefs, folk traditions of sharing and cooperation, and the songs, stories, and prayers of María Elena's childhood. Together they form the major substance of the interpretive system from which her creative efforts and political undertakings have evolved.

María Elena's deep mysticism, which informs all her actions and fuels her strength, was profoundly influenced by her grandmother's indigenous religious beliefs. María Elena also learned the dominant Mexican folk Catholicism of her mother and the other women in her community, a religion that was a direct product of the mestizo blend of forced Catholicism and native religions. This intensely spiritual belief system taught that faith and life are one, that health comes from harmony with the environment and other people, and that manifestations of the divine—the Saints, the Virgins, Jesus Christ, Mother Earth, and God—are accessible and immediate to the most humble of people. María Elena and others often address the deities by the diminutive, more intimate forms of their names: *Diosito, Mi Virgencita.*[55]

Folk Catholicism also celebrates a mystical closeness to *la tierra,* the earth, "Mother Earth," as María Elena often names her. To María Elena, as well as many others, this source of communion is always available. She need only step outside her trailer door, look up at the sky, feel the wind, or touch a plant to experience the divine presence.

In traditional Mexican folk Catholicism, acts of worship frequently center around prayers and devotion to specific saints and various manifestations of the Virgin or Christ, images that represent approachable mediators with the divine. Many homes contain an altar where devotions take place, a center to which the problems of *la familia* are taken. Lit by flickering candles, an image of the Virgin of Guadalupe or the Virgin of San Juan, a crucifix, other saints, the Sacred Heart, and perhaps a picture of John F. Kennedy create a sacred corner. There family members light candles, place flowers, recite prayers, petitions, and laments, and sometimes simply sit and talk to these intimate, concerned emissaries of the deity.[56]

Removed from male authority, both that of the local priest and the hierarchy in Rome, the daily religious practices give the poorest of traditional Mexican and Mexican American women a sense of some power. Many such women believe in their ability to bargain concretely with fate and to influence the forces that shape their destiny; their religion helps them survive.

Women carefully craft *promesas,* promises made to the sacred in exchange for divine assistance when a family member is ill, crossing the border, drinking or using drugs, or hungry and out of work. Such vows require meaningful sacrifice on the part of the supplicant, especially if the problem is substantial. For example, María Elena has given up a food she loves for a year and undertaken a painful pilgrimage, on foot or on her knees, to one of the shrines frequented by the faithful.

Also, as providers for the family, poor women often have to make triagelike moral decisions. Women must ultimately choose how scarce family resources will be used and how more resources will be acquired. Though the agonizing decisions they must make about such issues as prostitution, smuggling, abortion, or how to deal with a violent family member are often condemned by church and community standards, Mexican folk Catholicism also offers a mechanism of forgiveness for those who must make a choice. And this redemptive process can occur without priest or confessional. Through penances, petitions, *promesas,* and an acknowledgment of perceived wrongdoing, distraught believers can be assured of forgiveness.

Women may also claim direct religious and spiritual power. Midwives are able to baptize infants in emergency conditions. Continuing indigenous traditions, both male and female healers claim divine authority for the practice of their profession. And María Elena has responded to what she believes is a divine call to action against the force of oppression. By sidestepping male hierarchies, such beliefs offer women modes of empowerment.

Mexican folk Catholicism also represents the possibility of female divinity. Female saints, Mother Earth, and the Virgin provide an alternative system of spiritual authority. Probably the most important of these symbols both to María Elena's theology and to her political ideology is the Virgin of Guadalupe.

According to Mexican religious mythology, shortly after the bloody Spanish conquest, the brown-skinned Virgin of Guadalupe appeared to Juan Diego, a poor Aztec. Materializing on the hill of Tepeyac in Mexico where Tonantzin, the Aztec mother of the gods, had been worshipped, she became associated with the moon, as was the goddess Tonantzin and perhaps even the goddess Coatlicue, before her.

Because she appeared to a poor object of the conquest, the new cult of the Virgin of Guadalupe spread quickly among the indigenous, mestizo, and mixed-black population. By 1695 the popularity of the Virgin forced church officials to build a cathedral to serve the devoted Mexican pilgrims, and during the Wars of Independence (1810–1821) and the Mexican Revolution (1910–1917), the image of Guadalupe flew high on banners carried into battles by Mexican rebels.[57]

This symbol of divine aid and righteousness has accompanied the Mexican American people through the United States Southwest. Mothers going through childbirth stare at the image, undocumented refugees carry it with them as they attempt to cross the border, people on the picket line carry it on banners, and families in hiding tack drawings of the Virgin on their walls. In the 1960s, César Chávez, one of the most influential people in María Elena's life, evoked the Virgin of Guadalupe as he roused migrant workers to join together in a union, the United Farm Workers, to attempt to change their lives.

Yet the Virgin of Guadalupe and other virgins do not necessarily lead to the empowerment of Mexican American women. Much of her revolutionary potential has been appropriated by male hierarchies. In reality poor women are urged to imitate the Virgin as she appears on her portraits—eyes downcast and hands folded in patient prayer.

In contrast to the meek and quiet Virgin of Guadalupe is Doña Marina, the mistress of Cortés, who became La Malinche, also known as "La Lengua" ("The Tongue"), because she translated for Cortés and helped design the strategy for the conquest.[58] Thereafter she served as a mythological symbol of female as traitor and whore, but also, paradoxically, the woman who, in her act of treachery and shame, became mother to her people. Thus, conflicting dualities are again reinforced, as the woman who speaks and the sexually active woman as mother are both condemned.[59]

Other oral traditions helped to form the symbolic systems of María Elena's childhood. Many of her diary entries are written in the cadences of the prayers, petitions, and laments recited daily by the females in her extended family. María Elena's writings reflect the Bible stories read to her by her father and by missionaries in migrant camps, and many of her characters are named after Bible figures. Her works contain elements of folk tales from the Brownsville area, of popular tales of the Mexican Revolution, and of the many songs of her childhood, primarily tangos and *corridos*. *Corridos* are stylized folk songs, especially beloved by rural campesinos (farm workers), that frequently tell of legendary deeds performed by Mexican heroes who triumph over oppressors or who sacrifice their lives for freedom and justice for their people; some of the most popular of these songs tell of the exploits of female soldiers and revolutionaries.[60]

Through all of these sources, María Elena inherited a rich, oral literary tradition. The stories, songs, and petitions of her people not only expressed their longings and gave mythological explanations to their history, but these traditions provided entertainment and moral examples, offered remedies for various problems and sufferings, and inspired hope that poor men, and even poor women, equipped with enough courage and commitment, could ride forth into heroic battle with the forces of evil.

Traditions of Struggle

Farm workers of Mexican heritage engaged in spontaneous labor strikes and walkouts throughout their history as an exploited source of farm labor.[61] For example, in 1937 the United Cannery, Agricultural, Packing, and Allied Workers of America (UCPAWA), a highly democratic union that included many women of Mexican heritage, expanded from its base in the canneries and packing industries and entered the fields of California to negotiate the first union contract ever signed in the history of California agriculture.[62] Despite the frequent militancy of migrant field workers, however, grower violence, World War II, the advent of McCarthyism, and the bracero program prevented subsequent union victories until, finally, the United Farm Workers struggled successfully in the late 1960s.

In early 1962, the young César Chávez moved with his wife Helen and his family to Delano, California, to begin community organizing of the Mexican American farm workers among whom he had spent his childhood. Chávez had been trained by Fred Ross of the Community Service

Organization (CSO), a group practicing the multi-issue theory of community organization developed by Saul Alinsky among Chicago stockyard workers. To this theory, Chávez added the mutual-benefit model developed by the Catholic church and the Mexican American *mutualistas*. Dolores Huerta and Gil Padilla, also of CSO background, served as close advisors and supporters. Working patiently door to door, Chávez and his assistants built an organizational base and founded group-improvement associations. In 1964 the bracero program ended. When in 1965 Filipino farm workers in Delano struck against grape growers, they were joined by Chávez and his fellow Mexican Americans, who envisioned the farm workers' struggle as part of the national movement for civil rights.[63]

In the tradition of Martin Luther King, Jr., Chávez, a devout Catholic, appealed to the religious identity of his people, depicting their nonviolent effort as a sacred struggle against the forces of oppression. Chávez's brother designed a red flag with a black eagle shaped in the form of a thunderbird as the symbol of the struggle.[64]

The United Farm Workers (UFW) both drew upon and inspired the emerging Chicano movement, and *La Causa* tapped into the national social conscience of the turbulent 1960s. Individuals, groups, and religious leaders traveled to Delano from across the nation and volunteered their support. In 1965, when the growers refused to negotiate with the striking workers, Chávez and his companions organized a national consumer boycott of grapes picked by nonunion workers. Finally, in 1970 the UFW signed major grape contracts.

Following the grape victory, the UFW turned its attention to the lettuce fields, where growers had already signed sweetheart contracts with the Teamsters' Union. Violence erupted, Chávez was jailed, and the political alliance between growers, the Teamsters, and the Republican administration in Washington grew stronger. As the battle progressed, UFW workers were murdered, and membership in the union plummeted.[65]

Nevertheless, the UFW's effort had gained better wages for field workers and had resulted in more progressive state laws. The union remains the symbol of farm worker needs and issues, bringing such problems as pesticide poisoning to the attention of the nation. Chávez, Dolores Huerta, and the others have not relinquished their fight, and they continue to be a source of inspiration for Chicano and Chicana activists such as María Elena.

The late 1960s also marked the beginning of farm-labor activism in the Midwest. Inspired by the events in California, workers in Wisconsin, Michigan, Indiana, and Ohio, who tended crops contracted primarily by Hunt, Campbell Soup, Libby, McNeil, Vlasic, and Heinz, rose to demand better living and working conditions.

In 1968, Baldemar Velásquez, a twenty-one-year-old Chicano activist, organized a march of farm workers to the Campbell Soup plant. With the assistance of migrants who had "settled out" into northern cities, Velásquez and others formed the Farm Labor Organizing Committee (FLOC), and, through a series of strikes, negotiated contracts with twenty-two individual farmers.

FLOC understood that while signing contracts with growers was good for farm worker morale, growers' contracts with the food processors really determined wages and living and working conditions for the midwestern farm laborers. Consequently, FLOC aimed to conduct three-way negotiations between farm worker unions, growers, and food processors such as Campbell Soup and Heinz.[66]

Aware that mechanization has eliminated countless farm worker jobs, Baldemar Velásquez and other FLOC leaders have continued to maintain contact with workers settling out into midwestern cities, and to serve as spokespeople for general Chicano concerns. Presently, FLOC also organizes actively in Florida, another major farm-working region and the winter home for thousands of migrants who travel north each summer.[67]

Organizing within the Texas Valley has been notoriously difficult. Extreme racism, brutal and deadly repression, threats of deportation, the exportation of resources, and the ease with which strike breaking labor can be brought across the border combine to repeatedly crush attempts at resistance. In 1966, Eugene Nelson, trained under César Chávez, led a strike against La Casita Farms outside of Rio Grande City, an event that became a symbol of the possibility of resistance to people in the Valley.[68]

Since that time, various community efforts have continued, among them the San Juan Service Center, sponsored by the UFW, and shelters for battered women and other victims of family violence.[69] Also, throughout this whole period, Chicanas in the Southwest have had a rich history of labor activism outside the farm worker movement, especially among cannery and garment workers.[70]

María Elena's activism began in the late 1970s, when, unaware of the UFW and their struggles, or of theories of labor and political organizing, she and other poor farm workers in Onarga, Illinois, banded together as a community to change their living conditions. When Olgha Sierra Sandman, leader of the Illinois Farm Worker Ministry, became aware of the Onarga group, she introduced María Elena to the theology and political practices of the National Farm Worker Ministry (a group associated with the National Council of Churches), the UFW, César Chávez, and Dolores Huerta. Within this group, María Elena finally acquired a framework for her developing belief systems, and, nurtured by this community, she transformed her religious and political symbols into an ideology of action and change.

Eventually she joined FLOC, and in the summer of 1985, she and other women from Onarga worked in its successful campaign against Campbell Soup. By then an impassioned believer in the need for political action, María Elena traveled to many communities and spoke to thousands of people as a grass-roots organizer for farm worker concerns; she also wrote and directed short plays in which farm workers acted out their political awakening and clamor for justice.[71] Today, although she is no longer organizing on a formal basis, her support of FLOC, the UFW, and their ideals remains strong.

After agonizing over the decision, María Elena has decided to speak out about the gender discrimination she experienced from the leadership of FLOC.[72] While considering her decision, María Elena felt trapped in a condition faced by a multitude of women in progressive movements. To criticize aspects of the movement is to risk that these criticisms will be used by forces wishing to discredit the movement itself. However, to remain silent is to sentence other women activists in similar situations to the belief that they are alone, and to blunt the potential for equality.

Virtually all modern social change movements that include both men and women, such as the civil rights movement and the new left, have marginalized their female members. In fact, it would be exceptional among organized struggles if María Elena had not experienced sex or gender discrimination.[73]

An additional problem arises because María Elena's material sets the two male leaders of UFW and FLOC in sharp contrast. María Elena speaks frankly about the human limitations of Baldemar Velásquez, the leader of FLOC, with whom she had daily interaction, at the same time that her poems and the symbols she employs elevate César Chávez to almost a mythological level. The two men entered her life at different times and played different roles in her developing political consciousness.

In her more recent reflections, she has begun to wonder if comparable daily contact with César Chávez or other leaders such as Jesse Jackson would have revealed similar personal weaknesses and organizational problems.

The movement promises improvements. The UFW is known for its effort to include all family members in the union drive,[74] and Olgha Sierra Sandman, in recent personal discussions and letters, has assured me that FLOC has become increasingly sensitized to the need for female leadership. She also explained that the summer of 1985, the period during which María Elena remembers being subjected to strict discipline, was a time of tremendous stress for FLOC leaders as they entered the final stages of their eight-year campaign.[75] For María Elena, however, bias against women in the movement and her own individual struggles with the men in her family have prevented her from exercising her full leadership potential.

Since the early 1970s, a strong Chicana feminist movement has been developing. Arising first from within Chicano student and other activist organizations, the Chicanas formed a variety of caucuses and organizations, and today many Chicanas have joined coalitions of African American, Asian American, and indigenous women, calling for a simultaneous struggle against the forces of race, class, gender, and sexual oppression. As María Elena's document so eloquently demonstrates, Chicana feminism is not some sort of imitation of white, middle-class feminism, but it is instead a richly textured product of its own heritage and creation.[76]

The Issue of Male Violence

The people who arrived in the Valley during the early decades of the century to become part of the family wage system of the North brought with them the feudal culture of parts of Mexico. The rural social order—in which the dominance of a land-owning elite over peons, and, frequently, of men over women, was institutionalized—was perpetuated in the fields of South Texas. For the women especially, life in the Valley offered no escape from subordination: the family labor contract, the isolation of Mexican families within labor camps, the Anglo farmers' perceptions of proper gender roles, and the continual infusion of various Mexican peasant family ideals by new immigrants ensured that most women in the fields would remain subservient.[77] Indeed, in the hierarchy of oppression that assured the economic viability of the agricultural system of the region, poor Mexican American women were at the very bottom. This legacy shaped the world into which María Elena was born.

In that world, in which behavior common to many cultures was exacerbated by misery, males were frequently more highly valued than females, a woman's worth was measured by her virginity before marriage, her fidelity in marriage, and her reproductive abilities, and deviation from the ideal of female submissiveness was severely punished. That punishment came in many forms, as María Elena's testimony shows.

We must keep in mind, as we read her life story, that when María Elena talks about "Mexican men," *machismo,* and women's support of a system of male dominance, she is discussing the problems of a specific class of people of Mexican heritage, a class existing within a specific historical context. She is not describing all Chicano or Mexican families, but rather the people she has known, a subjugated people from an impoverished peasant background who live very difficult lives. Recent studies have illustrated the diversity of Mexican American people,[78] and examinations of families in Mexico have shown that machismo is a stereotype, whereas real behavior varies according to "social class, economic status, ethnic identity, and degree of urbanization."[79]

In María Elena's life, violence toward women is commonplace. The acts of violence she describes in her document fall into several patterns. One is her father's abusive behavior. María Elena interprets his violence both as an indication of emotional disorder and as a form of behavior control, although she also stresses the tensions under which he tried to provide for and protect his family.

Another category of violence consists of instances of sexual harassment, attempted sexual assault, and actual rape. While all women are potential victims of such crimes, the women in María Elena's accounts are especially vulnerable and have little social recourse or protection. And their assailants come from all sides. They are Mexican American and Anglos; they are family, strangers, bosses, and agents of the government.

A third pattern implies that some violence against women is a form of bonding among men, as well as a means of teaching women their proper roles.[80] María Elena's first husband was instructed by his brothers to go out frequently without her, even with other women, and to hit her when she objected. In time, his cruel violence became life threatening.

Finally, there is the indirect but very real violence committed by the leaders of agribusiness towards the migrant women who labor in their fields, and by other people in powerful positions who perpetuate systems that impoverish hundreds of thousands of women, forcing them into violent relationships, near-starvation, repeated childbirth, and prostitution.

The violence experienced by María Elena was closely associated with her sexuality. Males attempted to communicate and struggle with each other using María Elena's sexual expression, the fruits of her labor, and her children. María Elena's "purity" before marriage and fidelity after became a means by which the men could compare their relative power and sexual prowess with each other, and they seemed almost oblivious to the suffering their battles caused María Elena. In some way, violence itself seemed to become eroticized to a group of both Anglo and Mexican heritage men.

The violence described in this document leaves us with several disturbing questions. What mechanisms allow men to see women's sexuality as a weapon they can use to injure each other? How can we hold economic structures and rulers responsible for the suffering by women and children at the bottom? How can women, whose sexuality is so full of cultural meaning to others, claim their sexuality for themselves and control the use of their own bodies?

In the face of such formidable antagonists, María Elena chose to rebel. Ostracized by the suspicious, she devised her own methods of survival. And, although derided for doing so, she made the extraordinary decision to keep a record of her life.

Poetry is the Theory: Documents of Resistance

Throughout her life, usually in crowded conditions where three adults slept in a single bed, María Elena lay at night with a flashlight under a blanket, writing poetry and letters to God. These letters to God, written on scraps of papers and old notebooks, became the major substance of her diaries. Her writing was almost always disrupted so the works she created are in segments—fragments of attempts to explain and record her world and to give directions for resistance.[81] Audre Lorde, an African American literary critic, states that poor and working-class women's lives usually don't allow them time to produce lengthy written works such as novels, works of theology, or political theory. Instead, poetry—work taking up

little physical space, work that may be carried around in the mind—
functions as:

> . . . a quality of light within which we predicate our hopes and dreams
> toward survival and change, first made into language, then into idea,
> then into more tangible action. Poetry is the way we help give name
> to the nameless so it can be thought.[82]

So it is for the actors in María Elena's poems and songs who give names
to the nameless so they can be known; so it is for the metaphors she
employs to represent her political theory; so it is for the narratives she
presents to interpret for her people and to give them hope.

María Elena and the women like her have struggled most of their
lives against interlocking repressive social structures, a conflict recorded
throughout this document. Many women begin their daily battles of
resistance by refusing to be destroyed by all of the layers of suffering that
bears down on them and their families. Throughout this process, they
labor heroically to maintain life and meaning for their families, continu-
ally pushing against the bands of poverty and violence that encircled their
lives.

Many of these women also fight overtly with various power structures, struggling on behalf of their families and community or work net-
works to win concessions that make life more bearable. To do all of this,
women fashion a variety of techniques for such resistance: cooperating
with each other quietly; helping each other flee from violence; challenging
schools, churches, and government agencies to live up to their stated
objectives; protesting in strikes and other public actions; and generally
sowing disorder in the systems meant to keep them under control. Some
of the women, gaining confidence through group successes, also begin to
struggle for themselves as individuals and as poor women of Mexican
heritage.

In this resistance, María Elena and the other women tell each other
stories, stories to inspire, to entertain, and to build bonds between each
other. They tell stories about the material constraints on their lives, stories
about their acts of rebellion, humorous stories that help them laugh and
strip power away from those above them, and stories about male and
female heroes. The stories they tell explain the control mechanisms in

which they are trapped and hint of weaknesses in those systems, flaws that can be exploited for change. The women's tales about outsmarting *la migra*, stories about winning concessions from employers, elaborate jokes about the frailty of landlords, and stories about out-maneuvering husbands often are accompanied by the healing balm of group laughter.

María Elena engaged in all of these forms of protest, often providing leadership, but she also started recording, enlarging, and giving alternative meanings to narratives and spiritual forces in the lives of the women she loved. In the process, she created diary entries, poems, songs, and short plays—writings that she began to believe might someday contribute to a history for her people.

The seeds of María Elena's visions, explanations, and protest actions lay within the conflicting and contested meanings of the symbols, beliefs, and legends of her childhood. These seeds were nurtured by the harsh, but fertile interactions between the ethical systems of her people and their starkly difficult material lives. They ripened in a terrain of contesting images of what it meant to be poor, Mexican American, and female in the context of María Elena's childhood.

For María Elena as a child, danger and safety, food and hunger, love and cruelty, faith and horror, and innocence and heart-breaking knowledge coexisted in a turbulent mixture requiring her to make constant adaptations and to engage in often conflicting behaviors. For example, at the same time that the child María Elena struggled with her anger toward her father, any rebellious word brought immediate reprisals. At the same time that the young María Elena was expected to scavenge in the streets, sites of constant sexual danger, her father and husband demanded purity and seclusion, battering her at any hint of impropriety. At the same time that commercial agriculture relied on her people to be available for labor at any moment, María Elena's people were supposed to live nearly hidden lives, exacting no resources or acknowledgments from the larger society. And, throughout María Elena's life, in mutually exclusive ways, various institutions and groups competed for the control of her sexuality, for the fruits of her body, and for her mind—attempting to define and limit her personhood for her in the process.

Cultural visions—such as songs of revolutionary women, stories of the Virgin of Guadalupe, the saints, and La Malinche, combined with Anglo tales, legends, and values—provided María Elena with symbols and a vocabulary with which to communicate meaning; however, these representations also gave conflicting accounts of what is good and how social changes could be made. Socially constructed ideas about color were a constant source of conflict. María Elena was relatively light and called *la Güerita* (the Blond One) by a care taker, but in a public world, she was labeled as dark, i.e., inferior and so potentially polluting that those labeled white used different water fountains. Her family, community, and missionaries told her to love an omnipresent Jesus, but Jesus was represented as blond and Anglo, and consequently far removed from her. In a similar fashion, María Elena learned songs about women fighting for their people in the Mexican Revolution, but whenever she tried to point out what she saw as unjust, she was charged with being a potential witch or a traitor, like La Malinche.

At the same time that María Elena tried to meet her own developmental needs, she wrestled to reconcile such conflicting values. In the process, she was rocked by alternating waves of rebellion and acceptance as she asked unanswered questions: Why won't, or can't, mothers protect their daughters? How do you love violent husbands and fathers? If my people work so hard, why do they have so little? Why are Mexicans considered dirty? How can we express our love of nature and beauty? Why, if God is good, why do so many people suffer? María Elena never questioned the existence of a mystical world, but throughout her life, she warred with evasions of her questions and with unexamined interpretations.

As María Elena came of age, these conflicting priorities converged and bore down upon her, giving competing meanings to the world and her role in it. That she survived at all and raised her children was a triumph of resistance. But she accomplished more. Out of these conflicting ingredients and, eventually, within communities encouraging reflection and an ideology of change, she organized for political action, exploited vulnerable cracks in meaning systems, and forged an alternative religious and political theory. Her documents attest to these altered visions.

She gives meaning to her concrete material experience, with all its racial, class, and gender dimensions, by placing it in a sacred, mythical landscape. When she dreams about leading undocumented workers across the Rio Grande during a flood, the event becomes a baptism; when farm workers are kept in the fields too long, their sweat becomes eucharistic blood and the wine that makes rich men sing; and when explaining why women should be respected, she says that God also must be partially female. Look at the night sky, she instructs. Consider the majesty of human creation. With our small eyes, we can see the stars, but the stars, in all their splendor, can not see us back.

With her poems and other writings, María Elena tells her people to take heart, that the forces of the earth are on their side. She tells them that by joining together they can survive; that leadership will come from unexpected places, perhaps even from a woman; that the divine is not only concerned with humble people but is also physically suffering with them on a daily basis, making a sin against them also a sin against God. Using these representations, she provides a revised vision of significance and hope for her people.

Her analysis of the interaction of her material and spiritual worlds informed her search for explanations of the social systems she observed. How and why, she asked, when we live in such a beautiful world, did it turn out like this? This struggle to understand moved her to analyze how events and forces change over time. Then, using the language and symbol systems of her heritage, María Elena constructed a new history for her people, recorded in her diaries, plays, songs, and poems. It is from such material that she hopes she and others might begin to fashion her Third Testament of the People.

María Elena's vision of history, like her poetry and other creative works, involves intricate interactions between divine and material beings—forces that struggle throughout time in a battle between good and evil. Thus, Adam and Eve become the first farm workers; Moses and Jesus are early organizers in a path of political prophets leading up to the black civil rights movement and eventually to César Chávez. Likewise, when farm workers hold a union convention, a resurrected martyr appears to make the most important proposal; and when a woman needs strength, the Virgin of Guadalupe is transformed from a meek and passive being into a pregnant campesina holding a document guaranteeing human rights in one arm and a rifle, standing for enforcement, in the other.

María Elena created this fictive, narrated history, this deeply symbolic interpretation, from both her personal reflections and group explanations from the farm worker movement. If María Elena's history had been simply an outgrowth of stories she heard while being trained as a union organizer, it might have become a somewhat standardized "movement" view of historical events and moral significance. However, María Elena also told stories of women's suffering and resistance and asked questions about gender roles and violence against women. These questions required her quest to function at another, more radical level.

María Elena's work, and her stories about resistance, leave us with questions about the meaning systems of activist women. How do questions of gender or race disrupt what might become somewhat orthodox histories of a movement and enable thinkers like María Elena to create new historical narratives from the interactions of poetic, symbolic, and material realities? Is it possible that for some working-class women, religious language is the only language of meaning available? If so, how can the languages of such belief systems simultaneously give power to organizers and present them with limitations?

Like the many others who have laid claim to María Elena's mind, spirit, and body, those of us who hear her story or read her words will attempt to incorporate her ideas for our purposes. Yet no one and nothing has been able to appropriate her being. While she wrestles with those who seek to contain her mind and spirit, in some, perhaps subtle, manner, she changes them, she changes us, and she changes how we view the world.

Claiming María Elena's Story for History

Listening to the stories of many women, I have come to the conclusion that memory itself is a political event. Social structures are often so powerful that they actually format memory into accepted boundaries, denying the validity of experiences outside the parameters of accepted social interpretations and distorting and fragmenting experience. Consequently, creating spaces for re-memory may be a profoundly liberating and energizing experience. This reconstitution of memory often takes place within relationships, and her relationship with the undocumented women of Onarga, with Olgha Sierra Sandman, with the farm worker movement, and eventually with me helped María Elena reinterpret her past.[83]

The life history María Elena and I present was constructed within such a relationship and is an act of collaboration, reflecting eleven years of friendship and cooperation. I never approached my time with María Elena as an unimpassioned outside observer, although I have tried to set her story within a social and historical context. My major contribution to this project has been my ability to interview people in an open-ended manner, following the subject's interests and concerns. I have largely attempted to follow, not lead, our discussions.

María Elena and I met in 1981 because of our shared political goals. At that time she was active in the farm worker movement, and I was compiling a collection of oral life histories of poor and working-class women. María Elena became the subject of the last chapter in that book.[84]

For years I had felt compelled to function as a witness and to try to provide a forum through which poor women could speak about the conditions of their survival. That compulsion can be traced to a number of events in my life. In order to exist as a single mother with three children under five and almost no family or resources, I lived with other single mothers and their children, moving from place to place, just weeks or days ahead of being homeless. I will never forget the friendship we shared or the terror of not having food, medical care, or a place to stay. Then, when I went on welfare in 1971, I joined with several other welfare mothers to form a Women's Crisis and Information Center, one of the earliest advocacy programs in the country. Running the program taught me much about the complexities of poor women's oppressions, the many faces of resistance, and the great need for political action. However, the insights I gained did not adequately protect me.

When I was twenty-eight, I was advised to have a hysterectomy by the only doctor in town who would take welfare clients. High on drugs, he botched the surgery, which turned out to have been unnecessary in the first place. I now believe he wanted the welfare payment and felt the sterilization of a welfare mother was socially beneficial.[85]

Years of infections, great pain, follow-up operations, and many additional surgical procedures without anesthetic, because I could not pay for it, left me permanently wounded and deeply in debt. They also left me filled with an understanding of the vulnerability of poor women with little social power. Later, when I met María Elena, although I was not Latina and had never worked as a migrant worker, I did not feel like a total outsider to the perils of her life.

The techniques by which we would carry out our working relationship were established during my first extended visit in Illinois. We began our tape recording sitting at her kitchen table, but within minutes she was interrupted by people who needed her assistance, and I quickly learned to record under extraordinary circumstances.

After we completed our early work in 1982, we traveled hundreds of miles just to see each other as friends, going back and forth between Wisconsin, Illinois, Texas, and, later, Arizona. At times we talked vaguely about doing a book-length life history that would highlight her experiences as a migrant worker and union organizer, but it was not until María Elena's poisoning in March of 1988 that we began to work urgently on our project.

When I visited María Elena, I usually brought a functioning automobile, a precious resource to people in her situation, so most of the recording took place while we were driving, and providing rides became a way I could thank María Elena's people. María Elena and I cried together when the material we discussed or what we observed was too painful; we laughed and celebrated when our children succeeded or victories were won; and we had great adventures. Finally, I was dazed and astonished as I slowly discovered the artist in María Elena, and chagrined as I listened and realized how close we had come to losing her talent. María Elena took me on paths I had never expected to follow.

In between our visits I transcribed our tapes, read background material, and developed lists of questions for our next meeting, although each time we were together, María Elena brought up additional topics. Slowly, I came to recognize the depth of the conflicts in her background and in the social and symbolic systems upon which she drew to portray her vision. Eventually, about half of the material on the tapes was transcribed into some thirteen hundred pages, and María Elena gave me access to another nine hundred pages of her written materials. I finally outlined all the data, then I began the difficult task of editing the document.

In most of the oral histories I have collected, speech patterns have tended to be repetitive, working back over and over again to important, pivotal memories. In this case, because the original tapes and transcripts will be placed in the Schlesinger Library of American Women to be used by future scholars, I was able to edit out much of the repetition. I have also occasionally summarized, added transitional phrases, identified vague pronouns, placed the material in chronological order, and—because the data had been collected over many years—tried to make consistent use of present and past tenses. In so doing, I know I have deprived the material of some of its original nature, and I refer interested scholars to the tapes.

I also decided to weave parts of her original writings and excerpts from her written and taped diary into the oral history, sometimes out of chronological sequence, because I feel they give extra depth and highlight the multiple dimensions of her feelings. After I had experimented with that technique throughout the section on her childhood and early marriage, I read sections of the text out loud to María Elena and asked for her feedback. She responded enthusiastically and gave me further directions and suggestions and provided her own translations of the Spanish excerpts. We also made a joint decision to correct the spelling in several of her writings, but other than that, the excerpts remain essentially as they appear in the original documents.

Throughout our collaboration I worried about problems the manuscript might cause her—with her family, with others, perhaps legally. We checked with a lawyer and had someone knowledgeable read the information about undocumented people to ensure their anonymity and safety. When I finally completed the entire manuscript, I rated the sections according to their sensitivity and possibility for causing problems in María Elena's life. Then I took the manuscript to her and read approximately 60 percent of the total work out loud to her, beginning with all the sensitive sections. I read for hours and María Elena cried soundlessly through most of it, stopping me periodically to clarify or change a section, occasionally making changes in the choice of written materials to be interspersed with oral testimony. Finally, having listened to all the material that might cause problems, she asked me to stop reading.

Then, to complete the process, we changed names. We kept her name, Pablo's, and those of her children and grandchildren, of union officials, and of her three close friends from Onarga, her heroic women—Gloria Chiquita Carmona, Lucia Carmona, and Meche Barbosa. Finally, we made the legal arrangements regarding royalties and copyrights. The tapes, manuscripts, diaries, photographs, and written materials will be placed in the archives, but some of the tapes, including personal material that might cause embarrassment to individuals, will be held back from scholarly use for twenty years.

Although memory slants, rearranges, and sets priorities with material, it is a significant source of information. Oral documents such as María Elena's provide a deep evocation of the thoughts and belief systems of people generally disenfranchised from historical memory. Others will weave that information into frameworks created with additional forms of social data.[86]

That María Elena kept diaries is remarkable. I have located no similar record among other women with her background, although such documents probably exist. Throughout her life, María Elena has been driven by a creative force that has never let her rest. To have denied such a person access to books, to have nearly extinguished the radiance of her mind and spirit, is a crime. That she continues to write, that she has kept faith in her struggle, and that she shares her story in these pages—these are María Elena's gifts to us.

NOTES

1. The complexity of terms I use to identify women of Mexican heritage reflects the heterogeneity of the people of Mexican descent (or heritage) in the United States. The term *Latina* (Latino for a male) refers to a large population, including such groups as Puerto Ricans, Cubans, Mexicans, Mexican Americans, Central Americans, and South Americans. The term Mexican American is used to refer to people of Mexican heritage who are strongly identified with the United States, either through birth, upbringing, or specified choice. The term *Chicana* (Chicano for a male) is similar; however, it reflects a conscious self-labeling among activists who identify themselves politically with laborers and farm workers. I tend to use Chicana to express María Elena's self-identification as a politically active person.

   I use the term *Mexican* in two ways: first, to refer to people who were born in Mexico and primarily identify with Mexico as their home country and, second, to represent a specific label used in a racial ideology existing in South Texas from the early part of this century up until about World War II. At that point, the term Mexican referred to anyone of Mexican heritage, even if they had been United States citizens for generations, and the term white applied to those of Anglo-American heritage, despite the fact that Mexicans were listed as white in most census data. As with other human labels, Anglo-American is also an imprecise term, a term that is generally used to describe "white" Americans of a European, especially Northern European, descent.

   Finally, I use the term Mexican heritage when I refer both to people who are recent immigrants from Mexico and those Mexican Americans who have been in the United States for several generations. For further discussion see Margarita B. Melville's introduction to *Twice a Minority: Mexican American Women,* ed., Margarita B. Melville (St. Louis: C. V. Mosby, 1980), 4–5.

2. Quotations from the play in the main body of this book are taken from María Elena's spoken interpretation: her translation of her original version, written in Spanish, appears in the Appendix.

3. *Indocumentados* is Spanish for "undocumented [workers]," a term for people working in the United States without the legal documents that would give them permission to be here. The term also indicates that such people consider themselves part of a culture not arbitrarily divided by the formal United States—Mexican border. Pejorative terms for such people include illegal aliens, wetbacks, or *mojados.* See Alan Weisman, *La Frontera: The United States Border with Mexico* (New York: Harcourt Brace Jovanovich, 1986), preface.

4. See Paul Schuster Taylor, *An American-Mexican Frontier: Nueces County, Texas* (Chapel Hill: University of North Carolina Press, 1934), 194–97.
5. I use the term gender to refer to socially constructed male and female sex roles.
6. Phil Gramm, "Gramm Unveils Plan to Fight River Pollution," *Brownsville Herald,* August 17, 1987. Quoted by Robert Lee Maril, *Poorest of Americans: The Mexican Americans of the Lower Rio Grande Valley of Texas* (Notre Dame, Ind.: University of Notre Dame Press, 1989), 201.
7. See Georgia Tasker, "Central America's Dying Children," *Arizona Daily Star,* August 27, 1990, 17; Michael Massing, "The New Game in Guatemala," *New York Review of Books,* October 25, 1990, 53–57.
8. Edward R. F. Sheehan, "The Open Border," *New York Review of Books,* March 15, 1990, 35.
9. Ibid.
10. Maril, *Poorest of Americans,* 4–5.
11. Sheehan, "Open Border," 34.
12. Maril, *Poorest of Americans,* 10, 14–15. For a general discussion on the feminization of poverty, see Joan Smith, "The Paradox of Women's Poverty: Wage-earning Women and Economic Transformation," *Signs: Journal of Women in Culture and Society* 10, no.2 (Winter 1984), 291–310.

    Even women who are employed are likely to be under the poverty level. Patricia Zavella, in *Women's Work and Chicano Families: Cannery Workers of the Santa Clara Valley* (Ithaca and London: Cornell University Press, 1987), 10–11, states that Chicanos have remained on the bottom strata of the working class for over a century, and Chicana wages are even worse than those of their husbands and fathers. Yet, Chicanas have experienced some of the same processes as other women within the labor force. Except for their work in migrant labor, they have also been concentrated in sex-segregated "women's work," such as domestic labor, garment manufacturing, low-level factory operatives, cannery employment, and, when lucky, clerical labor. Today, working-class Chicanas are concentrated in food processing, electronics, and garments. All of the industries tend to pay minimum wage. They have virtually no advancement opportunities, they are segregated by gender, and their employment is seasonable and sporadic.
13. Maril, *Poorest of Americans,* 138–46; U.S. Department of Health and Human Services, *Health Needs Assessment Survey for Brownsville, Texas: A U.S.–Mexico Border Community Case Study, 1983–1985* (Brownsville, Texas: South Texas Institute of Latin and Mexican-American Research, Texas Southmost College, 1985), Introduction and 42–45.
14. In 1989, according to the Bureau of Census of the United States Department of Agriculture, a single person who lived alone and was younger than sixty-five was considered to be poor if she or he earned less than $6,451. A family of four, under similar circumstances, was considered poor if the members

earned less than $12,674 in total. *World Almanac and Book of Facts 1992* (New York: Pharos Books, 1991), 135.

15. The *Health Needs Assessment Survey for Brownsville* describes details of this tenuous existence and its effect on mental health, 46–47.

16. See Fran Leeper Buss, *La Partera: Story of a Midwife* (Ann Arbor: University of Michigan Press, 1980), for an understanding of the multiple religious roles of Mexican American midwifery, and see Robert T. Trotter II and Juan Antonio Chavira, *Curanderismo: Mexican American Folk Healing* (Athens: University of Georgia Press, 1981), 53–55, for general information about parteras in the Texas Valley.

17. See Matt S. Meier and Feliciano Rivera, *The Chicanos: A History of Mexican Americans* (New York: Hill and Wang, 1972), 10, and E. Bradford Burns, *Latin America: A Concise Interpretive History* (Englewood Cliffs, New Jersey: Prentice-Hall, 1972), 14–20.

18. At the time of the Conquest, both Spanish and Aztec societies were organized according to stratified class lines and the institutionalized power of males over females. Of course, Northern European societies, colonizing North America at about the same time, were also hierarchal and male dominated. Nevertheless, the specifics among the various societies were different. For a brief description of the patterns of ownership and military development in Spain at the time of the conquest, see Eric R. Wolf, *Europe and the People Without History* (Berkeley: University of California Press, 1982), 112–14. For a discussion of the strict limits on women's social power in Spain at the time of the conquest, see Electa Arenal and Stacey Schlau, *Untold Sisters: Hispanic Nuns in Their Own Words,* trans. Armanda Powell (Albuquerque: University of New Mexico Press, 1989), 1–6. For a discussion of Aztec hierarchies, see Meier and Rivera, *The Chicanos,* 8–10, and for a description of the power relationships between males and females in Aztec society, see Cordelia Candelaria, "La Malinche, Feminist Prototype," *Frontiers: A Journal of Women Studies* 5, no. 2 (Summer 1980), 2–3.

19. Cordelia Candelaria, "La Malinche," 1–7.

20. Arenal and Schlau, *Untold Sisters,* 337.

21. For a discussion of the *hacendado* system, see Michael C. Meyer and William L. Sherman, *The Course of Mexican History,* 3d ed. (New York and Oxford: Oxford University Press, 1987), 266–68, 457–60.

22. See David Montejano, *Anglos and Mexicans in the Making of Texas, 1836–1986* (Austin: University of Texas Press, 1987), 15–21; Antonio N. Zavaleta, "'The Twin Cities': A Historical Synthesis of the Socio-Economic Interdependence of the Brownsville-Matamoros Border Community," in *Studies in Brownsville History,* ed. Milo Kearney (Brownsville: Pan American University at Brownsville, 1986), 135–45; and Meier and Rivera, *The Chicanos,* 57–65.

23. Raquel Rubio-Goldsmith, "Oral History: Considerations and Problems for Its Use in the History of Mexicanas in the United States," in *Between Borders:*

Essays on Mexicana/Chicana History, ed. Adelaida R. Del Castillo (Encino, Calif.: Floricanto Press, La Mujer Latina Series, 1990), 163–64.

24. As part of this process, southern emigrants pushed their settlements across eastern Texas, bringing with them "a cotton-slave economy" and an idea of race that defined Mexican Americans as only slightly different from blacks. See David J. Weber, ed., *Foreigners in their Native Land: Historical Roots of the Mexican Americans*, foreword by Ramón Eduardo Ruiz (Albuquerque: University of New Mexico Press, 1973), 152.

25. Montejano, *Anglos and Mexicans*, 197–201.

26. Taylor, *An American-Mexican Frontier*, 300.

27. This new order began in about 1920 and lasted until its gradual breakup following World War II. Montejano, *Anglos and Mexicans*, 159–61, 259–61.

28. Ibid., 197–213.

29. Ibid., 160.

30. John Higham defined "nativism" as a certain type of aggressive nationalism and "intensive opposition to an internal minority on the grounds of its foreign (i.e. 'un-American') connections." [*Strangers in the Land: Patterns of American Nativism 1860–1925*, corrected and with new preface (New York: Atheneum, 1972), 4.] Higham identifies three major focuses of this expression in American life: anti-Catholicism, a fear of foreign radicals, and a concept that the United States belonged to the superior, Anglo-Saxon "race." (See pages 3–9.)

31. For a description of the so-called scientific theories of race, see Thomas F. Gossett, *Race: The History of an Idea in America* (Dallas: Southern Methodist University Press, 1963), especially chapter XV, "Racism in the 1920s," 370–408.

32. Montejano, *Anglos and Mexicans*, 225–28.

33. Ruth Alice Allen, *The Labor of Women in the Production of Cotton* (Chicago: University of Chicago Library private edition, 1933, reprinted by Arno Press, 1975), 71 and 64, respectively. Excerpts used with permission of Arno Press, Inc. Quoted in Rosalinda González, "Chicanas and Mexican Immigrant Families 1920–1940: Women's Subordination and Family Exploitation," in *Decades of Discontent: The Women's Movement, 1920–1940*, ed. Lois Scharf and Joan M. Jensen (Westport, Conn. and London: Greenwood Press, Contributions in Women's Studies, no. 28, 1983), 63. See also Ruth Allen, "Mexican Peon Women in Texas," *Sociology and Social Research: An International Journal* 16, no. 2 (Nov.–Dec. 1931), 131–42. In addition, many of the farmers quoted by Paul Taylor state that they require large families.

34. *Child Labor and the Work of Mothers in the Beet Fields of Colorado and Michigan*, U.S. Department of Labor, Children's Bureau (Washington Government Printing Office: Bureau Publication 115, 1923), 25–26, 111. The fact that many desperate families resorted to some sort of physical punishment or violence to keep protesting or exhausted children working in the fields for long hours has been confirmed to me by private conversations with ex-mi-

grants over the past nine years. Also, four of the five migrant women interviewed by Kristina Lindborg and Carlos J. Ovando talk about their parents' use of physical punishments during their childhood. See Lindborg and Ovando, *Five Mexican-American Women in Transition: A Case Study of Migrants in the Midwest* (San Francisco: R and E Research Associate, 1977), and Joy Hintz, *Poverty, Prejudice, Power, Politics: Migrants Speak About Their Lives* (Columbus, Ohio: Avonelle Associates, 1981).

35. See *The Life Story of the Mexican Immigrant,* autobiographical documents collected by Manuel Gamio, with a new introduction by Paul S. Taylor (New York: Dover Publications, 1971), unabridged republication of the work originally published by the University of Chicago Press, 1931, under the title, *The Mexican Immigrant: His Life-Story;* Selden C. Menefee and Orin C. Cassmore, *The Pecan Shellers of San Antonio: The Problem of Underpaid and Unemployed Mexican Labor* (Washington D.C.: U.S. Government Printing Office, U.S. Work Projects Administration, 1940); and Taylor, *An American-Mexican Frontier,* 158–161.

36. For the experiences of women of Mexican heritage, see John D'Emilio and Estelle B. Freedman, *Intimate Matters: A History of Sexuality in America* (New York and Cambridge: Harper and Row, 1988), 91.

37. Certainly, somewhat similar exaggerated beliefs about sexual performance and availability are part of the history of the use of racism against African American women, and poor women of all races have been assumed to be sexually available by men in more dominant positions. See Josephine, Darlene, Lee, Mary, Mildred, and María Elena's stories in *Dignity: Lower Income Women Tell of Their Lives and Struggles,* compiled by Fran Leeper Buss (Ann Arbor: University of Michigan Press, 1985) and D'Emilio and Freedman, *Intimate Matters,* especially introduction, 85–87, and 131–38.

38. Marian Moses, M.D., "Pesticide-Related Health Problems and Farmworkers," *Official Journal of the American Association of Occupational Health Nurses* 37, no. 3 (March 1989), 115.

39. Mark Reisler, *By the Sweat of Their Brow: Mexican Immigrant Labor in the United States, 1900–1940* (Westport, Conn. and London: Greenwood Press, 1976), 260.

40. For basic interpretations of such forms of economic displacement, see Claude Meillasoux, *Maidens, Meal, and Money: Capitalism and Domestic Community* (Cambridge: Cambridge University Press, 1981), 91–119 and Harold Wolpe, "The Theory of Internal Colonialism: The South African Case," in *Beyond the Sociology of Development: Economy and Society in Latin America and Africa,* ed. Ivar Oxaal, Tony Barnett, and David Booth (London: Routledge and Paul, 1975), 229–52. See also, María Patricia Fernández-Kelly, *For We Are Sold, I and My People: Women and Industry in Mexico's Frontier* (Albany: State University of New York Press, 1983).

41. Eventually, three migrant streams developed among U.S. migrant workers. The workers of the east coast stream moved north from Florida. The workers

of the west coast stream were based in California, and the central, midcontinental stream was based in the Rio Grande Valley and traveled north to the Midwest. Goldfarb, Ronald L. *Migrant Workers: A Caste of Despair* (Ames: Iowa State University Press, 1981), 10.

42. Moses, "Health Problems," 115.
43. *New Harvest/Old Shame,* 1990. Produced by Hector Galan, "60 Minutes," Frontline Series. (Video).
44. See Goldfarb, *A Caste of Despair,* chapter 3, for more details.
45. Dr. Marian Moses, the foremost national advocate for farm workers suffering from pesticide poisoning, states that "only 10% to 15% of applied pesticides actually reach the target pest, with the remaining 85% to 90% dispersed off-target to air, soil, and water . . . " Moses, "Health Problems," 116.
46. Ibid., 117–27. Although workers are exposed throughout the country, only California requires mandatory reporting of pesticide-related illness. Even there the frequency of exposure is hard to determine because frightened workers often do not seek medical care and doctors frequently misdiagnose. One estimate of the numbers of workers affected by pesticides in the United States each year is approximately three hundred thousand. [R. F. Wasserstrom and R. Wiles, "Field Duty: U.S. Farmworkers and Pesticide Safety." (Washington D.C.: World Resources Institute, July 1985).] Quoted in Moses, "Health Problems," 117.
47. For exact figures, see Maril, *Poorest of Americans,* 58–59.
48. For a history of women's employment in the low-paying clothing industry, see Joan M. Jensen and Sue Davidson, eds., *A Needle, A Bobbin, A Strike: Women Needleworkers in America* (Philadelphia: Temple University Press, 1984).
49. Raul A. Fernández, *The United States-Mexico Border: A Politico-Economic Profile* (Notre Dame and London: University of Notre Dame Press, 1977), 134–36, and Patricia Marin and Cecilia Rodríguez, "Working on Racism: Centro Obrero, El Paso," in *Of Common Cloth: Women in the Global Textile Industry,* ed. Wendy Chapkis and Cynthia Enloe (Amsterdam and Washington D.C.: Transnational Institute, 1983), 81.
50. The number of plants in Matamoros increased from three in 1967 to thirty-seven in 1985. See Maril, *Poorest of Americans,* 67.
51. For specific information concerning the effects of such work on young women's lives, see Vicki L. Ruiz and Susan Tiano, eds., *Women on the U.S.-Mexico Border: Responses to Change,* (Boston: Alley and Unwin, 1987).
52. Maril, *Poorest of Americans,* 87–89.
53. When Mario Barrera speaks of these people, he talks about the possible emergence of a "marginal mass" of more or less permanently unemployed, almost left-over people, people with no real hope for stable employment. Some writers call these people an "underclass." See Mario Barrera, *Race and Class in the Southwest: A Theory of Racial Inequality* (Notre Dame and London: University of Notre Dame Press, 1979), 128. For a discussion of writers on

the "underclass" and a critique of their work, see Linda Gordon, "Feminism and the 'Underclass,'" *Against the Current*, January/February 1989, 42–43.

54. Arenal and Schlau, *Untold Sisters*, 339.

55. Paula Gunn Allen, in *Grandmothers of the Light: A Medicine Woman's Sourcebook* (Boston: Beacon Press, 1991), 3–7, discusses such mysticism in indigenous religions, and Gloria Anzaldúa writes of a similar mystical realm, poetically depicting what she calls "pagan elements" of the folk Catholicism of her family in the Texas Valley. See Anzaldúa, *Borderlands/La Frontera: The New Mestiza* (San Francisco: Spinsters/Aunt Lute, 1987), especially p. 27.

Anzaldúa also writes vividly about the consequences of forcing Catholicism onto indigenous religions at the time of the Conquest, a process during which earlier Mesoamerican fertility and Earth goddesses were severed and revised until they became the adored la Virgen de Guadalupe and the despised la Chingada, 27–31. Roberto M. Salmón and Juanita Elizondo Garza write of the culture of the Coahuiltecan people who lived in South Texas before the Spanish and the Mexicans arrived. Aspects of their traditions entered the religious beliefs of the Brownsville people despite the dispersal and absorption of the Coahuiltecan people. See "The Coahuiltecan Legacy of South Texas," in *Studies in Brownsville History*, 41–44. Finally, Edward H. Spicer, in *Cycles of Conquest: The Impact of Spain, Mexico, and the United States on the Indians of the Southwest, 1533–1960* (Tucson: University of Arizona Press, 1962), 504–17, gives helpful details about a similar process among three indigenous cultures in the United States Southwest.

56. Virgilio Elizondo, *Galilean Journey: The Mexican-American Promise* (Maryknoll, N.Y.: Orgis, 1983), 39.

57. See María Herrera-Sobek, *The Mexican Corrido: A Feminist Analysis* (Bloomington and Indianapolis: Indiana University Press, 1990), 34–35, 42, Andrés G. Guerrero, *A Chicano Theology* (Maryknoll, New York: Orbis Books, 1987), 96–98, and, again, Anzaldúa, *Borderlands*, 27–31.

58. Herrera-Sobek, *The Mexican Corrido*, 68.

59. Recently, feminist Chicanas have been reclaiming Doña Marina, describing her as a remarkable woman who created new possibilities out of slavery, death, and destruction, but the labels La Malinche and the related stigmatized female, *la chingada*, continue to be hurled at vocal women of Mexican descent in efforts to keep them quiet. See Adelaida R. Del Castillo, "Malintzin Tenépal: A Preliminary Look into a New Perspective," in *Essays on la Mujer*, ed. Rosaura Sánchez and Rosa Martínez Cruz (Los Angeles: University of California, Chicano Studies Center Publications, 1977), 124–49.

60. See Anzaldúa, *Borderlands*, 61; Herrera-Sobek, *The Mexican Corrido*, xix, 84, 92–93.

61. Although similar struggles took place in all major farm working regions, the battles between farm workers and growers in California can be historically traced to María Elena's first exposure to the farm worker movement. In 1903 Japanese and Mexican workers cooperated in the Oxnard Strike in California.

Then, in 1933, workers of Mexican heritage composed ninety-five percent of the twelve to twenty thousand strikers rebelling in the San Joaquin Valley Cotton Strikes. The strikers won partial wage increases and gained organizing experience that can be traced to the United Farm Workers and María Elena's own resistance. For more details, see Vicki L. Ruiz, *Cannery Women/Cannery Lives: Mexican Women, Unionization, and the California Food Processing Industry, 1930–1950* (Albuquerque: University of New Mexico Press, 1987), 49–50. Also see Devra Anne Weber, "Mexican Women On Strike: Memory, History and Oral Narratives," in *Between Borders,* ed. Adelaida R. Castillo, 175–200. Weber's article both highlights the importance of women to the events of 1933 and explores the manner in which a particular woman's memory ranks significant group values and actions.

62. See Ruiz, *Canning Women,* for a complete history of UCPAWA.

63. J. Craig Jenkins, *The Politics of Insurgency: The Farm Worker Movement in the 1960s* (New York: Columbia University Press, 1985), x, and Rodolfo Acuña, *Occupied America: A History of Chicanos,* 2d ed. (New York: Harper and Row, 1981), 268–69.

64. The farm workers framed their religious vision in terms used by the black civil rights movement and the developing liberation theology of Latin America, emphasizing social justice and the Exodus story of the Hebrew people's journey from slavery to freedom. See also Gustavo Gutierrez, *A Theology of Liberation: Liberation, Politics, and Salvation* (Maryknoll, New York: Orbis, 1973) and Vincent Harding, *There Is a River: The Black Struggle for Freedom in America* (New York: Vintage, 1981). Liberal churches, and the National Farm Worker Ministry under the National Council of Churches, provided psychological and financial backing to the crusade. Jenkins describes the Migrant Ministry's change from a somewhat charitable organization to a group supportive of political demands (*Politics of Insurgency,* 137–38).

65. See Acuña, *Occupied America,* 271–75.

66. Ibid., 278–79.

67. See the pamphlet, "For Justice: Farm Labor Organizing Committee," published by FLOC, 714 1/2 S. St. Clair St., Toledo, OH, 43609.

68. Acuña, *Occupied America,* 284–87 and Maril, *Poorest of Americans,* 46, 100–101.

69. Laura Friar, Director of Friendship of Women (a Brownsville shelter for victims of family violence), personal interview, July 31, 1990. Brownsville, Texas.

70. See Ruiz, *Cannery Women/Cannery Lives;* Lauri Coyle, Gail Hershatters, and Emily Honig, "Women at Farah: An Unfinished Story," 117–44 and Douglas Monroy, "La Costura en Los Angeles, 1933–1939: The ILGWU and the Politics of Domination," 171–80, both in *Mexican Women in the United States: Struggles Past and Present,* ed. Magdalena Mora and Adelaida R. Castillo (Los Angeles: Chicano Studies Research Center Publications, University of California, Occasional Paper No. 2, 1980); Acuña, 280; and

the condescending article by George Green, "ILGWU in Texas, 1930–1970," *Journal of Mexican American History* 1 (1973): 144–69.

71. Skits and plays had been used to rally workers in many other union-organizing settings, although María Elena was unaware of that practice. Also unknown to María Elena, Luis Valdez, a child of migrant workers, developed what he called "El Teatro Campesino," a farm workers' theater, as part of UFW organizing efforts in 1965. For more information, see Theodore J. Shank, "El Teatro Campesino: The Farmworkers' Theater," in *Theatre for Working-Class Audiences in the United States, 1830–1980*, ed. Bruce A. McConachie and Daniel Friedman (Westport, Conn. and London: Greenwood Press, 1983), 185–95.

72. As for the UFW, in a 1974 interview, Dolores Huerta discussed the ambivalent and sometimes contradictory attitudes towards women as leaders within the farm worker movement:

I really believe what the feminists stand for. There is an undercurrent of discrimination against women in our own organization, even though César goes out of his way to see that women have leadership positions. César always felt strongly about women in the movement. This time, no married man went out on the boycott unless he took his wife. We find day care in the cities so the women can be on the picket line with the men. It's a great chance for participation. Of course we take it for granted now that women will want to be as involved as men. But in the beginning, at the first meetings, there were only men. And a certain discrimination still exists. César—and other men—treat us differently. César's stricter with the women, he demands more of us. But the more I think of it, the more I'm convinced that the women have gotten stronger because he expects so much of us. You could even say it's gotten lopsided . . . women are stronger than men.

Barbara Baer and Glenna Matthews, "The Women of the Boycott," *Nation*, February 23, 1974, quoted in *America's Working Women: A Documentary History—1600 to the Present*, ed. Rosalyn Baxandall, Linda Gordon, Susan Reverby (New York: Vintage Books, 1976), 366.

73. Sara Evans, "Black Power—Catalyst for Feminism," in *Personal Politics: The Roots of Women's Liberation in the Civil Rights Movement and the New Left* (New York: Vintage Books, 1979), 83–101; Ilene J. Philipson and Karen V. Hansen, eds., "Women, Class, and the Feminist Imagination: An Introduction," in *Women, Class, and the Feminist Imagination: A Socialist-Feminist Reader* (Philadelphia: Temple University Press, 1990), 4–12; and Jensen and Davidson, *Women Needleworkers*, xviii–xix.

74. Patricia Zavella, *Women's Work*, 9.

75. See personal correspondence, January 21, 1990.

76. See Alma M. Garcia, "The Development of Chicana Feminist Discourse, 1970–1980," in *Unequal Sisters: A Multi-Cultural Reader in U.S. Women's*

History, ed. Ellen Carol DuBois and Vicki L. Ruiz (New York and London: Routledge, 1990), 418–31; and Anzaldúa, *Borderlands.*

77. González, "Chicanas," 72.

78. Zavella, *Women's Work,* 13.

79. Lindborg and Ovando, *Five Mexican-American Women in Transition,* 17.

80. For other examples of males from varying ethnic groups using violence towards women as a means of communicating with each other, see Peggy Reeves Sanday, *Fraternity Gang Rape: Sex, Brotherhood, and Privilege on Campus* (New York and London: New York University Press, 1990) and Ann Whitehead, "Sexual Antagonism in Herefordshire," in *Dependence and Exploitation in Work and Marriage,* ed. Diana Leonard Barker and Sheila Allen (London: Longman, 1976), 168–203; and details of the 1991 so-called Tailhook Scandal in which several dozen Navy officers at a convention sexually assaulted Navy women. See *Newsweek,* August 10, 1992, 30–36.

81. Resistance is defined as active or passive opposition to some oppressive situation. It can include such actions as the French military resistance during World War II, the African American civil rights movement, or the quiet scheming of a poor mother trying to save enough money to send her daughter to high school. For an excellent discussion of a variety of women's types of resistance and for a work important to my thinking, see Bettina Aptheker, *Tapestries of Life: Women's Work, Women's Consciousness, and the Meaning of Daily Experience* (Amherst: University of Massachusetts Press, 1989).

82. Audre Lorde, *Sister/Outsider: Essays and Speeches* (Trumansburg, New York: The Crossing Press, 1984), 37.

83. I draw upon insights from African American history, the feminist movement, fifteen years of work on life histories, and the ideas of Michael Frisch, *A Shared Authority: Essays on the Craft and Meaning of Oral and Public History* (Albany: State University of New York Press, 1990), xxii–xxiii.

84. See Buss, *Dignity,* 245–81.

85. For an understanding of sterilization among poor women and Mexican American women, see Adelaida R. Del Castillo, "Sterilization: An Overview," in Magdalena Mora, *Mexican Women in the United States,* 65–91.

86. For more details about the theory and the complexities of compiling life histories, see Susan N. G. Geiger, "Women's Life Histories: Method and Content," *Signs: Journal of Women in Culture and Society* 11, no. 2 (Winter 1986), 334–51; the Personal Narratives Group, eds., *Interpreting Women's Lives: Feminist Theory and Personal Narratives* (Bloomington and Indianapolis: Indiana University Press, 1989); and Sherman Berger Gluck and Daphne Patai, eds., *Women's Words: The Feminist Practice of Oral History* (New York and London: Routledge, 1991).

PART ONE

The Making of a Farm Worker Woman

Prologue: Birth of a Metaphor

When I was a little girl, and we were working in Portage, Ohio, I remember that they had found workers stealing food from the *comisario*. These people were stealing because they didn't have food. We didn't have food either, but my father was always against that. He always taught us not to take nothing. Still, Daddy was very upset because they were in trouble, and he knew that it was not their fault. For some reason the grower didn't pay the people, and the people were in need of food, so that's why they stole it.

It was raining real hard. I was outside at the water pump getting water when I saw Daddy go into the woods. He was very upset and he was cursing and saying things, and he was hollering at God. I followed him. I hid behind a tree. I was scared and didn't know what was going on.

Then he was crying, and he was cursing God. He was saying, "Dammit, why? If we go and do our work, why do we always have crumbs?" So he just cursed God. He said, "Damn you, God." And he shook his fist at the sky. When he did it, there was lightning and thunder, a *centella*, lightning that goes around in a circle.

And I went, "Oh, my God!" I didn't know what was happening. I was so frightened, I ran back home before he discovered me because I would be in a lot of trouble.

Even though we wouldn't go to church, every night my father would read part of the Bible to us. We just had one room, one little shack, and it was a very special thing to be all together. That night, he came home, and we all sat as usual, and I asked him, "Well, are you going to read to us?"

He took the Bible and opened and looked at it. I asked him again, "Are you going to read?"

"No," he said. "God is dead." And he closed the Bible.

I went to my bunk bed. The beds were made out of hay, where you put straw and hay in a canvas bag; they were not real mattresses. We would pick cotton, and the beds were what you put the cotton into, like a big, long bag. It was real stormy, and I didn't sleep. Finally, the storm went away, then everything was pitch dark.

I kept wondering whether everything was going to be there in the morning since God was dead, since Daddy had made God die. Because, you see, all the plants and the flowers and the vegetation outside represented God. That's the way my father and my grandma and all those thought, that God represented all of Mother Nature—the sun, the sky. My grandmother had taught me that when I had blisters in my hands, all I had to do in the morning before I started to work was let the rays of the sunshine touch the palm of my hands, and God would heal them. And I kept thinking, everything's going to be gone, how awful! Now we've had it. Now what are we going to do? I was in anguish and so afraid all night.

But in the morning, when I saw the rays of the sunshine and the plants and tomatoes, I rejoiced. I said, "No, God's still here. God just died for my daddy." And he did, I guess, because Dad never again believed.

And I wrote that into a poem. I was such a small child, but I wrote it because I didn't have any other way of expressing, and I always did that. The poem was something like, "Daddy got mad." Like a child would write. "Daddy got mad. God died. Daddy caused the Crack in the Sky."

Later on, as I grew up, I saved the poem, and I would go to it and remember and cry sometimes, because of my dad. Every time Dad would mistreat us, I'd go back there and see it. Finally I wrote it into my final poem. I think it's a beautiful poem because it really happened.

The White Crack in the Sky

When Daddy raised his tight fist up in anger,
　　there was a terrible storm.
I thought he caused the thunder,
　　and the white crack in the sky.
And as I stood in helpless terror,
　　I saw my Daddy cry.

And to this day, I can't forget,
    he called on God and said,
"God! If it's true that you are God,
    Why can't you hear my prayer?
Why, if we toil this sacred land
    And plant our hearts in you
All we receive are crumbs of bread
    And plagues of misery too?"
That night, my Daddy closed
    Our old and worn-out Bible,
    And told us God was dead—
Then winter came, but hunger hit us harder,
    And dear Mom only wept.
And I cried all that winter.
    Each night, I laid in my straw bed,
I cried, but not for food,
    And not for shelter either.
I cried because I thought
    that God was surely dead.
The years have passed, and Dad has aged,
    And Mom looks tired now.
And as I toil the fields and cry,
    I pray my children never see me raise
My tight fist up in anger,
    to cause a white crack in the sky.

CHAPTER ONE

A Child of Promise

> My Grandmother taught me that the fields was a place of worship where
> we could sing and rejoice and also where we could cry out our anger at
> God and nobody would care.
>
> My grandmother would tell me we were Farm worker flowers and
> she would call me "My Dandelion" because she'd say we were like Dandeli-
> ons, that the wind would blow us into the drifting winds and we'd go all
> different directions and go land somewhere, only to start all over again.
>
> —Diary, July 20, 1984

I learned a lot about beauty from my grandma, my father's mother. My grandma would identify God in a drop of rain, in a drop of dew, in a little butterfly, in so many ways. She was the one who would tell me about the dandelions, and I would look at them and see they were like little feathers. She was very knowledgeable about herbs and plants and knew a lot about healing, about medicines. But I guess a lot of people in those days knew about home remedies, more than nowadays.

I don't know much about my grandma's background. All I know is that my grandfather would tell me she was an Indian woman and that when he met her, she was thirteen years old and couldn't speak any English and didn't know any Spanish at all. I think she was wandering on this side of the border, in the United States. Her people were bootleggers, so I guess that's the reason my grandpa would stop talking there.

Later, my family told me that she was either a Yaqui or Tarahumara or Tarascan woman. I don't know, but if we went down to the bridge that crosses the Rio Grande from Brownsville, Texas, into Mexico, I know there would be an Indian woman sitting on it that looks like my grandma. They all have the long hair, and it's in a braid, and the color of the skin is the same as my grandma's. That's the way my grandma looked, but she didn't dress like them.

She was dark and tiny, and my grandpa, he was an Anglo from Kentucky from a big, poor, hillbilly family, he was a very tall man with real blond hair and one blue eye and one green eye. In the blue eye, his eye pupil was elongated, so he looked like he had one cat's eye. He claimed he could see more and through and farther than most of the human race with that eye. Anyway, my granddaddy was much, much bigger than my grandma. I don't really remember him being a violent man, but I do remember them having arguments because of his drinking. He would drink all of the time, and my father would get mad with him. My father used to say that my grandpa was mean, so maybe there was some wife and child abuse.

My grandma had three or four sons that lived, but no daughters. I understand from my grandpa, and I don't know whether this was bragging or not, that she had three sets of twins and that she had one birth of four babies, but I think she lost them all. I understand she lost the four babies because of a great fight that she and my grandpa had. I guess the fight must have had something to do with drinking, 'cause I think they had a party and then got into a fight. The reason I remember is because I heard her say one time, "I was almost going to have the three wise men and one daughter." She was going to name the boys Gaspar, Baltazar, and a name I can't remember, and she was going to name the girl Mary Magdalene. But I think after that fight she must have miscarried. I know that when my father was very young, about seven or eight years old, he used to tramp the trains; he'd take off and roam, so something bad must have happened at home.

My mother's father would tell us stories, that he was an *Indiochichimeca,* and you could tell he was an Indian guy. He came from the state of Michoacan in Mexico, but my mom, she just looks like a Texas woman to me. Her mother had died from a hemorrhage when she was eight years old, and she was about fifteen years old when my daddy found her at a *charreada,* that's a Mexican celebration in Texas. I guess my mom didn't have much hair because she had sores on her head, and they had cut her hair off. So she was wearing a scarf, but she was pretty.

She was with an aunt, and she suffered a lot. That's what she tells us.

They'd get her up around 3:30 in the morning to start breakfast and everything, tortillas, and they were used to having cupcakes and things like that besides breakfast. She didn't go to school, I guess maybe to the third grade.

So my daddy met her and he asked her to marry him, and he took her to my grandma's house. Grandma didn't have any daughters, so she was thrilled. So there was some love there then, for my mother. My grandmother was like a mother to her.

Sometimes my grandmother would tell me, "You're not an *americana*, you're a Mexican. You were born in Matamoros, close to the sea. A *comadre*, a *partera*, was with your mother when you were born, and a scorpion fell on you and stung you and you made your first cry." But Mom says that Grandma must have been sick or joking because I was not born there. Either way, I was born on March 22, 1941, and when I was born, my grandmother loved me, and I loved my grandma. I wanted to be with her all the time, but I couldn't.

My mom must have been just sixteen when I was born, and she said she had a hard time with me. She says that I was a terrible kid when I was little, that I cried and was puny. She says that my dad used to take me out and walk me so I'd quiet down. I have images of when I was a baby, looking at the moon and the stars and just going to sleep. Mom says I walked when I was seven or eight months old, but I also cried and cried and wanted titty all the time.

I remember things from way back at a very early age. There used to be a water fountain in the plaza, and it had lots of water going up in many different colors. I remember being carried in my father's arms around it and him talking about the stars. I'd just stare and stare at the stars until I would go to sleep. I must have been very tiny.

My grandmother loved me very, very much. She used to love to dress me in red. Red was her favorite color, and she loved glittery things. She'd take me with her when she and my grandpa would go drinking. I remember this big, huge place, like a big warehouse, with a railroad track on this side, and the warehouse next to it, about thirty feet away from the railroad track. Up on top it was like a regular working place, but downstairs there was a basement, very concealed and very secret. People would go in there and drink. I remember my grandparents sitting me up on the counter and them drinking.

But when I was still very little, my daddy had to go to the service, right about the start of World War II. My younger brother and I were alone with my mommy in a house, and then I remember Daddy coming home all dressed up in his Navy suit. That was a very happy occasion, then he had to go again, and when he came back he was a different person. He'd been in the war and changed. Our problems started real bad at that time. We didn't have enough food and the winters were bad, and in the winter, we shared our house with lots of other folks, especially relatives.

I guess Daddy was very young when he joined the Navy. He was more like on his own since he was a little kid, but he was very intelligent. He says he learned to read English and Spanish from an encyclopedia he'd found in the garbage behind a store when he was eight, and it was from other books they threw out that he got his education. Anyway, he'd talk about politics and religion and other countries and geographical areas, and I used to listen to him and admire him, how much he knew about everything from the sea to the sky to the land, the vegetation. He'd talk to just about any person, and to me, that was very impressive.

But my dad went through some terrible things in the war. I know once they were on a big ship, and he was radio operator in communications. He said that all of a sudden, the bombs hit the ship. By the time he got to the deck, Navy men were running all over. He saw many of the guys, including his best friend, burn alive. He said he tried to help his friend, but it was too late. He says the young man managed to say, "Go see my wife and my mother," but he was all in flames. My daddy couldn't do anything. He burnt himself through the process of trying to help him but he couldn't. Also, he looked around in the water, and it was full of flames. I don't know how he escaped, but he was one of the ones that was alive. It was in the bombing of Pearl Harbor.

The last time he came out of the service, he was like a total stranger. I think it must have been real hard on my mother because they were so young, both of them. My daddy became cruel, especially to Mom. I can't say he was like that all the time. In many ways, he was a great daddy because he never quit worrying about food, and he was a provider, a hard-working man, and there were so many of us to take care of. I just guess when people suffer a lot and go through horrible things, it changes people. It can make you very bitter and a very mean person, or it can make you understanding so you try to help other people who have been in bad situations.

My father was totally against my mom drinking or using birth control, and he'd tell her, "If you dare, you'll be in trouble," and, "If I ever find out that you take anything for birth control, you're going to pay for it. You're going to be sorry." Later I understood more of the pressures he felt. So my mother had altogether sixteen kids. And there was another girl, by my father and another woman. I was the oldest and worried all the time about food.

When I was very little I'd go with my daddy and mom to the water port, and the big boats that carry shrimp would come to the docks. We used to go just about every day, probably before I was old enough to go to school. They'd have to put a big wooden box for me to stand on, and they taught me how to take the head off the shrimp. The head would go to the bucket, the body would go out to the stream of water. I'd do this mostly during the night. This way I could help provide food.

'Cause Mom kept having kids all the time, I'd have to take care of them. I'd do the dish washing, washing clothes, cleaning house, and taking care of children, and then going to school when I was old enough. My brother who was next was the same. All the oldest ones had to go through the same thing. And all the time we'd raid the garbage cans in the neighborhoods and just pick up anything we could.

Dad never wanted us to get government help for food. He's never allowed Mom to take food stamps, but my mom, she has done it behind his back. He never allowed us to go ask for a can of tomato or an onion or nothing, even if we didn't have enough.

That's one thing I'll say about my father. He never let us steal. He never let us do anything that was at all dishonest. In that way, he was a very good model.

I think I was very, very curious as a child because I studied a lot of things. I studied the clouds, and when it would rain, I'd say, "What makes it fall?" and, "Why does it feel wet?" I'd climb on the roof of our home to just gaze at things. But I also think that what makes a child do that is being neglected, because I felt very neglected, at least by my parents. But my grandma gave me something very precious because she loved me and she cared, and I stayed with her a lot.

I don't remember watching my grandma pick up a beer after I was about four years old. My mom says that she totally quit drinking. The only thing I remember doing was rolling up cigarettes for her. She'd say, "Taste it and let me know if it's good."

So every time I'd roll up a cigarette I'd say, "Yep, it's good,

Grandma."

I was my grandma's only love. She didn't reject the other kids, but it was obvious that I was her favorite grandchild. Because she'd only had sons, my mother was like her daughter, so that when I was born, I could feel that I was loved a lot.

When I take care of my granddaughters and comb their hair and caress them, I can see the same smile on their faces that I used to have. My mom says that I'm crazy, that I couldn't remember things about my grandma so well, but my mother wasn't as close to her as I was.

Every day Grandma would wash my hair and her hair, then she would braid my hair, and she would braid her hair into a long, long braid. Grandma reminded me of God.

Dear Mother God,
    I love you so much, you are so many things, beautiful *esencias* for me . . . and your mild gentle breeze feels like my Grandma's soft fingers softly drying my long hair when I was a child . . .
    —Diary, March 11, 1989

I learned English at home from my grandparents because my Anglo grandfather didn't make it a point of talking Spanish. He talked English, and my grandmother learned it, but her English was very chopped up, worse than my mom's and worse than mine. My grandpa taught me, and, also, my uncle, my dad's brother, he'd teach me Spanish and English when I was very little, maybe three or four. My dad talked more English than my mom did, and my dad sang in English; rarely did my mom sing in English, but when they talked to each other, it usually was in Spanish.

After she quit going to the tavern, my grandma was just a woman who stayed to herself. I never remember seeing anyone coming around to see her or her visiting anybody except for one old lady, but I don't think she was lonely. She certainly seemed very happy and was singing all the time.

I have a lot of beautiful memories with her, a lot of things we shared together, even though some things I was too young to understand. She was very fond of plants. Every day she'd go by the railroad tracks and pick wild flowers, *altamisa,* which is very fragrant, and a lot of other wild flowers that smell good. She would burn them or put them in water, like with rose petals and gardenias and jasmine. People would see her do things like this, and I guess they must have thought that she was a witch. Maybe she was alone because nobody could understand her way of living. She'd wash her floors with flower water and then wash my body and wash her hair with *amole,* which is a root, and she'd make colors for her face from the flowers. Whenever people see me doing things like that, they think I'm weird too. My mom and my father still think I'm strange.

My grandma loved to sing all the time. I guess when she'd sing, it was praying. She mentioned the word *terra,* probably like you and I would say *tierra,* and I think she meant the earth. She was very close to the earth and Mother Nature. She taught me that as Mother Nature does for us, we do for Mother Nature. We work together. She'd say, "Look at the bees," as they would go to the flowers and collect the pollen or the nectar. "Mother Nature at work," she'd say.

We'd lay down on the ground among all her flowers in her yard, and she'd say, "Shhh, be quiet. I want you to see something. They're working together—the plants and the bee—and they create something beautiful, *mi'ja,* they create honey."

At that time, it was just beautiful for me to see the bees and the flowers, but later on, as I watched the children work in the fields, I remembered that, and I thought, people and Mother Nature at work, working in harmony, creating something good. My grandma would actually talk to the flowers, and she'd show me things in response to what she was doing. Sometimes, about three o'clock in the morning, she'd get me up, and she'd say, "It's time to get up. I'm going to offer the mesquite pods to God." And we'd gather the mesquite pods that would fall from the trees around here, and, especially if the moon was full, she would make a big celebration. Oh, it was beautiful!

Then she'd dance and sing in a language I didn't understand, but she'd be singing and praying to the moon and waving her arms. She would make signs like when you're caressing a child. It was like Grandma would touch the stars and the moon and the flowers and praise God and thank God for everything. Then she'd unfold, like a flower, when she was singing at night. I thought it was beautiful, and I could never forget it.

A lot of people still remember what she'd do, and they would say, "She's a witch! She's a witch!" And people didn't come around her 'cause they thought she was dangerous or crazy, especially when they saw her at that hour, throwing the mesquites in the fire. But she was so, so beautiful, and the fire really brought nice odors.

It was just something wonderful the way she would touch the flowers, I mean she just loved plants. During the days, she'd tell me, "This one is sad. This one is dancing. This one is crying." She'd say, "The palm trees are so beautiful because they are the tallest ones. They're trying to reach the sky, to be close to God, but they can't." And she would tell me that the palm trees would waltz, and she'd say, "They can talk, and they'll show you that they're sad."

When she'd gather the flowers, for every flower she cut, she'd ask its permission, especially the dandelions. She loved the dandelions. And she sang constantly. She'd sing beautiful songs in, I don't think it was another language, but in different words, words that I couldn't understand, especially when she was singing and praying to the moon and weaving her arms.

I've done it sometimes myself at night, and some people think I'm crazy or a witch, but maybe all people dance like that, when you're alone sometime. You listen to music and you start moving. But for her, it was her own music. She'd sing so much, especially sing and dance when the moon was real big and the sky was so beautiful. She'd be out there, and I'd be with her.

I remember her little one-room house. She had a chimney with a fireplace, the old kind where you put wood inside of it and it's got like a skillet on top of it. You can put a coffee kettle on it or make tortillas, cook over it. There was only one bed in the room, which was supposed to be the living room and also where they slept.

In one corner, she had her firewood, and in the other corner, she had a big altar; maybe half the room was an altar. She had virgins and saints all over. She had Our Lady of San Juan and Our Lady of Guadalupe. She had San Martín de Porres. I think she had grass and water, like a little flower vase. And she had a big angel, a guardian angel, a beautiful picture. I think it must have been kind of old, from way back, because I've never seen another one like it. The angel's arms were spread out, and she was guarding two children. It was the largest picture and the most adored.

And she also kept marbles on the altar. I could see her pick the marbles up off the floor in the morning and set them back up there. She told me not to play with the marbles, and I obeyed her.

One time I asked her, "Why do you do that?"

She says, "I'm going to show you why." And I don't know whether I dreamed this or whether it really happened.

58   Forged under the Sun / Forjada bajo el sol

That night, she woke me up and said, "Don't be frightened, but I need to show you something very special."

And I said, "Yeah."

She whispered, "They're playing with the marbles. Look."

I remember sitting in the bed with her, and the kids had come down out of the guardian angel picture and were playing with the marbles.

Then she told me, "That is why I have the marbles, and you're never to touch them. And if you hear noises, it's them. You must not disturb them." Isn't that something? Sometimes I want to believe it. Because I saw it, I know I did. I wonder, were those things created by my imagination? Is it possible that two persons can have the same vision at the same time?

My grandmother would be very upset with my father every time he came to take me away from her. My mom would tell my daddy to go get me from her. I imagine my mom must have been afraid to make my grandma angry, so my daddy would come and get me. As soon as I saw my father coming, I'd tell my grandma, "Here he comes! I'm going to hide under the bed, and you tell him I'm not here."

And my grandma tried, but, of course, I couldn't fool him. I had to be around there someplace. He'd say, "You have to come because your mother needs you at home." That would be their excuse. I'd climb between my grandma's legs and grab her and cry and go under the bed, but, of course, she couldn't retain me by force, and I cried but I couldn't do anything.

I don't remember that my grandma ever knew that my dad was hurting me. The only time I remember my grandma very, very upset with them was when there was a real bad freeze. There was ice all over Brownsville, on the ground and the trees, like with Jack Frost. It was beautiful, but I remember that we had an old kerosene stove, and there were a lot of us in there, and Mom needed something, probably food or kerosene.

I must not have had shoes because they forced me to walk several blocks barefooted on the ice to my grandmother's house to get something, and when I got there, I couldn't feel my feet. It was real bad. I guess I had frostbite. That time, my grandmother was very mad at them for sending me over like that. I guess there was nobody else to go, so they had to send me. Being the oldest is always really hard because you have to take over a lot of responsibilities. My grandma did have a very strong temper, and one day she also got upset 'cause I was selling in the streets. I guess she thought it was bad for me out there.

I can remember my grandma fighting back with my grandpa once. My mother never fought back with my dad, but my grandma did. My grandpa would come home drunk. He was a very big man and she was a very tiny woman, and one day he was being pretty rough, pretty violent. He knocked the door down with one blow, and I guess she didn't know what to do. She grabbed the bottle he was drinking, the tequila, and she hit him on the head. He fell down—and slept till the next day. I guess she was worried that she'd hurt him, 'cause I remember her bending over him and checking. She never let him hurt her or intimidate her when I was there. So I didn't see him beat her up or anything bad.

There was a lady who lived with us at my mom's and dad's, her name was Ana, and she's still alive. This lady was such a wonderful person. She helped to provide a lot. She lost her husband and two kids in Mexico and she was all alone. She was a prostitute, but when I was real young, I didn't know it. I guess she went with men to have food, because as I grew older I realized that all she did was bring us food. Also, she'd go with my brother José and me to garbage cans, and we'd pick up a whole bunch of stuff, sometimes vegetables, fruit, clothes, and about everything that we could get. Mom never worried about her. She was real good and attached to us.

Ana says that the first time she saw me, I had a little bucket of tomatoes that I'd gone to scavenge from the warehouse. She called me the Blond One, *Güerita*, 'cause my hair used to be real light when I was little, it bleached in the sun.

I remember that when I was a little girl, she took me out to a place where there was water, but I'm not sure whether it was a *resaca* or part of the sea. There were pillars, and there was a little bridge, and we went with whoever was her boyfriend. We sat on the rocks, and I guess I began to feel so inspirational. I was inspired by what I was seeing, and I couldn't put it together—that the pillars and the water and the pebbles meant a lot to me.

Ana just kept saying, "What are you trying to tell me, Güerita?"

And I just couldn't ever put it together in words, words saying that I was very impressed. I'd say, "The sky. Look at the sky and the pillars and the water."

And she just laughed and laughed, and then she came home and told Mom, "La Güerita m'estaba tratando de decir una historia y nunca le entendí, Celia." The Blond One tried to tell me a story, and I could never understand her, Celia. That's my mom's name, Celia.

There are some happy memories from when we were little. When we used to have a real bad storm with a whole lot of water in the alley, all the kids in the neighborhood would smooth out the mud so we could slide around and around and around. The more the water sank into the mud, the more fun we had, with all the kids around the neighborhood scream-ing and crying and making noise. Then, as the mud dried, we made little horses and cows out of clay.

I used to love watching storms. I'd sit outside and watch the light-ning, and I'd sleep real peacefully with all the raindrops on the roof. When it was raining, I imagined that the raindrops on the roofs were little soldiers, marching, or lots of people in a parade. After the rain comes the other sounds, the musical sounds of the crickets and the frogs, and then everything starts again. It's beautiful, the sounds of Mother Nature.

I remember rainbows. Oh God, one of my favorite pastimes was to see the rainbows, and I used to listen to the stories of the leprechauns and the pot of gold. I imagined I could climb up that rainbow and find that pot of gold. Then, there was the song, "Somewhere over the rainbow, way up high." Oh, when I was sad, I used to sing that song all the time. "There's a land that I heard of, once in a lullaby."

I used to wish and dream that one day I'd cross the rainbow, and I used to even imagine the whole valley down below, a land where every-thing was so good and beautiful. I don't remember people waiting for me on the other side, I just remember the peaceful valley, filled with canyons and trees and colors. When I was sad, I used to sing that song all the time. There was another song that I even sang to my kids to put them to sleep. "Hush little baby, don't say a word. Mama's going to sing you a lullaby." I'd make up my own words.

My father used to tell us stories. There was a story he started to tell us, "The One Thousand and One Nights." But it was so complicated, I just remember that it was about a lady that had to keep the kids happy in order that she wouldn't get killed. I think my daddy wasn't really reading it to us as a fairy tale story, I think he was reading it to himself and maybe to Mom. And, of course, the Bible stories that he'd tell us.

My grandpa, my grandfather on my mother's side, the Indian, would tell us stories and sing us songs about the Mexican Revolution. He'd been a bracero and was very, very patriotic. And he would sing us songs, *corridos,* about women in the revolution. Songs about La Adelita and about La Valentina. La Chamuscada. Luzelena. There's more. Those are revolutionary songs.

According to the stories I heard about those women, they were leader women, not just followers and the ones who were cooking tortillas. See, there were a whole bunch of revolutionary women. A lot of them were just following their man and just cooking and having kids along the way, but there were some women in leadership positions, very few, but they were there. These leaders were ordinary women, not like wives of the politicians, brave women that had fought for their people, and my grandfather would tell their stories.

Sometimes he would sing the songs and say, "Huh! La Valentina did this, and La Valentina did that!" La Chamuscada was another story. Grandpa told us about how this girl, this woman, was with her father, and they were fighting together, and the soldiers killed her father and then she took over. It was like every guy would look up to those women and kind of praise them and put them in a very special place because they were brave enough to fight for their people and their country. So I had those songs and stories.

And when we were migrants, we used to hear that there were little people living out there in the woods called leprechauns, elves, and I really believed it. I imagined they were just like us, but little, little people. I used to think that they could swing on the ferns and the leaves and come down the river on leaves, and I thought, wow, I wish I was one of them.

Of course, we also heard stories that scared us. My mom, my grandma, and other people around me always were talking about La Llorona [the Weeping Woman], about how she was like a spirit woman who had [drowned] her kids and was out to steal the souls of other children. When I was a little girl, and we wouldn't go to sleep, they would say, "¡Duérmete, porque si no, sale La Llorona!" "Go to sleep unless you want the Llorona to come out and take you!" And we'd wiggle down in bed and close our eyes real tight.

Sometimes we were told, "Don't go out at night when it's raining. She'll come after you, any of you kids that are wandering in the street." Everywhere there was water, they'd make the sign of the cross so that she wouldn't come to that area, and it kept us scared. Also, when a baby was born but not baptized, it was against our beliefs to cross any water with the child because the baby's soul would be taken, not especially by the Llorona, but it would die. So we paid close attention.

But I never stayed too scared or too unhappy for real long. I'd start thinking about something else or doing other things. I'd use sticks and rocks and try to make the stars, try to copy the way the stars were in the sky. I'd use little sticks to connect them and figure out where there was some animal.

Also, I really loved my hat, and it was so worthless. I adored my blue straw hat 'cause I could put my braids up and mask, disguise myself, I could cover my face whenever I didn't want to see something or I didn't want somebody to see me. Whenever somebody was looking at me real weird, I'd pull my hat down. I even refused to take it off in school.

We used to walk about two miles to school, and sometimes I'd kick rocks and cans and stop and listen to the birds, just look at the *resacas,* the turtles that were in the *resacas,* and look at the flowers and grab mesquites, the fruit from the trees. Or I'd just take a twig and cut the leaves off it.

I didn't carry hardly any books with me, and as I grew older, I liked some boys, especially the kind of boys that I used to hang around with when I was selling in the streets, but I was always on the lookout for my father, because my father followed me several times. He'd made me a map, and if he didn't find me whenever he'd come by that route, I was in big trouble. He wasn't like that with the other girls. The first girl really suffers.

I'd make up my own little songs and complain through my songs. I'd sing a lot in the fields, and I'd try to let my problems out. We had so many problems. All the time we worried about food. All we could think of was, I wonder what we're going to eat tomorrow. I wrote a song about a little girl with those kinds of worries.

. . . Sahila Sahila Oh beautiful Sahila

Your dusty face and your sad brown eyes
give beauty, life, and grace
to the crops in the fields
that you water with tears
in your battle to survive . . .

(undated)

Sometimes, when we were up north working, we'd get rich eggs and milk and cheese and lots of vegetables and fruit, but once we were back in Texas, it was terrible. There was just very little. Sometimes, at the end of the summer, my daddy would have money from all the work we did, and he'd fill a whole wall with food, all kinds of vegetables and everything. My mom and dad would also can. So I remember that we'd all stand back and look at the wall and it was such a beautiful sight. Then when all the food started going and going, oh, it was sad.

After we would get back to Texas from up north, we'd spend our days getting cactus, *nopales*. We would clean them up and take the spines off and sell them in the street. Sometimes we'd sell bananas, sometimes fish, 'cause we caught fish. Different things. My mother would also trade, like clothes for eggs.

When I'd go through garbage cans, I'd think, God, what a beautiful home, and sometimes, as I'd be looking in the cans, little girls would come out of the houses. They'd have pony tails and bows and pretty clothes. It was fun to watch them, but it was something out of my reach.

There were times when the little girls would stand and look at me like, like I was a cat or garbage rat, probably. I just wonder if that was their reaction, like, "How can a child be a garbage scavenger?" There was some times when they'd just stop playing and stare. That would make me uncomfortable, and I'd move on to the next garbage can.

Sometimes grown-up people would come out and yell, "Get out of my garbage! Don't be digging in my garbage!" And I'd just move on. I was chased by dogs plenty of times and would have to take off running.

I especially liked to go through the garbage around Christmastime, when they threw away all the Christmas cards and pretty bows and wrapping paper. I loved to see the Christmas cards, I'd just go to the place in my mind. I'd see a beautiful little church—the lights are on and people are in the wagons in the snow and there's a little sled with a kid pulling it. I'd get lost in the winter scene, or Mother Mary, the birth of Christ, the manger, or the town of Bethlehem. And I loved cards with flowers, Mother's Day cards. I also adored empty bottles of perfume. I collected lots of them, and sometimes I'd find rhinestones and stationery with pretty designs, but the minute I got home, everything with me was put back into our garbage can again.

I remember it was real exciting to find good pieces of food behind grocery stores, especially a lot of lard and intestines. Those we ate. And good strawberries among the bad strawberries, tomatoes, pieces of good onions. It was very exciting to be able to take food home. Cracked watermelons, I'd eat them along the way. Mostly I looked for food, bottles of perfume, and little jars of talcum powder. I'd look for clothes, but I wasn't excited about that. Of course, if there was an old bike or an old chair, I'd take it home.

Sometimes I'd climb all the way inside the garbage cans. Once, a black and white dog bit my leg when I was in a can. You know what I did? I bit him back, real deep, and he let me go.

I'd go with the boys to the warehouses where they packed potatoes or tomatoes. The water would carry the little potatoes out to a big pond of water which flowed to somewhere else. I didn't know it was dangerous, and we'd get under all that equipment which came out of the factory. We'd dig for the new potatoes and fill up our baskets and then go wash the potatoes and sell them or cook them ourselves.

Another thing that I did too was to get on the freight trains and throw pineapples across to the other kids. I was a monkey, really. I was light at jumping and I guess I could smell the pineapples. Also, in the water port there was another section where they brought bananas in. I knew how to ask the workers and persuade the people to give us some. Maybe they just felt sorry for kids like myself. Also, I'd go to the banana boats and get bananas too.

My daddy would take us to the ocean and piers, to the jetties, to the docks to fish. The jetty is all rocks, and you can walk on it and fish from it. Sometimes Daddy would tie ropes to our waists and lower us under the water so we could go under to the rocks and fish oysters with a chisel. We couldn't really swim, but after he'd pull us out of the water, we'd take oysters out of the shell and put them into quarts. Also we'd do a lot of crab fishing. Then we'd sell fish in the streets.

Daddy usually didn't allow us to work the streets, but I was very sneaky, and sometimes he was gone to work. I was always dressed as a little boy on the streets, always. I wore my straw hat with my hair up, and I hung around with boys. Whatever we had, whether it was shoes, clothes, vegetables, or fruits or cactuses, I'd be in the street selling. You meet a lot of people in the streets, and you see and learn a lot of bad things, too. That's one reason I always tried to keep my kids from it, but it was hard to do. You also learn there's another way to survive, too, not just working in the fields, that you can work in the streets, selling. But there's a lot of stealing and other bad things too.

You don't see any girls in the streets, but people couldn't tell the difference with me because I was too little. The first time I smoked was with the Indian girls, when we were working the crops, but I smoked more in the streets, and while some of the boys went to steal bread and food, I'd sit there and wait and take care of the shoe-shine boxes or whatever they were selling, so they could do it. I took my share, too. Also, I learned how to say bad words, and I saw other bad things, like men who'd rub against girls. Sometimes we'd be all crowded on a bus, and I could see that older men would hurt and bother a girl, then they would just sit very innocent like they hadn't done nothing. I learned how to take care of myself in these things, like how to bite.

I dressed like a boy to be safe, but deep down inside me, I was a little girl, and some of the kids in the crowd knew it, so they kind of protected me. The only problem I had was going to the rest room, and when anybody wanted to pee, I had to play dumb.

I worked in the streets to about age nine or ten, when I began to grow into a girl. Also, it got so difficult to get out to the streets when my dad was around. We were very young when we'd hit the alleys and the garbage cans and go to the river front, *la boca del río,* where the river goes into the mouth of the sea. It's hard when you grow up in the streets. I don't know where I got the idea to protect myself, but it helped me.

I loved music, even then, especially a lady singer. At the time I was a little kid, I learned all her tangos, just about every one of them. I guess she would come on the radio every day and that way I picked up all her songs, 'cause I don't remember having any records.

The people would say, "María Elena, María Elena, sing me a tango," and they'd tell me which one, and I'd stand there and sing for them. That was my favorite—tangos, beautiful music. Her songs, they always say a story.

Ana knew that I liked to sing a lot. One day when I was about nine years old, Ana said, "María Elena, why don't we go to the amateur hour in the theater and you sing, and maybe you'll win a loaf of bread." The first time I did that, my legs trembled, I was so scared, but I never gave up, I still sang. I guess I must have been funny that first time, 'cause I won a loaf of bread. The first prize was two bags of groceries and next place was one of groceries and then maybe a five-dollar award and then a loaf of bread.

After that, I liked it and went every time we found a place, like the Mexico Theater in Brownsville where they had an amateur hour every week. I had to sneak out because of Daddy but I managed it. And when I was working in the fields, unless I was sick, I was always singing. A lot of other girls would sing too, sing together. We'd start competing against each other just for the fun of it and start imitating people.

Ay Diosito . . .
Si yo fuera chula, chula, chula, chula, chulaaa . . .
Con el cuerpo de Sirena,
y la cara de muñeca,
con la voz de Lucha Villa . . .

Tara-ran-tan-tan Rica, Rica, Ri-ca-ca
Tara-ran-tan-tan, Chula, Chula, Chi-chi-chi . . .

Ay, God . . .
If I was pretty, pretty, pretty, pretty, pretty . . .
With the figure of a mermaid,
and the face of a doll,
with the voice of Lucha Villa . . .

Tara-ran-tan-tan, Rich, Rich, Rich
Tara-ran-tan-tan, Pretty, Pretty, Pretty . . .

(May 14, 1983)

CHAPTER TWO

Girlhood in the Northern Fields

A slave girl. Yes, thats's right. I was a little farm worker slave girl. How did
I know I was a slave? My mother told me I was a farm worker slave girl
and she told me she too was a farm worker slave woman. I knew she was
right, for no woman could have suffered more or worked more . . .
—Diary, July 26, 1982

Sometimes, when we were home in Brownsville, a truck would come and
pick up all the kids to go work in the fields around here. Then, when we
were still little, my daddy started taking us all up north to work the crops
for the summers. We went to Michigan, Wisconsin, Ohio, Arkansas, Indiana, and as far as Montana. Around Idaho, South Dakota, North Dakota,
we were working the sugar beets and potatoes. I was such a strong girl,
my God, I was strong. I could pick up a basket and the baskets seemed
so big, but I could put one on my shoulder, with one knee on the ground
and the other one bent. I could also pick up a sack of cucumbers for pickles
and a sack of potatoes.

It was exciting sometimes, while we traveled on our way to someplace
new to work in the fields, but when we were working, my God, it was
terrible. Even then, lots of time we didn't have enough to eat, and we'd
have to go to a town and go through the garbage.

The trip north itself was dangerous. We had to travel with such old
cars. Sometimes we'd go with relatives, and it seemed like we were thousands of kids. I mean, it was super-crowded, and migrants have lots of
accidents 'cause their cars are so bad. One time we were in the camp by

Sturgeon Bay, Wisconsin, and, all of a sudden, we heard a loud noise, like you hit something real hard. Everybody started coming out and saying, "What happened? What was that?" Then we started running toward the road.

Oh my God, when we went out there, what a horrible sight! I'll never forget that as long as I live. These people, they were migrants coming to camp, and it was raining and foggy and their car skidded or slid and it slammed into a tree. And the lady, oh my goodness, her breasts were cut almost off and her chest was torn open, and she's going like a little doggy when it's a baby and it goes, "Mmmhh, mmmhhh, mmmhhh!" Just a sound, oh, horrible. The two children were thrown too and laying unconscious, but they weren't torn apart. The car was completely smashed, and one guy was laying on the ground and was awake and he was crying. The other man was cut and his eyes and expression were like his mind was gone, horrible.

I guess I must have been the first one to reach the scene 'cause I was always running. Anyway, the police came and my mom and my dad, and they said, "Hey, get María Elena out of here, and the other children." But I saw the lady. Her eyes were closed but for a while she was making that sound, like trying to cry, then they covered her all up. I didn't understand then but now I know that when they cover a body like they did, it's dead. They put her in the ambulance and the children too and took them away. So there were bad times for many people. You know, my story is not unique. I don't think it's really unusual. People die and their stories die.

When we traveled, we'd stop to rest and try to cook in parks, and the only difference between us and others in the parks was we were dressed like migrants, smelling like migrants. Other than that, we were just doing like any other people do when they go to the park to barbecue or spend some time, but we were doing it to rest. The kids would go around playing, and my father would rest on the bench, and my mom would start cooking. Then the police would come and say, "You can't do this in here. You have to get out. It's a public park."

We'd feel real scared when they were running us away, like when Immigration is following you, like somebody's hunting you down. I couldn't understand why we were kicked out. We were thrown out of just about everywhere, but what really made me feel bad was when we tried to go into a restaurant or a rest room downtown, and we were told, "No, you can't use it." The police would always come and say, "This is a public place, you have to get out, you're not allowed here."

So we'd have to go into a woods to cook. Sometimes we'd spend up to three or four hours so my father could sleep, and during that time, my mom wouldn't sleep, she'd cook with firewood using a big pot. We'd be kindling the fire and making tortillas and cooking beans and fixing rice and potatoes. Then we'd save some beans, and the next stop we'd get to a park, Mom would just heat the beans and tortillas up and give us something quick before the police could come. Lots of the time, we wouldn't do it fast enough. The police would get there and run us off before we could eat, so back again to the woods.

If we were traveling in a truck with lots of others, we'd sleep in it, but if my daddy had a car, we'd stop on the side of the road to sleep. He'd put a canvas on the ground and lay down army blankets all over us kids. We'd keep kind of warm because there were so many of us all together. Because Mom was always pregnant, she slept inside the car with the littlest one, and my father used to sleep on top of the hood to keep an eye on us.

Sometimes, when we'd stop along the road to eat, we'd all be bit by ants, and often when we'd go into the woods, it was super-infested with mosquitos, I mean it was terrible. We wore long shirts, long pants—but, oh, our faces, our hands, our bare feet—and mosquitos could even go through clothes. I used to think they were related to vampires. When we slept, we covered our whole body to keep them away. It was hard breathing like that, but it kept away the mosquitos.

We'd have car problems all of the time, especially with our old tires. We'd spend hours and hours on the side of the road while the men were fixing part of the car or changing tires. I think that my dad carried more tires than kids. The men would work on the cars real hard before we'd take off north, but still, the cars were all dumpy, junk.

We traveled in two cars, with my father, our family, and Ana in one, and my father's brother and his family in another. Believe me, I have no idea how we all managed to get into the car since altogether Mom had sixteen kids.

And it took forever, days and days and days. I remember that sometimes my father would turn around and would plead, "Please be quiet, please let me drive; 'cause if you don't, I'm going to stop the car and let you have it." We were afraid of him, we were very scared, so we minded most of the time, but it was hard, especially when we were trying to sleep. You'd be half asleep, then someone would kick you awake. And the crying, especially from the little ones. They were the ones that made most of the problems.

When we'd travel in the back of the crew leaders' big trucks, the trucks of the guys we called *troqueros,* we'd be crowded in with lots of families. We'd have to sleep in the back of the truck in a very small, crowded position. We'd be sleeping hip to hip with other men, women, children. Every truck I rode in was covered by canvas so we couldn't see out and people along the road wouldn't know we were in there.

It was always hot and dusty and stinky. And we had to go to the bathroom in a bucket inside the truck while traveling. Somebody would put a blanket over our heads for a little privacy. It was very embarrassing, very humiliating. I'll never forget how humiliating it was, totally gross. I don't know who to blame for that. Sometimes people riding in the back of the truck would start banging on the roof of the cab to get the attention of the *troquero,* but sometimes he couldn't stop. Also, everybody had all their daily belongings with them, things from their lifetime—skillets, washtubs, clothing, everything for cooking, bathing, and wearing. We'd stop along the road and just go into the woods to find water, like water in the ditch, so we'd get sick from the water. We'd get a lot of diarrhea, a lot of stomach problems, and a lot of throwing up, and all we'd have on the back of the crowded truck was the bucket.

My baby sister, Esmeralda, got so sick that by the time we got to Frankfurt, Michigan, she was hospitalized, and my mama nearly lost her from dehydration and diarrhea. See, we couldn't stop at a park, and there were no rest areas, no camps. The water we'd find would taste so bad. Esmeralda had started with diarrhea on the road, and it just got worse. I know that the priest came and baptized her, and I think he gave her last rites. He told my parents to be strong, that it looked like they were going to lose the little baby. I remember my mom being very sad, very anguished over it. She told me, "Your little sister is very sick. Please take care of the kids for me." But, finally, she got better.

If it was later in the season and we were driving our own car and sleeping along the road, there would be frost and it'd be cold. My brother was sick for many years, sick in his chest with a chronic cold. His nose was always running.

My little sister Norma had some rare sickness when she was real little and suffered a lot. She was real pale, real skinny, with a big stomach, almost like with worms. We all thought she was going to die, but they took her to the hospital in Galveston, Texas, and she got better. Then, once, when we were working in the fields and she was about four, she ate something that had been in a container, then she ate some of our lunch and went back to the fields. I think she was trying to climb a tree to pick some fruit when she had an attack. She started foaming from the mouth. The doctors said it was food poisoning, but I think that the field was being sprayed and someone left the containers out there. Norma had convulsions after that.

When we drank bad water, then we bent down under the sun, it made us feel like we were going to throw up all over. You feel real feverish when you're working out there in the fields. You may be wearing a hat, but you feel like you've got a high temperature. And the sun and the water combined make your stomach feel so upset, and that can go on for days and days and days. Of course, we wouldn't see a doctor or nothing. We'd just get over it with the medicine Mom had.

We lived in cabins the size of a small room. Sometimes there was bunk beds and some of us slept in the bunk beds with straw mattresses and the rest on boards or the floor. I wouldn't really feel rested the next morning, I'd feel terrible. And I was just a girl, not an old woman! Sometimes we used horse stables, old hay barns, and chicken coops with three walls and then an open place. I remember being just out in the open in Texas when we were working in straw. Usually we cooked outside. We had a tub and we'd burn wood in it. If we had food, we'd come back from the fields and cook tortillas, a pot of beans, coffee, and then meat and potatoes.

There was a lot of scurvy and sores and head lice and the rest. One time my little brother picked up a bad infection. His genitals swelled up real bad, and he was really, really sick. And you couldn't really keep the kids clean, not in the camps. My daddy, wherever we were at, he and some other guys would make a big hole that was especially to burn garbage to keep it cleaner, and he was very strict about being clean. He wanted no flies because of the food and the baby bottles. So my mommy had to work very, very hard to keep us healthy. Daddy, he was constantly keeping us on the ball. "Don't let any flies in." "Wash up before you eat." Food had to be very clean, our utensils, everything. We worked extra hard, but it kept us from getting too sick.

My dad would take us out early in the morning so we could work for a few hours, and as soon as the sun would begin to get real hot, we'd quit working. Then we'd go back, like after two o'clock, and work the evening. This seems to be a system that the people have developed.

There was always danger if you had to stay behind in camp while the others were working in the fields. This lady in Arkansas stayed in the camp, and by the time the people got back, she'd been assaulted and raped. So we knew that if most of the people were going to work, everybody would have to go. Also, we had to be careful with the single guys. Most were good, but you could never tell, especially when they'd get drunk and forget there were families there.

Sometimes we'd work with just our family and sometimes under a crew leader with others. The crew leader wouldn't have to do any work, just see that the work was being done. He'd take the people to the field and back to the camp, and he'd be in the fields checking your work and seeing that you didn't take too much time to go to the woods or to the rest room. He'd keep on the parents so the kids would do the work right and keep up the same pace as the other workers.

The crew leaders would get paid good. They'd get a certain amount per person, then transportation, and they'd get some out of the work you did, part of your earnings. Like for every hamper of tomatoes you'd pick, they'd take a few pennies. They were pretty good to you if you'd keep up, but if you were slow or something they'd push and push and push. It was not likely that they'd get on the kids directly, they'd get on the parents. So the parents put a lot of pressure on the kids.

I remember that sometimes we wouldn't get paid. The crew leader would give us some money every week to go buy what we needed, soap and whatever. Then at the end of the season he'd give us all the money that we earned, but then we'd have to pay him for the transportation, and we'd have to pay him how much we owed for necessities. That didn't leave too much money. That's why my dad, he bought a car for ninety dollars, so we could travel on our own, but still he had very little left when we got home.

I remember overhearing the talking between the ranchero and the workers. It was always the men. Women were not included, and, of course, children had to stand aside and listen. If my mom was pregnant or had just had a baby, the grower would say, "Great, Manny." My dad's name was Manuel. "Another baby. That's good," the grower would say.

"Keep it up. Eat a lot of mayonnaise and onions and give your wife a lot of it too." Then he'd laugh.

Onions and mayonnaise were considered to be something good for the woman to keep on having kids, and the kids were prohibited from eating onions and too much mayonnaise because that was considered to be sexual. The grower would also recommend it to the guys in the camp. He'd say, "Give your wives a lot of mayonnaise and onions." But I was the one who had to carry the load from all of Mama's babies, so I hated mayonnaise and onions because I thought that's what gave Mom all those kids.

The bigger families were better because that way the mom and dad were responsible for their own kids and could have better control and that meant better-quality work, more labor for the grower. When my dad would go talk to a ranchero, Dad would say, "I have seven or eight kids or ten or eleven kids and so many working hands." The ranchero would say, "The bigger, the better." That way the grower wouldn't have to worry about hiring a whole bunch of different people. So we would take a large portion of the *rancho,* the farm, and work it ourselves, and other big families would take other parts. There was also less of a problem in housing, in fights, with drinking, with garbage, and all that. If there had just been single men, some of them might be good workers and some might not, but if you have a mother and father with eight or nine kids, they'd all be desperate to eat, so they'd have to get up in the morning and work. It was true, the greater the number of kids, the greater chance of getting better jobs up north and better living for survival. That's how come Mama had a whole lot of kids. If each kid made five dollars a day, it's not the same as one person or two or three persons making five dollars a day.

And my dad did try to make sure that when my mom was pregnant, she ate good, even though we were so poor. Daddy would bring her liver, and I could see that my mom would sit down to eat. But other pregnant women didn't look as if they'd eaten that good.

I could see the ladies, all pregnant, working in the fields, doing stoop labor or whatever, but they'd try to let up on the work a little when they were far along. Like, if it was tomatoes, most likely the husband, he'd carry the basket across the rows to the road to be picked up. If it was pickles or potatoes, she wouldn't drag too much. If it was the kind of work when you're planting, it was easier, but when it was with a hoe, that was hard.

When a woman had a baby while she was working the fields, a *partera,* or just another woman, would help her, then she'd stay in camp 'till she got on her feet again. Three days later she'd be up doing housework, not heavy work, and nursing the baby or feeding him the bottle, whichever. Then probably in one month, she'd be in the fields. I know Mom, she didn't take too long. Mom wouldn't, and later I didn't either. Mom would get up on the third day, and she'd start housework and to recuperate real fast. Then, when she was back working in the fields, she'd stop every so often and go to the truck and cool a little bit and nurse a baby and then go back to the fields.

I remember seeing my mother in the fields crying. She'd be pregnant and dragging a bag of cotton. I remember her bent over picking tomatoes or working with a short-handle hoe. The reason they used a short handle was to make sure that we were doing the job. If they looked out and we were standing straight up, they thought that meant we weren't working. How terrible! Isn't that terrible? They made us do stoop labor when we didn't need to. Even pregnant women. My neck would hurt a lot and I was just a little girl. My back would ache and ache at night. I can imagine how Mommy felt, being so many years older and pregnant so much and doing stoop labor.

When we were in the fields, we were told you had to stay working all of the time. If it was wet, Mom would say, "Well, the sun will be shining soon." You get wet with the dew, but she'd say, "We'll get dry." Then, when it was so hot that I think if you put a thermometer between your hat and your head it would really register a high temperature, she'd say, "Well, we'll put water on our heads to cool off." We'd wet our hats and put them back on. It felt like your eyes would get real red and irritated, and the dust, it was uncomfortable.

My mom and dad were constantly behind us saying, "You're not doing that right. This is the kind you have to pick." Or, "The tomatoes are not ripe enough." Or, "You don't take the husk, you just pull the clean cotton." So they were right there supervising. And if anything went wrong, the grower would come straight to the father. He'd say, "Manny, the kids are not doing a good job. You have to get after them." Then Dad would get after Mom, and Mom would get after us, and so on. It was better work for the grower that way.

My daddy'd always say, "Pay attention and learn to work because one of these days this is what you're going to be living on and you're going to have to know it." He probably figured that with all the discrimination, it was going to be like that forever.

I remember one farm we worked on. The farmer's wife was very Catholic. She eventually managed to get Mommy and Daddy married through the Catholic church, against Daddy's wishes and will. I also think that woman baptized a whole bunch of my brothers and sisters, and she was constantly there with Mom. She'd help Mom a lot, give her clothes.

Daddy'd worked for those people for several years when one day, it rained. He was with other farm workers, and they'd gone to town to get groceries when their truck went into a ditch. One member of the farmer's family, I think his son, was right across from them with a tractor, and Daddy went up to him and said, "Would you please come for five minutes and pull us out?"

But the man said, "Nope, I don't want to waste my time." So Dad had to walk about five miles in the rain to get help when that man was right there and could have helped them.

When Dad saw the farmer, he was very upset and said, "You're not really my friend. What your son did wasn't right." So that was the last year Daddy went to work there.

He'd try to teach us. He'd go into the woods and say, "This is an apple tree. This is a pear tree. And this root is good to eat and this weed is good to eat." So we learned a lot of different weeds that you could have if you were real hungry. He was very strict, so he'd grab us and say, "Listen to me. Pay close attention. One of these days you're going to need it." It was constantly a worry to find food and how to get a little money to get food. It was always the same thing.

Every time we went up north, it seemed to get harder. It was awful. I didn't understand why I was told to go where the blacks were supposed to go. There were "colored only" and "whites only" signs all over. In restaurants, one side would be for whites, and on the other side, after all the cooking facilities, it'd be for blacks. The same with the rest rooms. I made plenty of mistakes before I could understand.

We were supposed to do what blacks did, but at first I didn't even know who blacks were. The first Christmas that I remember, my mother gave me a little black doll. I don't know why, but when I uncovered it and saw it was dark, I was shocked and thought it was burned. I was just like paralyzed. To me it was a dead little doll, and I couldn't get over that feeling. I wrapped it back again and rejected it because I thought it was dead and had been burned. Maybe I'd seen somebody burned, and I didn't really know there were black people.

It was in Newport, Arkansas, when I first saw real black people. I remember looking at a beautiful woman, black with green eyes, tall and slim. I guess if I'd have been a boy I'd have fallen in love with her. Then I remember being parked near someplace like a church in an all-black neighborhood. A black woman came over to the car with biscuits and gave us food. She was so nice and good, and the way she talked amused me, the accent, it was so different. She turned and touched me and said, "Ah, you're such a beautiful little thing." And she gave us biscuits and other food she'd fixed. She must have known we were migrants and hungry.

My Anglo granddaddy would try to warn me about prejudice. He used to tell me, "Don't ever take any bullshit from Anglo people. We're a bunch of bad people." He didn't say exactly those words, but that's what he meant. He'd say, "We've come to make *peones,* as in peee-ons, of the Mexican people."

But, of course, my grandpa got along very good with some other Anglos, and I'd sometimes overhear them talking and joking. I didn't understand what they meant when I was younger, but I'd hear the Anglo men say, "Hey, I've heard that Mexican women are the best." And, "If you want your first time to start out on the right track, go out with a Mexican señorita." And now my father says that sometimes my granddaddy bragged about my grandma to the other Anglos because she was a Mexican Indian woman.

Indians were looked down upon in a lot of ways. My grandpa on my mom's side, he's Indian, and he used to drink a lot, and the neighbors made comments like, "The old Indian is doing it again." Then, when we were in Montana, I saw that Indians were looked down on very, very bad. They lived on the reservation, and they were not allowed in the stores. It was like they were criminals, like savages. Up in Montana, that's where I saw prejudice against Indians more than I was used to.

One time we lived on an Indian reservation, in San Xavier, Montana, with the Crow Indians. We went to work there in trucks with a crew leader. I remember the Indian girls who were on the reservation. I had a real nice friend named Dorothea. She spoke English 'cause she was the daughter of an Anglo and an Indian woman. We lived right between the two reservations, the Blackfoot and the Crow, but really with the Crow.

I was very curious about everything the Indians did. I'd go into their hut and see that they worked very hard. I could see that the men sat down and smoked and drinked, and the women did the work. The women chopped the wood, they carried the children, they sewed their moccasins. The young Indian boys would ride their horses and throw spears real hard. I guess they hunted, though. The women, they worked terrible, the girls, everybody. Dorothea would criticize the Indian guys because she'd say, "All they do is sit and drink and smoke, and we do all the work."

I got to see the Indians get dressed with animal skins and moccasins. Of course, I didn't dress that way, but I was part of them. I went to their homes, I went to their camps, I was part of what they did, like taking a bath out in the creek all naked. After the bath they put up a tepee, and the women went naked into it for a steam bath and then came back out into the fresh air, shaking their hair. I wouldn't do it, but they did it. Then the men took the steam bath. I was impressed by everything. The first time I smoked was with the Indian girls. That's how I learned to hold a cigarette. I had beautiful times with them.

Then, one time, we got to go to Kentucky where the hillbillies live. My granddaddy, who was from around there, hadn't seen his folks for forty years, so they didn't even know if he was alive. My aunt was going to have a baby, and when she got sick, started labor, my granddaddy went to find his brothers. When we got to where the directions sent us, he knocked on the door, and the man who opened the door, Ed, says, "Oh, my God. You're my brother Ray." And, oh gosh, they started hugging and kissing.

He was real, real poor. He lived in a little shack, and he had a wooden stove so you had to burn wood so you could cook. Later we learned that they'd never had any tortillas or Spanish food at all, nothing.

My aunt was very sick with labor. There was no beds or nothing in the cabin, only sacks of burlap. All they could do is throw a lot of burlap on the floor, and my mom threw a bedspread and more covers on it. We could barely get my aunt inside. My mom delivered the baby, so I saw when Emilia was born, and I was very excited. Emilia, the hillbilly.

Then that night we slept in the cemetery. It was just next door. There was no place in the house, so we slept there on the ground, but I wasn't afraid at all. I was watching the stars and thinking how beautiful it was.

There were some good times while we were working the fields. Sometimes, when we had about twenty-something more hampers to pick, Dad would encourage us by saying, "After we get done here, I'm taking you for an ice cream cone and for a dip in the lake." So that was like a boost. We'd lick the ice cream cone, then go straight to the lake, and play in the water in our work clothes. I imagine that we contaminated the lake, but we loved it. And I really loved to wade in creeks because the sand and the water was so clean and clear. There would be lots of green plants, aquatic plants, in the running water. So it just looked like a beautiful paradise. There were also a lot of bullfrogs, the kind where you'd eat the legs. We'd go after these frogs, and the legs tasted something like chicken too. I didn't like to do that, but it was like bringing food home.

Sometimes we'd have a chance to play, but not very, very often. In the cherry fields, we'd be singing, and I really enjoyed picking cherries. We'd climb up the tree and just eat and eat. Eating cherries was expected from kids.

If my dad would have to go out of the fields and we stayed in the fields working, we'd have a ball. My brothers and I and my sisters, we'd start playing and running.

I remember one time we were in a tomato field, and green tomatoes can hit you pretty hard when you throw them like a rock, so we had a tomato fight. Of course, that was destroying tomatoes and was a serious thing, because the grower gets after the crew leader real bad, and then the crew leader gets after the parents. But when my daddy wasn't there, they couldn't keep us quiet, my brother and I and a couple of other kids. We were having a blast throwing tomatoes back and forth at each other. But, finally, they caught us and then when my dad got there, oh boy, we got a spanking for doing that.

My father was the one who sang a lot in the fields, American songs mostly. He sang in the fields and sometimes at home when he was happy, but most of the time, he was bitter. My brother José would make up songs, but whenever Daddy found José writing or caught José with a paper, he'd look at it and criticize it and tell José it was a waste of time. He really put José down. I don't think my mom sang too much; maybe life was just too hard.

Sometimes if we were working close to the *patrona*'s [farmwife's] house, like maybe a hundred feet away, we could hear the *patrona* humming or singing as she was doing her dishes in her beautiful sink. You could tell her body, her mind was at ease. Then you could turn around, and one of the sisters would be crying. And you'd wonder, why does it have to be like this?

> ¿Por qué canta la patrona?
> ¿Por qué llora mi mamá?
> La patrona tiene techo
> y mi pobre madre
> nunca lo tendrá.

> [Why does the farmwife sing?
> Why does my mother cry?
> The farmwife has a roof
> and my poor mother
> shall never have one.]

(ca. 1982)

CHAPTER THREE

In the Back of the Class

When we came back to Brownsville from the north every year, we lived in little old shacks, very run-down places. Then they built the Point Sierra Project, a housing project, and it was like, oh gosh, fancy. It was brick apartments with two bedrooms, a hall, and a rest room with your tub, then your kitchen and your living room, and a place to eat. It was very nice. It was built especially for low-income people so we were able to move in there.

You know, when you're very little and you live under poverty, you don't really know that it's not right or that it could be different. It was not until I was in school and older that I'd see other kids wearing nice shoes, nice dresses, nice things, being able to go to the movies, having nice birthdays. Then I realized that they were better off than I was, that there was a big difference.

I was very shy when we weren't working and went to school. I only had one little friend that I talked to. Francés was from Mexico and was very friendly. She couldn't speak English very good, and stayed there just a short time and then left. She was very poor too because she had very old and patched clothes. You could tell it was sewed up. I felt sorry for her. She was so good, but she looked sad all of the time, yet she was so pretty. She was light-complected and her eyes were big, with curly lashes, and she had a beautiful mouth. I was a kid, but I paid attention to everything.

The other friend in school was Rosalda. That was before I quit school forever. I guess Rosalda felt sorry for me because she was not really my friend. She didn't talk to me all the time like girls do with each other, but at lunchtime she'd come and sit with me and offer me some of her food. She probably saw that I didn't have any food, and I'd sit at the top of the stairs away from other kids when it was lunchtime. She'd come to me and she'd say, "Here, you want some of mine? I don't like it." She was always saying, "I don't want it," or "It's too much." In the beginning, I wouldn't take any, but when she did that every day, I began to look forward to it. I grew to like her a lot.

Also, school was hard 'cause I'd always be taken out to work the fields three months before school was out, and I remember going to school three months late all the time. Sometimes I'd have to go to school barefooted, and at times it was very cold and I didn't have a sweater, just a shirt and pants. I remember how my skin felt, walking all that way. There were just a few other barefooted children. It was very difficult to find charitable places in Brownsville then. If there had been any, they probably would have had two-thirds of Brownsville lined up.

There were not very many Anglo kids down in the Valley, but I had Anglo teachers, and there certainly was a difference in the children. A lot of the little girls would dress with those shiny shoes, patent leather, and socks and ponytails and petticoats and real pretty dresses, but I wore my dirty old hat and boys' clothes, and they'd make me sit in the back of the class. They wanted me to take my hat off too, but I wouldn't, and if they forced me, I'd put it on after school and go back home with my hat. It got kind of torn up, the straw was worn, but I sure loved it. I was just so shy at school, I didn't say anything, and the teacher put us real poor kids in the back.

When we were up north working in the fields, we kids had cans of Carnation and Pet milk. We'd empty those out and make a slit in the can to save dimes in. Then Daddy'd give us a few dimes all during the harvest season, and by the end of the season, the can was always filled. When we were working, Daddy'd say, "This is your savings. You worked for it, and it's yours. When we get home, you can use it for clothes and supplies for school." But after several times, I learned that my father wasn't keeping his word. I ended up getting one pencil and a Big Chief writing notebook, and maybe a pair of socks and sometimes shoes and a couple of panties and that was it. For some reason I knew that there should be money to buy more things, and I'd get very upset. Later, after I grew up a little bit more, I didn't want any money to save. I thought, no, they can keep it and do whatever they want to with it because I have no say anyhow. After the pencil and the paper was gone, that was it.

So, usually, when I went to school, I'd have to beg around for a pencil and paper, and I'd get embarrassed 'cause everybody gave me a dirty look. Then the teacher would say, "Can't your parents get you a pencil and notebook? Just go back to the back seat. I'll give you something." Sometimes she'd say, "If you'd like to paint or draw, here is some pencil and paper and colors." She didn't even try to teach me. I did go through some of those books with Dick and Jane and Sally, and I wasn't the only one that sat at the back of the room.

School was so hard being put in the back of the classroom all the time. It could have been because I was poorly dressed—I mean, what else could it have been for? There were other little children that were Mexicans also, but a lot of them were dressed nicely. Maybe involvement of parents helped, my parents never got involved. My father cared about my work when I came home. I remember being beaten up by him a lot because I couldn't ever understand some things, but they never got involved with school. Just three times my mom went to school.

One time was when I was sent home because a little girl said I was stinking. I know I bathed that morning because I remember, and they made such a big thing about it at school. I was so embarrassed. Lydia, the girl who accused me, was one of those little girls who would wear beautiful coats with pretty socks and shiny shoes and their hair all nicely done. I noticed how they dressed because I couldn't wear anything like that, so I felt like I was a loner. I'd stay to myself. I wasn't part of anything. That's the only reason I could think of why I was put in the back of the room. It must have been because I was not at the level of the other children.

The morning it happened, there was an empty chair up with the other children. I don't remember if it was by Lydia's side, but it was close to her. I decided I was going to sit up where the other kids were sitting, and I went and sat in the empty chair. I didn't really do anything to get Lydia's anger. It just must have angered her when I sat there.

She got upset and started saying, "María Elena stinks." That I smelled like pee, like urine.

The teacher called me and said, "Come here." I went up, then the teacher says in front of the class, "How long has it been since you took a bath?"

I said, "This morning."

She says, "Did you change your panties?" I started crying. I knew that I'd taken a bath and that I wasn't wet in my panties.

Then the teacher says, "Well, Lydia says you stink and that you're going to make her sick." So they sent me home. I was in second grade, maybe.

I remember my mom got upset and went to talk to the principal. She said we were poor but she bathed me.

One teacher noticed how hard school was for me. His name was Mr. Ramírez. One time, I don't know what happened to me, but I started crying and I couldn't stop, and then I was laughing and crying, and everybody looked. It happened in a classroom.

Mr. Ramírez took me outside the room and asked me, "Are you having problems at home? Did you have any food to eat today? How often do you eat?" But I didn't want to talk to him about anything, and I don't know what I told him. But there were many times when I hadn't eaten. Often. A lot of the times there were just potatoes or beans and tortillas, and I usually didn't have anything to eat in the mornings.

I guess Daddy also prevented us from learning about outside things. One time he found me with a book. And, boy, he really grabbed me by the hair and hit me and said, "I never again want to see you with another book." So I can't remember ever having books to read.

But I used crayolas, I used pencils, I used any kind of paper I could get my hands on to write my poems and draw my pictures. And I dug underneath the floor of the house, sort of like a little cave, and I drew on the dirt and buried my things. Because my grandma, she used to do that. She'd say the safest way to keep your money is to bury it, so I'd bury my nickels and pennies and special stuff. Then I'd go back and wouldn't find it, but it was my secret place.

When we were drawing or writing, my daddy criticized us pretty bad, especially José, my brother. Because by the age of eleven years old, José was already composing songs. But whenever José got caught writing, my father would take it and curse him and criticize him, and I think several times he tore up José's work. My brother would just look down at the floor and drop his head, very sad. I'd be very disgusted. I think José probably could have become a great composer and a great musician. His heart was all in there. Instead he got married young and started his family and worked the fields.

So I was careful not to let Daddy get into my work or see me do too much. Daddy thought our work was valuable time taken from them, from our chores. Any time that I spent doing anything else, I wasn't contributing to the household, to the babysitting, so I'd hide my work under my mattress or in my cave under the floor.

I must have been a very emotional or sensitive child, because I still am sensitive. To bring back these memories, it's still painful to remember. Sometimes I thought that maybe I wasn't their daughter. I have a sister Patsy who wasn't my mom's, so, I thought, maybe I'm not either. Maybe one of them is not my parent. Because I was punished constantly, and my brother José also had it bad, but, for some reason, my mom took more sides with the boys, always. I was the oldest one, but she always took sides with José, regardless of who was right. Even now, it is the same.

One other time I got in trouble in school. I was probably about twelve, and there was a gang of girls. Back in those days, there used to be gangs called *pachucas* for the girls and *pachucos* for the men. It was a gang of real mean girls who always were picking on the rest of the girls. They were very tough and the ones that took the better seats in the classroom. I was always walking in fear because one time they threw me all the way down the stairs.

They especially picked on a little girl, probably about two years younger than us, she was named Rosalinda. Rosalinda was real chubby and ran real funny. Just out of meanness, the *pachucas* were putting bugs in Rosalinda's hair and calling her "Ti-ling, Ti-ling," like when you ring a bell.

There was one big girl in the gang who was fully developed and would paint a mole on her face and fix herself up and smoke. And it seemed like this big girl just didn't like Rosalinda. Every time Rosalinda would go to the water to wash up, she'd pick on her. We were all so worried because the *pachucas* would take bugs from other people and put them in an envelope and then take them out and keep them in their hands. Then, when you were trying to drink water, they'd throw them over your head. We'd warn each other, "Be careful." But this big girl was always picking on Rosalinda, hitting her, pushing her, and grabbing her by the hair and yelling, "Hey, move over. I'm going to drink water." Or "Hey, I'm going to wash up."

This time, Rosalinda was drinking water, and the big girl grabbed her and rammed her head in the water. And I don't know what came over me, because I knew I couldn't stand up to that girl. There was no way, but I was so upset, I turned and told her, "Pick on somebody your size."

Then, as she slapped my face, I grabbed her hand and shoved her finger into my mouth. God, I'd have liked to tear it off. I sunk my teeth all around it, and blood was dripping, but it was out of fear that I wouldn't let go. I didn't let go until Mr. Ramírez, the good teacher, came running and pulled me away. Not until I saw him and the other teachers did I release her, because only then did I know I was safe. There was a big fuss over it, but that girl never again bothered me or Rosalinda.

I didn't get much more out of school, but I learned a poem that stayed with me, and I made it into a song to sing to my kids as a lullaby. It was by some guy named Stephen Foster. It said, "Some children sleep in palaces behind an iron gate and go to sleep in beds of gold whenever it gets late." Later on I'd sing it to my kids, "But way up north the children sleep in houses built of ice, and their beds made out of fur are really very nice." I love the part that says, "Someday I think I'll travel around and visit every place and learn to speak the language that a child can understand. They'll try to ask me questions then and I will ask them others, until at last we understand like sisters and like brothers."

The last time I remember Mom going to my school was to face the superintendent of schools so that I could be withdrawn and go to work. I was in sixth grade and twelve years old. He wanted to know why they were going to withdraw me, and she said that I needed to go to work, to help support the family. So the superintendent agreed. They didn't give Mom a hard time because back in those days, they weren't very hard on people to make their kids go to school.

So I got a job at a hotel, as a bus girl. The lady that was the manager at the hotel knew about our situation and how bad it was at home, so she gave me a job. At first I went to school in the morning, but it was about a two-mile walk and I wasn't learning much. So pretty soon, I quit going. I think I only had three total years of school 'cause I was gone so much working the crops.

CHAPTER FOUR

Take Your Pleadings to the Lord

Religion helped me all the time when I was young. I especially loved the *procesiones,* the distribution of the roses. The little girls would take flowers in a procession to Our Lady. We'd pass out flowers on the way to the Virgin. I got to do it several times, then my daddy stopped it. That was after the time in Portage, Ohio, when he told us God was dead.

But Mom kept praying all the time. She was very close to God and that way she kept us close too. Mother Mary and Our Lady of Guadalupe and Our Lady of San Juan and the Lady of Refugio were very important to us. When there was a thunderstorm or a bad crisis in the family, the people would say, "Mother of Refugio is the one that you just call. She's the one that helps." Ever since I was very, very little, Mom was lighting candles and praying at home and making *mandas,* promises to God. I was going to make my first communion, I even had a Godmother, but my dad said I couldn't make it.

Mom would teach us prayers and Dad would criticize her, but he let her do it. He'd say, "Oh, there you go again praying." She'd look at him with angry eyes and say, "Well, you don't believe it, but let us," and he'd just turn around and walk away. But before he quit believing, he'd told us such beautiful Bible stories, like about Abraham.

I have a poem and song, "Plegaria." I don't know how to say it in English, like pleading. It's a word that you use when you take your *plegaria* to God. And we have *lamentaciónes,* when you feel sorrow and when you're expressing lamentations. They are what I grew up with, in the neighborhood, because I lived in a very poor neighborhood. I heard laments from my mom forever and ever. And *plegarias*, from women that would go to church. Take your pleadings to the Lord.

I always had my mom's beliefs and my grandma's beliefs in me. I think I was a child when I first thought of God as female. Probably what happened was that I was very oppressed by my father, and I saw him as a male oppressor, but not using those words. I probably began to think that way 'cause I wanted to reach up for someone who was female. My mom never did help me, so I probably looked at God as female to come to my aid. And I had the Virgins and Mother Nature. God to me was more Mother Nature than even people. Now I often see God in people. I can see God in a child, in a young girl I care about, the little Mary Magdalene of the present, or in an old man that's an alcoholic or somebody who's sick or an orphan. But at that time, when I wasn't having my grandma anymore, probably that's when I started seeing God as someone to lean on, someone like a mother.

> Dear Mother Nature,
> There's a beautiful mysterious timeless heaven all around us, and little tiny Goddess you, unique, only, rare, mother of life, favorite daughter of Energy . . . you are the only womb from which I came. . . (Diary, April, 26, 1983)

I know by then I thought that God was my color, brown, but I'll tell you one thing, whenever I went to a church, the saints and everybody else in the statues and pictures didn't look brown. They were white. So when they said that God was everywhere and we were made in the image of God, I wondered if He was striped or what color He really was. Then finally, I decided that He was the color of everybody. So that's how come I say He's the color of my skin too.

Also, I was afraid to go to church up north because I kept thinking, God's there, I know, but I wonder what color He is. Missionaries came and invited us to their church, but they were white, so I just kept quiet and didn't want to go. I thought, we're not allowed this place and that, and everywhere there's one place for whites and another for blacks. So I thought, even if God's in there, maybe He'll be white and not want us.

But I knew at home in Texas that the priests weren't always good either. I remember one time when I was pretty little, Mom and I went to church to ask for help. It was very cold and I was wearing boys' clothes and my straw hat and my braids. It wasn't even inside the church. It happened at the house where the priest lived and he scolded me. He said that I should know better than to walk into the house of God dressed like that.

I was real hurt because this was coming from a priest, and it wasn't even the house of God. That's what I kept saying to myself, this is not the house of God. Anyway, I had to step outside and I was ready to answer back, but my mom said, "María Elena, go outside and wait." Oh, it was so cold. My mom was going to ask for five dollars. I don't even know if she got it.

On our way back home, I was arguing with Mom. I could complain to Mom some; to my dad I couldn't, not one word. Most of the time we wouldn't talk with Daddy; he'd just say to do something or to correct something, but we wouldn't get into talking. Anyway, after we saw that priest and as we were walking home, I told Mom, "Oh, Mommy, that's wrong. That's not the house of God. The house of God is next door in the church."

She said, "Oh, it's all right. Don't pay attention to the priest."

I said, "No, I don't like that. It's bad, Mother."

In my union-organizing play, *Flor Campesina,,* the priest, he also oppresses the main character.[1] Rosamaría is a farm worker woman whose husband is out drinking and spending all their money. Late at night, she remembers when she went to the priest to ask him how to deal with her husband and her boss. The priest puts her down and says:

> My daughter, my daughter,
> it is a sin to blaspheme, to complain,
> The *patrón* has the right
> to be rich and to enjoy . . .
>
> I know we are going through
> hard and bad times,
> but we must be patient,
> and live like Christians.
>
> Go now and pray a Rosary
> in front of the altar.
> This is your penance
> for complaining and blasphemy.

---

1. The entire play appears in the Appendix.

Serve your husband well,
and be good in your work.
Your *patrón* is a very good man.
He cares for you a lot and I do too.

(1983)

I could understand things like that about people, even priests. I was able to catch what was evil or good, I guess 'cause I'd been so hurt.

My daddy did do some good things for us when we were little, like when he tried to teach us skills and what wild food we could eat. And he did help my cousins. My mother had one brother and these were kids of his ex-wife. My uncle left his wife for another woman. He left her with three girls and a forty-day-old baby, so my cousins grew up very, very poor.

You can tell when kids don't eat. They look at you with big eyes and stare at your food and don't ask for nothing. Sometimes they put their head down. You know that for that child, there is something wrong. My cousins were like this, withdrawn and so poor. So my mom always looked after that sister-in-law. During the wintertime, Mom and Dad would take my aunt and the kids into their home and share food and beds and everything. And I remember that very often my father would take a big sack of sweet bread to my aunt. And I guess they also helped with a little money.

All the people that I've known in Texas and even in Mexico, it's all a family thing. Brothers and sisters, the grandpa and grandma, they take care of each other. Like when one gets sick, we all share in the suffering and the struggles of each other. Also, everybody is very protective of the little ones. That's why my parents tried so hard to help my cousins. Even if you're not too close to each other or have differences, if there's problems for the children, you have to protect them.

But Dad was very hard on us and Mom. When he was upset, we couldn't say one word. Sometimes we couldn't even look at his eyes. We'd have to look down and not give our faces. It's hard for me to remember, I get so emotional. It's hard to talk about it.

I think Dad tried to keep me isolated because he didn't want any boys to see me when I was growing up, and when I was a little girl, he was probably trying to protect me from strangers. And I think my father was so mad partly because my mother was always so friendly and so social, and he was never able to control too much of her. But he was mean to her, and with us, he was strict.

Even though José was younger than me, José had to hold my hand wherever we walked together—to the store, to school, anyplace—and I'd have to look down all the time. If I raised my head, my brother would tell my father, and my father would whip me. Brothers are to be the guardian angels of their sisters. But José and I were constantly getting into fights with one another because I stood up to protect myself. I didn't want his type of protection.

I remember the hard time in Ohio, the time when Daddy told us God was dead. That time the whole camp was upset, I think because we weren't getting paid, and we weren't getting food, and the farmer wasn't responding. For whatever reason, my father was upset in those days, and my father got very mad at my mom. I don't remember if it was because she didn't cook the food maybe fast enough or on time or what happened, but he was very upset. That's when he took a broom and beat my mom. He got very violent.

Also, there was a whole struggle to wash dishes. You had to go look for water, get it in a pan, bring it inside, and if the dishes were very greasy, which they usually were, you'd have to warm the water on the stove and then wash the dishes. Dad also got very mad at me that time because I had to wash the dishes and hadn't done it because it was raining real hard. When he sent me out in the rain to pump water for the dishes, lightning hit the pump, and the impact threw me on the ground. All I could see was light all over. For maybe a few seconds it was white, then blue, then black. When I opened my eyes, I was laying down on the ground in the mud and water.

Mom says my father never touched her to hurt her. When I remind her of the times he did, she says, "Oh, that was just like a push. Your father has never, ever hurt me." She always takes pride in saying that she's been an obedient wife and she was never bad enough for her husband to hurt her. So it seems like she's trying to send messages to herself to be a good wife. And she feels like she set her daughters a good example by taking so much abuse. That is what a good woman does.

I never heard my father getting upset or scolding Ana, but I know that when my father mistreated my mother, even Ana would go to the corner with the rest of us and grieve. I think even Ana must have been afraid of my father.

All I can remember about Mom was that she always was a very meek person, always crying and never answering back. It seems like after he'd be mean, Daddy'd come and love her to death, and I wondered if she just liked that so much that she kept her mouth shut. It could be that she just knew he was going to get over it. He'd be so good to her at times. I mean, he mistreated her terrible, except that he'd turn around and kiss her and love her. He'd strike and then kiss her. I thought she just loved it. I don't know. Maybe she loved him a lot and just put up with all that he told her. I remember him hugging her and kissing her. He treated her very kindly, very beautiful. But when he was upset with us every day, he'd become the devil. He was a cruel man, mean. He should have stopped.

I resented it very much because as far as Mom would go in sticking up for us would be pleading for him not to hurt us. She wouldn't help us, she'd just plead. I think Mom was also scared of Dad. I think she was frightened because she'd just drop her head and her arms would be down. She'd look at him like, if I say anything or do anything, he'll strike me. So he hurt us in an animalistic way, beating us up.

I still remember it very strongly, I can't forget. He'd beat me 'cause I couldn't remember arithmetic, and the more he'd beat me, the more I couldn't remember. There's times when especially my older brothers and I sit down and start remembering. It's painful to remember that he blindfolded me and made me kneel in gravel for so long, that he made me stretch out my arms and hold a brick in each hand while we kneeled there. And he made us do those kind of punishments where we had to run around and around the outside of our house, blindfolded and carrying bricks.

We lived in a neighborhood with all *compadres* and *comadres* [godparents] and brothers and sisters, and everybody knew each other very well, so others must have known. But there was a wooden fence—maybe it was too tall. And I don't ever remember seeing my mom when he was punishing us in those ways.

Later, when we moved to the projects, he made us bang our heads against the cement walls so hard he could hear the sound from the outside. I don't know why I never thought of getting a stone and hitting it against the walls. I did it, we did it, with our heads. My brother and I, we actually hit ourselves into the wall, over and over. I just wonder that we didn't go crazy or end up with brain damage. I think my father must have been a sick person.

I think when that was happening, Mom was there, and she never stood up to say, "Hey, this is enough." She never did. So I guess I resented my mom a lot for not protecting us. And I still resent her because I still see what she does for the boys, and she doesn't do for the girls, like putting down one of my sisters and dictating her life.

One time, my mom advised me to run away for a few days, but not to disappear. She sent me to a friend's home, first to an aunt's and then to her *comadre*'s. She sent me because my father had beaten me up so bad that I was bleeding in the temples. I don't know why my father beat me that time or why he beat me in the temples. I can't even remember.

Something must have gone wrong, but I never did know when I was doing something wrong. He was the type that if there was a fly in the house, all of a sudden he would strike me on the back, and I didn't know why. Then he would say, "You know we're not supposed to have flies in the house, damn you!" Then I knew why he had hit me. I was like always waiting, not ever knowing when I was going to be struck. I'd be washing dishes, and I'd always be on guard with that one *sentido*, with one sense of fear or worry. I was always waiting to be struck by him.

So that time, I don't know what happened, but he beat me up real bad with the metal part of the belt. Everywhere, anywhere it would land. I went to Mom's room and my mom says, "Open the window and run. Go to my sister's house and stay there for a few days because I want him to worry about you."

So I did. I opened the window, and I ran and ran and ran. When I got to my aunt's house, they told me to go up to the attic, so I went up there and stayed. I'd just come down to eat. After I'd hidden in the attic for a few days, I was told by my aunt that I could go home. When I went back, Daddy wasn't there.

In my anguish, when Daddy was so cruel, I'd always ask God why. Why? And, why, Daddy, why do you do this to me? I'd try so hard to understand. Sometimes I'd think about my "Crack in the Sky" poem and go over it in my mind.

I can talk about it now, but back then I didn't have anybody to turn to. I'd stayed close to my grandma and loved her so much when I was little, but when I was about eight, she had a stroke and was paralyzed. I think my mom took my grandma to live with us for a short period of time, but Mom was pregnant, and it was hard. And they didn't want me to go into her room. Also, I think my uncle was already married by that time, and his wife didn't want to take care of her. So my uncle hired Ana and promised her he'd pay her to take care of my grandma. Ana said, "I never did get paid, but it was like paying her back." Ana felt like a family member since Grandma would take her in and help her out. Grandma kept seeing a woman, like a vision, but Grandpa was with her and didn't see anyone. Grandma started telling my grandpa, "She's trying to hurt me."

She was disabled for maybe two more years, and all that time, I wasn't allowed to see her or get close to her. My mom and dad didn't want me with her. They thought maybe my grandma's spirit was trying to invade my body and that's the reason I was so strange, why I'd complain and make pictures and write poems. But I think I was like her just 'cause I loved her and saw a lot of what she did. I still can't see anything wrong in the way she prayed and the way she sometimes sang at three o'clock in the morning. Maybe they were afraid I'd suffer when she died. My mom certainly thought that after my grandma died, she was going to come back for me, that maybe I'd become possessed.

But, anyway, I'd sneak out and go and see her. Her hair had turned totally white, and I'd comb it and roll her tobacco. One time I was caught. My father didn't want me to go there. After she died, I wasn't going to be allowed to go to the funeral or to the wake, to attend the burial, nothing. So I just sneaked out to see her body. It was night, around ten o'clock, and a long way to the funeral home. I don't think the building was locked because I was able to get in, and I can't remember how I done that.

They'd cut her hair, right before she died. It was short and wavy, but I wanted her to have her braid. I just looked and looked at her, and she wasn't there. That was the first time I felt what it's like to see a dead body. Her body was there, but she was gone. So, I cried and cried, I was all alone. Then I said, "Good-bye."

But now I know she stayed with me, in Mother Nature, in my poems, and in the way I see the dandelion. And in the way I love and miss people.

> Feel very gently the rays
> of the sunshine
> Touch the palms of your
> hands and heal
> Heal the wounds made from
> thorns and sorrows.

(Diary, 1983)

CHAPTER FIVE

Tamed by the Monkey Demon

So I lost my grandma, and Mom and I had some big problems 'cause I resented all the babies. I didn't understand at all about how Mom got pregnant, but I did see Mom and Dad cuddle up together, and there came a day that I began to realize that somehow Mommy was getting all those tummies, all those babies. The time I saw Emilia's birth in Kentucky, that time I finally knew how babies would come out, but at the time I got married, I still didn't understand about the sex part. But I knew it had to do a lot with my father. So every time I saw Mom's stomach growing, I'd say, "Oh, my God, another baby." Poor babies. Poor brothers and sisters. There were so many.

I think that the biggest problem between Mom and me was that I felt that resentment toward her for getting pregnant. I'd say, "Mom, why do you keep having babies when we can't eat right and Daddy's so mean?"

A big part of my resentment was that I had to take care of the babies and see that they were alright. It was very hard work. We were working in the fields, and at the same time you had to keep an eye on the children and then make lunch for so many, my God, it was terrible, cooking for so many kids. I had to help Mom a whole lot, making tortillas and cooking beans, mostly from scratch. Most migrant farm worker ladies, they still cook from scratch.

We bought tubs for washing in Brownsville. We'd put one tub full of soap and water and the other one to rinse on a little wooden bench. If the clothes were real dirty, you'd make a fire and put a tub of water with soap and bleach in there to soak it real good. Then Mom always carried her tubs with her to the migrant camps, and inside the tub she'd put all the dishes and the *molcajete* [mortar for making tortillas] and the rolling pin and big pots. I did the same thing, too, after I married because I learned from her. Then we'd set up our own little place under a tree and take our washing there.

The babies smelled bad, and I hated to wash diapers and baby clothes. I hated to change the kids. I'd say to Mom, "It isn't my fault. I didn't have anything to do with you having babies. You should do it."

I don't remember my dad changing diapers. One thing, he liked to bake pies and has always been a food lover, but I don't remember my father helping like that with the kids. Well, Ana went with us up north, so Ana and I'd do a lot of the work. All those babies was always a problem between Mom and me.

One time when Mom was up north, she almost lost her life when she had the twins. She had a bad hemorrhage. We were lucky to keep her. After that, one last baby was born, and the doctor finally said, "No more." She had to have a hysterectomy, but that was when my kids were already getting older.

When we were in Texas, Mom would take the kids to the city clinic, for shots, for flu, for diarrhea, everything. She'd have to stay all day long to wait for her turn or to get medicine. She'd take a blanket and put it in the grass and take sandwiches or *taquitos,* tortillas, and we'd eat there and entertain the kids. I'd say there were well over one hundred people waiting there every time we went. It was an all-day event.

Mom started being a midwife while we were working in the fields. I think it started in Portage, Ohio, where there was this lady who was real heavy set, real big. She was in labor and there was nobody else, an emergency. My mom had to deliver that baby, and she had a terrible time doing it, too, because it was a very big baby. By the time they got the doctor, the baby was already born, and my mom had taken care of it. Then my mom started delivering in the camps.

After she delivered the first baby, it'd happen again and again. I guess she gained self-confidence. Then every time we were away working or would be in the camps, they'd just go and get her, talk to her, and have her check them and massage them or whatever. They'd ask her to deliver the baby and she would.

In some cases, when I was older, I helped Mom by getting hot water and being around when she need me. I could see the pain the ladies were going through, but I wasn't afraid because it was just something that was normal with my mom having so many kids. Now Mom's been a midwife for so many years, and she's got a certificate. She had to go to some kind of training. It wasn't against the law to be a midwife in my younger days, but nowadays they're very strict. She's got a little place like a clinic, with beds and cooking facilities, so when she delivers babies, she not only brings the baby, but for a whole week she takes care of the baby so the mother can recuperate. If she's got too many, she's got friends to take over. She really takes care of the ladies—she feeds them, she makes home-made soups. Despite the problems Mom and I've had, I really respect her. And she's got the gift.

> On Christmas Eve, my mom delivered a baby boy. He was born "dead." . . . Mom said, My God, I know you're going to give this baby life. . . . My mom turned into a Miracle Maker, a Magician really. She was so fast I was totally amazed and filled with wonder as I watched her work on the baby. My mom breathed life into that baby's body. I am totally convinced God has blessed her with the Gift of Life and Deliverance . . . (Diary, December 28, 1983)

But when I was little, Mom and I had several kinds of problems. For one thing, she thought I had demons in me. She thought that it wasn't right for me to imagine things, to create things.

The things I did with clay or drawing, they were a way of letting out my anguish because I didn't have any outlet. I'd get clay or mud and mold things. I think my frustration, my anger, my anxiety went into things like that. I'd just make, for example, my father. I don't know how many times I made little devils and he was my father, 'cause that's what I saw. I'd create people into these things, and this is what I guess they'd call abnormal and crazy or being possessed, but actually, I think I was shaping my anger at what I saw in people with clay.

I remember one time I showed Mom a drawing, and she looked at it like, "Oh, my God, the work of the devil!" Whenever she saw my things, she had this expression on her face that I saw many times, like when you look at something that's very awkward or very weird, that you're afraid of.

But how could it be that I had demons? It was impossible. I had no knowledge of any satanic things other than my grandma's way of praying and singing and having saints. And my grandma was not a witch, she was not satanic. She was nothing like that, but that's what they used to call her. And I never saw my grandma draw anything. But Mom thought there was something wrong with me, that I was possessed.

One day I overheard her talking to another woman, saying she was going to take me to a *curandero,* a medicine man, to see what was wrong with me because I was so different, so weird, and she didn't understand what was going on with me. It's true, I could see things she couldn't ever see, like when you look at clouds and there is so many different forms and shapes. She just couldn't understand how I was able to come up with images. Where did they come from? Among our people they call that voodoo, the devil's work. They thought my grandma's spirit had come to get me.

So Mom came to me and said that she was going to take me out. I was frightened when Mom took me to the place, it was the first time I'd gone to any place like that. See, my mom also cursed me a lot when I was a little girl, that she hoped the devil would come and teach me a lesson, so I couldn't figure out what they were going to do with me.

On the outside, where we went was like any house. On the inside, it was different, full of candles. It was very dark, with lots of people, very quiet, but they were praying and there was chanting and strange smells. They had lots of saints and pictures and all kinds of weird things, braids, hangings on the wall, occult offerings. See, when you go to the temple of Our Lady of San Juan, here in San Juan, Texas, and also in San Juan, Mexico, they have the same thing, lots of pictures and things, braids, and they offer these things for the miracle that the Virgin is going to perform.

This *curandero* was a man, and he and the others had me look into these great big glass jars, and they wanted me to say I was seeing something in there, but I said, "No, I don't see nothing." So they got very upset.

According to the people in there, the man changed into a *tatapedrito* [Little Saint Peter], or whatever. According to them it was a saint. And they wanted me to say, "Yes, I can see you. You're *fulano de tal,* so and so."

They wanted to put the words in my mouth. "Can you see *tatapedrito* there?" Or the name of the person that was supposed to have taken the place of the *curandero.*

And I'd say, "No, I can't see nothing."

So they said something was wrong with me, that I was a naughty girl, that I was possessed. I was very young and frustrated. They wanted me to say, "Yes, I can see this person and he's holy, he's a saint." They wanted me to lie about the work they were doing.

When I got home I drew a picture of the *curandero,* and he was an octopus under the sea, and I showed it to my mom. My mom didn't know what it was, but he had the face of a man and the body of an octopus. And she went, "Oh, my God! My God!"

So they took me to a *curandera,* a woman. According to them, this lady had El Niño Fidencio[1] come into her body. While I was watching, this woman's voice changed, and she was having like an epileptic seizure, her body would like jump, and when her body quit trembling and jumping, her voice sort of changed, and she said, "Welcome, this is Niño Fidencio."

Then they had me stand up in front of her, and she said that I was a naughty girl and had some kind of demon, that I was possessed. She said something was wrong with me, that I was a bad girl.

I think everybody did this because I was like my grandma. It's true, I was like her, but I also did things I never saw her do, like draw. She did pray to the moon at night, but she wasn't a witch.

In those days, I was very upset at Mom, and every time she was getting pregnant, I'd get very depressed. I never cursed and I never did really say anything back to Mom. I never was a bad mouth, but I kept complaining.

My mom resented me for all these things, and she'd say, *"Uno de estos días se te va a aparecer el diablo."* One of these days you're going to see the devil. And this went on for days and years. "The devil is going to appear to you, and the devil is going to take you," or "You're going to see the devil in a hole." In so many ways she'd put it. Sometimes it really scared me.

When I was about eleven years old and always nagging her about being pregnant and me doing the hard stuff, she says, "You're going to have to stay at home because I'm going to the store."

I said, "I want to go too, Mom. I don't want to stay alone."

---

1. El Niño Fidencio was a saintlike male figure, popular along the border, who was said to appear to certain female healers. While these healers were in a trancelike state, they would speak with his male voice and give healing instructions. For details see June Macklin, "All the Good and Bad in this World: Women, Traditional Medicine, and Mexican American Culture," in *Twice a Minority: Mexican American Women,* ed. Margarita B. Melville (St. Louis: C. V. Mosby, 1980), 127–63.—Ed.

"No, you're going to stay and take care of the house." So she took everybody else but left me there.

I never answered back or said a bad word, but, that time, after they left, I began to think, I want to be dead. Why don't you take me, God? I was very mad, and I said, I don't want to be here anymore, God. I just want to go.

Then I thought, if you can't take me, why can't you take Mom and Dad? I don't want to be with them anymore.

At that time, I was in the living room by the window to the backyard. I was sitting on a wooden chair, just sort of leaning back on it against the wall. You could see as clear as day. All of a sudden, in the window, I began to see like nails, like big long cat nails. At first I didn't know what I was seeing, but there was one set of claws closer and one set still out there.

I really paid attention, but I couldn't make out what it was. Then a monkey started to take shape, and then that monkey began to [jump and pant]. And I saw fire in his eyes and white slime in his mouth.

I couldn't move. My whole body felt numb. I couldn't even close my eyes. It was like my heart stopped, like everything stopped. Then, a few seconds later, I thought about God, and the minute I thought about God, I could close my eyes. So I closed my eyes and began to pray, Our Father who art in heaven, and as soon as I began to pray, my circulation came back, I felt my blood move again.

Then I told God, "Oh, I'm never, never going to curse Mommy and Daddy again. Whatever they do, I'll never wish that they were dead, and I'll never go against my parents like I did. I promise, I'll never forget what happened today." And I never have.

When I opened my eyes, there was nothing there anymore, so I undone the latch to the door and went out running, just running and running. Then I saw my mom about a block and a half or two blocks away. So I stopped running, put my hands in my pockets, and tried to straighten up. I was terribly, terribly frightened that the thing was going to come and grab me, but I walked real straight and tried to whistle, because I didn't want my mom to see what shape I was in. But I couldn't even whistle.

When my mom was closer, she said, "María Elena, I thought I told you to stay inside."

I said, "Yes, Mom, but I saw you walking and I thought I'd come and meet you." I pretended like nothing was wrong. Then we went home, but, I tell you, from that day on I changed. I even talked softly to my mom. I just couldn't be the same anymore.

That night, I just couldn't go to sleep. I felt sick all over and my stomach was bad. So I went to Ana and said, "May I sleep with you?"

She said, "What's the matter, Güerita?"

"Nothing, but I just want to sleep with you."

For three days I was strange, and they began to say, "She's very pale." Of course, I couldn't see myself how pale I was, but then Ana and I went for a walk to the back alleys to collect garbage like we did very often, and Ana noticed how quiet I was; I'd always been so active.

She said, "Can you tell me what's wrong with you, Güerita? I promise, I swear to God, I won't tell nobody." So I told her what had happened, and she said, "You know what, let's go to church."

So we went to church, and she talked to the priest, and the priest talked with me. He began to question me, and I told him about all my dreams about being caught between God and the devil. He said, "It seems to me, little girl, like God pulls you one way, and the devil wants to pull you another way. But I'm going to tell you what. I'm going to bless you, and you pray a lot, and this won't ever happen." And he says, "Remember, it can only happen if you let it happen." This is where I learned that a person can open the gates to heaven and a person can open the gates to hell. Then he says, "There's nothing wrong with you." So he got holy water and he [blessed me].

After that I was always aware, I was very conscious, I was afraid that if I got very upset, I could create something bad. There had been nothing out that window, not a garbage can, not a clothesline, nothing, and I saw something. Whatever created that, my imagination, whatever, it was horrible. The priest told me that God would pull my right hand in one direction and that the devil would pull my left hand in the other way, that behind me was hell and ahead of me was heaven. I told the priest, "But I try to pull with God." And it's true. In all my dreams back then, I always tried to pull with God. And it was constantly a battle between God and I, because I knew that God was out there and God was everywhere, and I had nobody else to call, so I continued to call Him.

Years later, I tried to express that pulling back and forth when I wrote my play. The farm worker woman Rosamaría becomes a poor widow who still has to work in the fields. The narrator says that she carries her cross to the fields from one harvest to the next harvest, from one state to another state, from summer to winter. Life beats at her with hunger and misery, gnawing at her mind.

Finally, she falls on the ground and starts crying. She feels nothing more can happen, and she calls out to God and says, "No, no, it can't be possible, my God. . . . Why have you forsaken me if I never offended you? Answer me. Whose God are you? Answer me!" Rosemaría says it the way I felt it all those years while I was growing.

Yes, I changed how I acted after I thought I saw the devil. I repented. For some reason I understood that it was wrong to curse my parents or to wish death upon somebody else. I guess I also changed because I realized there was something evil within myself or out there someplace that could be brought inside. I was more obedient, more submissive. I guess I didn't nag as much. I never quit thinking about getting out of the situation I was in, but I wasn't as rebellious as before.

CHAPTER SIX

Coming of Age: Shame and Terror

Dear Women, Sisters: Listen to my story and then tell it to your sister,
friend. Tell it to your daughters, tell it to your Granddaughters, and forever
pass it on . . .

—July 26, 1982

. . . I pray some day all women organize to abolish all this male wickedness
and their double standards.
    Curse man's wicked ways!
    Made in the Image of Satan

—April 23, 1983

Of course, all those years I was growing, I was also learning about men's
evil ways. When I was about eight and we were in Indiana, the ladies, we
all took a bath in the same place. Women, little girls, no privacy. And my
uncle, my father's brother, came to me, and he asked me, "Do you take a
bath all together? Your mom and the *comadre* and the other lady?"
    I said, "Yes, Uncle."
    "Oh, and does María and Viviana take a bath with you also?"
    "Yes, Uncle."
    "Do you all take all your clothes off when you take a bath?"
    "Yes, Uncle."
    "Can you see their bodies?"
    "Yes, Uncle."
    "Oh, what part of the bodies do you see?"
    And I thought about it, and then he started asking me, "Would you

show me your body? Would you show me up there?" And he pointed to part of me.

I think I felt like my stomach turned, like when, all of a sudden, you get nauseated. I felt something bad inside, something bad about my body. So I knew that I had to protect myself from men. From then on I knew there was something about my body that was meaningful to him. It was just an instinct, but I felt awful.

And another time I went into this store downtown with Ana. I guess I must have just been developing my boobs. A man in the store looked at my chest, and he touched one of my breasts. He was just being nasty, but, again, I felt the same horrible thing come over me. When I was working at the hotel, I got followed home by six men at night, and I was so scared. And when I'd been out on the streets and dressed like a boy, I'd watched men and listened to them make comments on women's bodies.

My mom would let me go out to babysit because I'd get fifty cents or whatever, and, one time, when I was about twelve, I went to babysit with a neighbor girl, Aurora. She was about two years older than me. I was just supposed to keep her company at her house.

When I got there, she started locking the doors and shutting the windows. I said, "Why are you locking all the doors and windows?"

She said, "I just want to lock the house up so we can watch TV quietly."

"OK."

Then, all of a sudden, she let her cousin in. His name was Roy, and, my God, I'd never gone through so much. It was terrible. He tried to rape me. I didn't know a person, a man, could be so vicious. I didn't know that kind of cruelty. I'd been hurt by my dad, I'd been abused a lot, but not in this way.

He slapped me and pulled my hair. He pulled my clothes up, just pulling me apart. I fought and crawled under the bed, and both he and Aurora were tearing at me. She was doing it so he could abuse me. I was under the bed, grabbing the spring in the center, just like a spider or something, an insect under there. So they got sticks, I think one was a broom, and poked me all over and moved the bed one way and the other and poked me pretty bad. So, finally, I was so hurt that I couldn't hold on anymore, and they pulled me out.

Next he pulled me to the rest room, and I kept fighting and biting him, but he was too strong for me. He got me on the floor and was choking me, with his arm over my throat.

Then somebody started banging on the outside door. It was Aurora's brother, Nono, that's what I called him. I guess he noticed that his sister was puffing, and he called, "Hey, what's the matter?"

She said, "Nothing's the matter."

He said, "Hey, something's wrong."

Eventually, he started opening up his way through the hallway, and he heard my moaning or whatever sound from underneath Roy's hand. Then he broke into the bathroom and grabbed Roy, and he beat him up. He beat him like you wouldn't believe and said, "You dirty dog."

When I got home, my mom was laying down with a whole bunch of kids all over her as usual, and I was crying and trying to talk to her, "Mommy, Mommy, do you know what happened, Mommy?"

But in her sleep, she was saying, "Go to bed. Say nice things. Don't say things like that." I guess she didn't . . . couldn't . . . I guess she was just too tired.

I was so afraid my father was going to find out, and I was totally in shock, very, very cold. I was shivering. It was hot outside, but I was cold. So I took my clothes off and made sure I'd put them way down in the garbage so nobody would ever see them, and the next day, my mom was just my mom—nothing was said.

I would have never imagined something like that, even if I'd had any knowledge of sex, but I didn't even have that. I could tell you if there was malice in a person, in a guy's eyes, but I really didn't understand it. And I had nightmares for the longest time.

Also, I'd already felt bad about my body. I had a girl cousin when I was young, and she'd always embarrass me and put me down because of my body, that I was built wrong. I don't think she meant to hurt me, but I was conscious about how I looked. She was a few years older, and she'd constantly put me down, saying that I was ugly, I wasn't pretty. She'd say it in a way to try to help me. I can't remember ever seeing myself in a mirror, but I felt different, and I felt I didn't belong. I guess I felt ugly.

I didn't know about periods either. One day I was scrubbing and waxing Mom's floor on my hands and knees, when I leaned back on my heels and suddenly felt something warm and wet. I was wearing a dress, a wraparound, and one of my distant aunts noticed and said, "What is that on your dress?" When I turned my dress around, I saw blood, and I ran to the rest room.

When I got there, my panties and my dress were stained, so I washed them hard and put toilet tissue against me. I was really worried, I thought, oh my God, why is it coming out? What am I going to tell them? What is happening to me?

Then I thought, I'll tell them I cut my knees while I was scrubbing, and that's why I have blood on my clothes. So I scrubbed my knees till they bled, and I felt safe that it looked like the blood came out from them. I didn't know what was going to happen if they saw blood on my panties. I just didn't know how they'd react to that.

For about three days, I couldn't sleep I was so anguished because it wouldn't stop. Finally, I think it was Ana who asked me about it. I think I made her swear and promise that she wouldn't tell nobody, and she told me my aunt had Kotex up in the closet.

So I started taking my aunt's Kotex, and I guess I'd taken about three, when my aunt, she went up to her closet and noticed that the box was open. So she got Mom and everybody together. See, Ana was pregnant, and my mom wasn't on her period, so they cornered me and asked if I knew who had taken some Kotex from up in the box.

I said, "No, I don't know," but my aunt knew I was lying because I was so scared.

So she told my mom and Ana to leave me alone with her, and she grabbed a belt and said, "I'm going to beat the living daylights out of you if you don't talk." And she was mean. I wouldn't talk, but finally I told her.

She said, "Well, why didn't you say so?"

I said, "Because I was afraid. When my father finds out, that's going to be the end of my life. What's going to happen to me? What are you going to do?"

She said, "Well, I'm going to fix some tea for you." I was so surprised. Then she said, "From now on, you don't have to steal them. You can take them." But after I drank the tea, she said, "OK, you can get your butt up, and it's time to go back to work. This is nothing to be worried about, and I'm not going to tell your mom or anyone else."

So I thought it was a secret, but I think it wasn't. I think she told my mom. But I never told Mom that I was on my period, that I was sick, nobody. I just kept it to myself. I went through a lot of toilet tissue so I wouldn't have to ask for those things called Kotex.

I confided in a little girl, finally, and she told me that wearing Kotex was bad, that your part wasn't supposed to be touched at all, that it was like committing a sin to wear something there, to put anything even close. So I would constantly wear toilet tissue instead of Kotex.

I think it was Ana who said, "You're going to be having this the rest of your life." She said that I could take aspirins and was not to eat this and not to eat that. But, of course, I didn't pay any attention to that. I didn't connect down there with my mouth, so I ate anything I wanted to when we had it.

The worst times were when I was in the field. It was bad because your back hurts. I never really suffered from cramps up front, but from backaches and carrying those heavy hampers of tomatoes and cucumbers, which was what we worked mostly. And there was no privacy in the rest rooms in the camps. It was awful, when I was on my period and having to be around other little girls who were younger and older females who were just watching your body and what you were doing, sometimes just waiting for you there or trying to hurry you up. I'd be trying to have privacy. It was awful. So sometimes, to avoid going through that embarrassment, I'd go into the woods so I could change in there.

It was horrible in the migrant camps. You still see places like those all over, taking a bath or sharing the same toilets without any doors. I always carried toilet tissue under my panties or in my bra, and I was always scared I was going to bleed in front of somebody.

I tried to talk to my daughters about it, to make them feel at ease and to know that it was alright. A lot of people still think it's wrong to tell your daughters. There's a lot of people that don't want their kids to know about sex and menstruation.

And my father seemed to keep getting stricter. I was in a migrant camp, and this little girl named Reina Andrade gave me a beautiful, emerald-green, two-piece bathing suit. I was about eleven. Dad didn't find out about the bathing suit until one day when we went to a lake and I came out of the bath house in the suit. Well, I didn't even make it to the water. He just dragged me away and whipped me real bad.

Then, when I was older, my girl cousin, the one who was always putting me down for being so skinny and bowlegged and dressing stupid, wanted me to go with her to a dance. She was already going to get married, and she went to my dad and asked if I could go to the dance with her.

My dad said, "María Elena can only go if the whole family's going to be there."

She said, "Yes, Uncle Manuel. We'll do it that way."

Then my father said, "OK, but I'm going to come around there, and you all better not be dancing because if I see you dancing, you're going to get it."

So we went to the dance, but the whole family wasn't there, and this boy came up and invited me to dance. The boy, who was real nice, asked me, "Where are you from?"

I said, "From Brownsville," and that's as far as I got when my father walked into the room. My God, he came in, grabbed me by the hair, and pulled me out. He said, "I told you that I better not catch you." And he almost hit my cousin too. Then he took us in the car and said, "This is the last time that María Elena goes with you, 'cause you're not going to make a fool of me."

I was so scared, I can't even remember what happened after that, but he didn't ever let me go out again. I'd dance at home, like with "La Bamba" on the radio, but not ever any real dancing.

When I was twelve, something happened. One time I'd gone with Ana to a junkyard. There was an old man there, his name was Che. That's when I started to understand that what Ana was doing was selling her body for food. I stayed in a near room while she went someplace else with the man. I thought, what is she going to do out there with that guy? And, all of a sudden, even though I didn't really understand the sex act, I realized that she was being a prostitute.

Then we had a real bad time at home and were really hungry. There was no food. Most of the time, it was beans, tortillas, butter, and potatoes, but this time was really bad. Ana went to my mom and asked for permission to take me to the movies.

My mom knew I'd never been out to a movie and didn't pay much attention, so she says, "Yeah, go ahead."

So this boyfriend of Ana's came up and instead of going to the movies, we went out in the country. They had another young man along with them in the back seat. We went far into the woods, and I told Ana, "Hey, why are we here? Why aren't we in the movies?"

Then she took off with her boyfriend in one direction, and I was left alone with this other guy. This young man said, "Do you know why you're here?"

And I said, "No, I don't," but I knew something was wrong, and I was scared.

He said, "If your mom and your dad knew where you were, this lady would be in a lot of trouble. I know the reason she's doing it is to provide food for the rest of the family, but this is not the right thing to do." He said, "She came to sell you to me, and I was supposed to pay her."

That's when I really understood. But he was nice and said, "I'm not going to hurt you. Don't be afraid." He didn't even touch me.

I think Ana took about two hours, a long time, and it was raining too. So when she came back we were still sitting in the back seat talking. I was talking, but I was so scared too. Ana was surprised to see me just sitting there. I guess maybe she expected to see me in another condition.

I really don't remember at that time what kind of emotional reaction I was having, but I'd been so close to Ana. She was like a family member. I know I was upset and I was hurt, so I guess I must have lost my trust with her because I never went out with her again. To this day, I think Ana still thinks that something happened to me, which it didn't. I think she was just trying to get extra money home because whatever she made she'd bring as food, and this was just another way.

Also, Ana knew how terrified I was of my father and that I'd never, ever open my mouth to tell him something like that. She also probably saw that Mom was so easy, so negligent, that she didn't keep up. I mean there were so many kids that I don't blame Mom. Ana probably figured, well, Celia's never going to know. She won't even notice anything. And Ana probably thought about me, well, you're a girl. Maybe this will help a bit more. Learn to sell your body.

> The child grows into a woman
> > Spring is gone, winter pierces her heart
> The black eagle flies high while it watches and waits
> > Love turns to hate, hate to rebellion
> The black eagle strikes, the woman goes to war
> > Guerrillera!
> From the mountains the echoes are heard
> All the way deep down where the miners work
> > Guerrillera!
> The machete hisses as it cuts the cold wind
> The flame burns with despair
> > And the Guerrillera with anger cries

Fly, black eagle, Fly
Deliver unto men and women on earth
    my sorrowful plight!

(Diary, October 30, 1987)

CHAPTER SEVEN

The Child Weds: Learning to Think like a Married Woman

If God made man in his image, this certainly confuses me . . .
—Diary, September 20, 1983

I met Andrés when I was fifteen. He was five years older than me and living right next door to us in the government projects. The first time I saw him, my brother José had stuck a nail in his foot, and Andrés came out to help. He said, "Hi, let me help you." Either he tried to help me carry José or stop the bleeding, it just happened real fast. But I remember already dreaming about a man who looked like him, that we were married and had a child.

The second time I saw him, there was a big screen with movies outside the projects, and I was sitting down on his porch with his sister, then she went in and Andrés came out. He sat down on the porch sort of close to me, and over about fifteen minutes, he kept scooting closer till he was sitting next to me. Then all of a sudden, he says, "Will you marry me? Be my wife?"

I looked at him and answered, "Yeah." It was a way out. I wanted to get married. It was like running away.

After he kissed me, Andrés said, "What's your name?"

I said, "María Elena." Then he kissed me and said, "Are you sure you'll marry me?" and I said, "Yeah," again. Then I thought, oh my God, think what you did.

113

It must have been about two or three days later that I saw him and said, "We're leaving. We're going to Ohio."

He said, "Can I write you?"

"Yeah, but I'm not sure of the address, so as soon as I get there, I'll write you a letter and tell you where."

Then he said again, "Are you still going to marry me?"

And I said, "Sure." It was a way out. I didn't even love him. I swear to God I had no idea what love was. The next day, we went to Ohio, and I told an aunt he was going to write me, and she went and got the mail so my daddy wouldn't get to it, because if Daddy got it, that was the end of me, probably.

In every letter, Andrés asked me, "Will you still marry me?"

And I answered back, "Yes."

But Andrés's family didn't want him to get married to me. There was another girl by the name of Evangelina from Mexico who was living in Matamoros. Her family had won a lottery, *la lotería mexicana,* and they were kind of wealthy and she was educated. According to them, I wasn't, I was just like what you'd call a dog. They tried to bribe him by saying they'd take him away to somewhere in Mexico, like Acapulco, Cuernavaca, Guadalajara, some place away so he'd forget me, but he didn't go. He wanted to marry me and I wanted to marry him.

Then, after I got back, he was in Monterrey, Mexico, so it was about a week before he came to see me. By then my father had gone back up to Ohio to work, and I thought, well, this is going to make it so much easier. It was easier to manipulate my mom.

So Andrés came and we kissed and we talked, and he says, "Well, I want to send the *portadores* to come and ask for your hand." These are the people that come to the parents and ask for a girl's hand in marriage. They are supposed to be very respectable and experienced people.

When they came, my mom said, "No, I can't say nothing. You talk to her father."

Well, my mom used to go to the pay phone at a certain hour once a week, and my dad would call her. The next time I went with her to the phone booth, and I reached it before she did. Then the phone rang, and Mom said, "Answer it."

So I did, but I had no idea that he was going to talk to me about the marriage. My dad says, "Hello, *mi'ja.* Oh, you should see how beautiful it is out here in Ohio. There are stars in the sky, it's real clear. There's a big full moon, and the snow glitters like diamonds, *mi'ja*."

I said, "Oh, yeah?"

He says, "Yeah, it's beautiful. You should just see this." Then, all of a sudden, he says, "*mi'ja*, they're telling me you want to get married."

"Oh," and I froze.

"Who is that *cabrón* that you want to get married to?"

"His name is Andrés, and he's the helper of a masonry, in construction."

"Oh, yeah, *mi'ja*? So you want to get married?"

"Yeah, Daddy."

He said, "OK, *mi'ja*, if you get married, don't ever, ever come to me with your problems or come to the house again. If you're married, you're dead, you're gone."

And that's what he told my mom. "Ella ya se casó, se murió." Meaning, "I don't even want to see her. She got married, she's dead." And so for over a year, I didn't see him at all. It stayed like that until I had Eva.

So Andrés's sister sewed up the gown, and his family bought the whole outfit for the wedding. It was just a civil ceremony on December 30, 1956. It was not the church, and I could tell by the look on their faces that Andrés's family was against me.

I still didn't understand totally about sex when I got married. I knew Mom's getting pregnant had a lot to do with my father, but I didn't exactly know how. Andrés and I went to one of his family's house right after the wedding. I didn't really know what I was getting into. I thought we were just going to live together, that we were going to kiss. I knew that felt good, but that's as far as I knew.

When he tried to touch me or unbutton my dress, I said, "No, what are you doing? Is this part of being married?" I said, "Oh, no, not with me. I didn't get married to get undressed."

He says, "What do you mean?"

I said, "Just what I'm saying. You can kiss me, but I'm not going to get undressed."

Mom didn't tell me anything about what was going to happen, nobody did. So, after three days of talking to me, he told me that was the way it was supposed to be, but I still didn't agree. I never did agree. It happened to me, but I didn't accept it. I was so embarrassed about my body.

I didn't marry him because I loved him. I didn't know what love was. I liked him, and he liked me, but you don't love from one day to the next, not the way I agreed to marry him.

I think I've tried to be very open with my daughters, talking to them. But I think we all try to be, not discreet, but there's things that we don't talk to anybody about, not even to your own mother. We have a tendency to be, not really conservative, but to just keep some things to yourself. My daughters seem very open, very frank, with me, and I try to advise them, but I wonder if they're saying everything because I couldn't have with my mother.

At that time, Andrés's family was living in Mexico, Matamoros, because his father was a Mexican. My mother-in-law always claimed she was born in the U.S., but I think she was actually born in Mexico, and some sister died, and she took the papers and claimed she was a U.S. citizen. Later, they told me two different dates for when Andrés was born, and I kept trying to clear up his legal status, but they'd say, "Your curiosity isn't good. It will just create problems." But when it finally came out, Andrés really had been born in Texas.

Anyway, when we got married, Andrés's father, may God bless his soul, was already sick and said he wanted to die in Mexico. So, of course, we went to live with them in Mexico. But they told me, "We're not going to introduce you to the family as Andrés's wife because it's not convenient right now. We don't want them to find out."

I was very young, so I said, "OK," and agreed with everything they said.

So when they introduced me to the family in Mexico, they said, "This is the new maid."

The maid they had, her name was Rebecca, and after I'd been there about a week, they started showing me the work that Rebecca was doing. Rebecca started like training me, and I didn't realize it. Then they let Rebecca go, and I took her place.

My in-laws made it very clear right away, when I first got married, that I didn't count at all. They made it clear that anything they said or did I had to accept, and every time I tried to talk to them, they thought I was crazy. As a matter of fact, many times my own husband would tell my kids, "Your mom's crazy."

By two weeks after I got married, I already regretted it. Andrés started being violent just about right away. Right away, his brothers came around and said that it was good practice to leave me within his mom's care, and that he could start going out very frequently so that I'd not be thinking that he was going to be there by my side. They said that a woman belongs to the home, and the man belongs to the streets. If he stayed with me and was nice to me, I'd get used to that, and then, whenever he wanted to go out and find someone else, there would be problems because I wasn't going to let him. They told him he should start practicing going out with other women right away, so I wouldn't think I was the only one.

And he did and that made me very sad, made me cry and be sorry that I'd ever gone with him. And when I let him know that I didn't want him to do that, he said, "You don't have any say-so. You don't have any rights. You married me. What I say or my mom and family say goes. Don't ever forget that."

So whenever I started crying, my mother-in-law would start in on me, and then I'd cry more. He'd come home, and she'd tell him, "I can't take this. She cries all the time. Look, *mi'jo,* you're going to have to straighten her out because she's got to learn that she's a woman and that this is her responsibility. She's in the house, and you're a man that has nothing to do with the house." She'd say, "You support her, and she should be happy that you're providing. Her family don't want her. They don't care about her." She'd repeat that very constantly. "She's got to learn to behave like a married woman." So that would get me in trouble and he'd start hitting me.

They were very jealous, too, in the sense that I think I must have been kind of pretty, and they didn't want me to be around anybody else. I was not allowed to go any place at all, not even to the grocery store. And I wasn't allowed to talk with anyone, and they always put me down. I had to adapt from one household's ways to another household's ways, and both were equally just as bad. In both of them, I just didn't count at all.

Sometimes I'd talk to one of my sister-in-laws and tell her stories. I was just a kid, and I'd tell her stories about when we were out raiding garbage and times like that. I'd tell her what I thought about this and that, and she would listen to me. But later on, I heard her laughing with the rest of them about my conversations. They were making jokes about me, making fun, and I decided not to ever talk to any of them about any of my experiences.

So sometimes I'd write things down, but I had to be very careful. I was worried because I'd write about how I felt, then I'd be afraid they'd find it and laugh about it or get upset. I wrote a lot of poems, and I'd just generally complain to my diary. It became my friend. It became what I could complain to, and nobody would laugh at me.

After Andrés would hit me or beat me, he'd continue to punish me by not talking to me, by not having anything to do with me. Even in our very early marriage, it was like he had to teach me he was the man of the house, that he was the boss and anything I had to say wasn't appreciated. I think that partly comes because even before they get married, other men tell them to do that. Even now, it's the same. My son Héctor had a baby without being married, and when Héctor went to baptize his baby, the guys that are married to the baby's mother's sisters said, "You have to teach her who's the boss." It's sort of joking, but it's done in a serious way. Many different ways they put that through, and men seem to accept it. They say, "Yeah, well, you're right." Like it's to please the other guys, too.

Andrés's parents had a lot to do with it, especially his mom. Many times, it seemed like if I was trying to go with Andrés wherever he was going, she'd right away interfere and say, "Well, listen, we have a lot of work to do here at home, María Elena. But God bless you, my son."

Women can get more authority when they become a mother-in-law, especially if the son is like Andrés and some of my brothers. If the man is nicer to his wife, then she has less control. I understand my mother-in-law got married when she was around thirteen years old. She used to say her mother-in-law was a wonderful person, that she loved her a lot. She'd tell me stories that sometimes her mother-in-law let her play like a little kid after she was married. She'd say that she was always at home with her mother-in-law and would always try to please her. In a way, it was a message to me. The better you behave, the better you act, the more you please me, the better your life will be, the better we will treat you.

That's very common among our culture when you get married. Nowadays, with the girls of this generation that are American-born, I see a great change. But a lot of people from the Mexican culture, the real Mexican people, that is still something that is very strong among the married couples. The girl gets married and goes home to the young man's parent's house to stay there and begin her life, and it's just like she takes over as a maid and they take over her life. They strip her of everything she was and make her into something that they want her to be. That can go on for years. It all hurt so much. I wasn't allowed to sit at the same table with Andrés to eat. My mother-in-law kept me away from him at all times.

After I got married, I hardly let Mom know anything about what was going on with me, but sometime I must have told her about Andrés hurting me. I guess Mom told Dad, then Dad came to me and said, "You were the one who wanted to get married. You wanted a man. Now you stay with him. That's your place. Don't think that we're ever going to take you back."

And I'd listen to my father tell my husband, "Any time that this bitch doesn't listen to you, beat her up. Any time this bitch gets out of line, hurt her bad." Ain't that terrible! I remember that.

A few months after I got married, it got unbearable. I wasn't allowed to talk or laugh or do nothing. "Stay out of the way, sit down, don't laugh, do nothing." By the second week we had been married, he had already slapped me around, and I was constantly punished in one way or another, for being dumb, for being ignorant. I'd tried to talk to my sister-in-laws, but I talked about childish things. I was a daydreamer and I didn't have any other things to talk about. I think I talked about beautiful things, but things they didn't talk about. I was interested in flowers and trees and the sea and songs, and they said it all was childish.

The only time I stood up and fought back was when I ran away. And that time I learned that if I answered back to my mother-in-law or defended myself in any way or tried to oppose any of the things they did, I'd really be in trouble with Andrés. One day we were cleaning house, and my mother-in-law was very upset, and she told me, "From now on you stay up until Andrés goes to bed, and when he goes to sleep, you go to sleep. And if there's company and they ask you anything, just don't answer. And if they laugh, I don't want you to laugh or talk or anything."

I felt terrible. I went into the main room and sat down and cried. There was a girl in there, and she looked at me with such sadness that I felt she could feel for me, and I turned and I told her, "They don't like me, do they?"

She says, "No, they don't."

Then, I guess, it was like it was revealed to me. That gave me the courage to stand up. I knew that my birth certificate was in a cupboard, and I opened the door to it and took it out. And Andrés had given me one nickel, one American nickel. I'd asked for that nickel because many guys would come around with little wagons selling snow cones. I'd asked Andrés, "Can I have a nickel so I can buy something from the wagon?"

So I took my nickel and birth certificate and just walked out as fast as I could. I didn't even have any shoes on. I walked at a very fast pace and was afraid to turn around because I felt like somebody bad was following me. And, sure enough, my mother-in-law caught up. She grabbed me and turned me around. She said, "I'm going to tell Andrés, and you're going to be sorry, and don't think that you're going to be coming back."

I just looked at her and I was scared, I was afraid, she was a big woman. She overpowered me real easy, not that I thought I could fight back or anything, but she was something like my father. Anyway, I told her, "I want to go home. Let me go."

She said, "You're going to be sorry," and she turned and left.

I kept walking, but it took two nickels to get the bus to the border. I ended up in the *mercado,* and I ran into my friend Francés from a long time before in school. She's the one who was so poor and pretty and who didn't speak much English. She was working as a salesgirl in the Mexican market, and I don't think she was married yet. I told her of my trouble, and she gave me another nickel so I could take the bus to the border. Then we said good-bye, and I never saw her again.

I took a bus to the border, then I walked across. I guess I must have looked pretty bad. People usually wore shoes to cross; I don't think I've ever seen anybody cross barefooted, but at least I could speak English.

I went to my aunt's house because my father had made it clear that I couldn't go to them. He never wanted to know anything about any of my problems. While I was at my aunt's house, Andrés and his sister came to talk to me. He told me, "You can't go home to your parents. If you stay here, don't ever expect to go to their house because they're not accepting you."

And his sister told me, "You're married. You're a woman, and women don't do things this way. You have to grow up. You have to learn that you're not a little girl anymore. You're already a married woman, and you need to think like one."

Finally, I was overpowered by them. I got in the car with Andrés, and when we got back to the house in Matamoros, there were about twenty-some people waiting for us, people I didn't even know. It was like the whole neighborhood went to the house to get me. One and another and another kept putting me down, telling me I wasn't allowed to do that kind of thing.

One time I did try to defend myself, and I told them that it seemed to me like they were ganging up on me and that wasn't fair. I don't remember whether he slapped me or what happened, but Andrés turned and in front of everybody said, "Don't you dare again, ever, ever again, open your mouth. The only one that has any right over you is my mother and I. You have no say. I don't even want you to say anything to my sisters."

At that moment, I realized he was not the only person that I was bound to, it was his family also. So I had no say over nothing, absolutely nothing. I was told, "Here are the dirty clothes. We want you to wash them and iron them. We want you to do this and to do that." No happiness, no kindness, no nothing. I realized then that I had gotten into something that I didn't know how to get out of. And I was just a little girl, really. I was just a kid. I didn't talk to them, I didn't have any friends, I just kept to myself.

There seemed to be no more running away, but I kept drawing and writing poems, and I was creative, and sometimes I still talked about beautiful things. Then Andrés's family would sigh and say, "What did he marry?" So they decided to take me to a *curandera*, because, according to them, I wasn't normal. They always judged me that way. I was dumb, I was stupid, and I was not normal. I was crazy. I'd hear them say this.

So they told me they were taking us to a lady at something like a little chapel or a church. They said it had to do with giving my wedding bouquet as an offering. We hadn't had a church wedding at that time, and the bride and groom has an offering to Our Lady of San Juan. Because it was to Our Lady, right away I agreed it was the right thing to do. As ignorant as I was, I responded to something related to God.

We went to a very poor *colonia* in Matamoros, and the building didn't look like any church to me. The boards of the little house were rotten with cracks, and it looked so quiet on the outside, I wasn't even sure this was the place we were going to. I thought maybe we just stopped here first.

When we opened the door, there was a big room full of people, but it was so dark you could barely see their faces. I thought it looked like a long time ago when someone died, and the body and wake would be at home. My mother-in-law said to be very quiet and to sit down. So I sat down and listened and watched what was going on. There was this big woman in the center of a place, and she was surrounded by candles and saints and objects and pictures and a big bowl of water. And flowers, like when there's been a funeral. And incense. Now I know it was incense because I know the word. And rosemary and garlic all over, a lot of different things.

Then this lady, they called her Chavelita, began trembling and jumping and her voice changed. She began to call some people forward, and another woman came in there and a man stood in the door. Sometimes they'd say, "So and so come forward," and that person would come forward and talk to her. I guess they'd tell her their problems, and she'd make signs on their heads.

My mother-in-law told me that I had to believe in the woman, and if I didn't believe, she'd know. So I thought, if I say, yes, I believe, whoever this woman is and whatever they're trying to do to me, they're going to find out the truth of how I feel. When it was my turn, my in-laws said, "Get up. That's you! Go to her." Andrés didn't go up to her with me. He just stayed with his mother.

So I went to her, but I didn't kneel down. I stood just straight, kind of stiff. Her eyes were closed and her voice seemed kind of hoarse, like when you have a sore throat. She looked weird, and I didn't trust any of them there. I guess I was frightened because I didn't know what they were trying to do.

Chavelita said, "So, you're María Elena. I know you, I know who you are. You're not behaving too good, and we're going to have to cure you of that demon inside of you." She said that I wasn't a very good person, that I wasn't going to make a good wife, something like I was going to need a lot of discipline because I was kind of wild and crazy, that I was going to have to let the family discipline me a lot because I wasn't normal.

Then she asked me, "Do you believe in me?"

"No. I don't know what you are or who you are." And that made things real bad. Everybody gasped, like, "Oh, my God!"

Chavelita was very upset, and she called someone and said they were going to *curarme,* to cure me of the bad spirits. I couldn't figure out what they meant. Then she said that I had to do everything that I was told. She said, "We're going to . . . *te vamos a dar una barrida.*" A "sweep." So this other lady and a man came and took me about two feet from her, and she told me, "Drop your blouse."

Even though I couldn't see them, the rest of the people were out there. I kept my front covered up, but my back was bare. Then they took out two whips, like from a willow tree because the whips could bend, but they didn't have no leaves. Then she took one in each hand, and she began to whip me with one hand and the other.

It was like a nightmare, like when you're having a nightmare and you can't wake up from it. My heart was pounding real fast, and I didn't know what was going on. I forgot about the crowd. All I wanted to do was to get out and see the daylight.

She whipped me, and she kept saying something like, "You're too hard and heavy." I don't know what she meant by that. And she'd say, *"No puedo, no puedo con ella."* I can't, I can't with her. She kept saying that there was something unholy about me, that where did I get all my ideas, and that I wasn't worthy of God. I think I was crying, and everybody saw her whip me. Then, when everything was over, I was taken to another room. There was light in that room, and they said, "Stand here and wait."

After about forty-five minutes, Chavelita came out and talked just like another person, her voice was changed again. Everybody was bringing her presents, and she was treated like royalty and like a holy kind of thing. I just stood and looked at her. Every once in a while, she'd look at me, and I don't think she looked at me with blessings. I guess it was obvious from my expression how I felt about her.

My mother-in-law was too busy pleasing her to notice how I was staring. I guess I was just studying Chavelita. I couldn't get over that they claimed she was a holy person, that the spirit would come into her body. I just looked at her, and I could tell that she was bothered by my expression. She'd turn and look at me and keep on being very nice to the people.

Then she came and sat with my mother-in-law and told her that they couldn't do nothing with me, that it was impossible, that I was just too strong. She said, "She's too much. I can't with her." I kept thinking, this must have something to do with witchcraft. They're claiming that this is a holy thing. There's nothing holy about it. They must be ignorant. It made me very angry, and I was glad I was too strong for them.

Then they told me I'd have to go back to continue the treatment, but the second time I was taken to her, she was kind of sick so she didn't do a lot. But she still tried to convince me I should be a good wife and do whatever my husband said, that I must always obey the family. She said that I had gotten married to a very good man.

The third time I heard about Chavelita, she was dead. Then another time I saw a newspaper story and realized that she had been a *curandera*. There had been raids, and people like her had been exposed to the public because they were exploiting people who'd pay money for miracles.

It didn't make me stop my poems and drawing. I'd draw the way my husband came to my mind, and they were usually pretty ugly, kind of demonlike, and it was kind of frightening to see that, 'cause it was like the devil really showing up. And I had so many things written down. I'd write little notes calling to God and asking why. I wanted to know what caused all this suffering. Of course, I was very afraid that if my husband found any of it, I'd really be in a lot of trouble, so I kept it hidden. It was like in my song:

> I was born a poor girl
> by the Gulf of Mexico,
> I was raised in the woods
> Off of chayote roots
>
> Ay, Santo Señor, sudando bajo el Sol.
> [Ay, Dear Lord, sweating under the sun]
>
> I became a woman
> when I should've been a child,
> Ay, Santo Señor, sudando bajo el Sol.
>
> I was made a woman
> when I should've been a child,
> Ay, Santo Señor, llorando bajo el Sol
> [Ay, Dear Lord, crying under the sun]
>
> Just the tumbling weeds
> that were blowing by,
> On that dusty windy day
> heard my helpless cry.
>
> Ay, Santo Señor, llorando bajo el Sol.

(October 12, 1983)

CHAPTER EIGHT

Motherhood and Misery

Using birth control never came up with Andrés, and before long I was pregnant. But my mother-in-law even controlled that. Every time I got pregnant, that was the end of sleeping together. So I learned to be that way. Andrés would do everything his mom said. I couldn't understand it. The rest of her daughter-in-laws always took off with their husbands and had privacy. But our marriage was something they didn't want to happen.

We were all very poor, so we left Mexico and went working as migrants again in Texas. I worked in the fields all the time when I was pregnant. I was pregnant and fifteen years old and dragging those bags of cotton. I also was barefoot. I lost my shoes in the field one time, and Andrés and his mom wouldn't get me any others. They said they were going to teach me not to be careless.

In Vanderbilt, Texas, we lived in a little shack with maybe four rooms. I slept in one room with my sister-in-law. My mother-in-law was sleeping somewhere else at that time, but most of the time, she slept with us. But I remember the crevices, the cracks between the boards of the walls, they were full of scorpions. At night we had to light a piece of wood with a rag soaked in kerosene like a torch, and brush all over the walls with flames to keep them away. I couldn't sleep good because I kept thinking that one of them was going to fall out. And in the outhouse it was so terrible. The first time I opened the door, it was filled with huge lizards, what I now think were iguanas. They started jumping and hissing. I thought they were attacking me and threw my arms up to protect myself. Even after the lizards were gone, there were scorpions. You could see them, one after another, and some of them were eating the mother. Also spiders. Even now, it's sometimes like that.

When I was pregnant that first time, it was so bad that we went for about three months with only oatmeal without sugar at ten o'clock in the morning and boiled potatoes around three or four o'clock in the afternoon. That was it. No tortillas, no bread, no nothing.

My mother-in-law made the decisions about who got what to eat. I didn't have to be told too many times, but when the food came in, she'd say, "Now, the men have to eat first because they're the ones that have to go out and work, and we women can do with anything." So that meant stay away from it, even if you were pregnant. It was always like that, even when there was enough for everyone.

I still don't understand how it happened one time, but I was very hungry. Very hungry. They had a cupboard, and I somehow saw hidden cookies in the cupboard, but there was really no way I could have seen them. Still, I saw cookies way up high, so I got up on a chair, and I put my hand through to the back of the cupboard, and, sure enough, there was a package of cookies. Chocolate cookies.

I was caught doing that, but my mother-in-law wasn't cruel about it. She just told me, "María Elena, you can't have those cookies. Those cookies are for Pepe and the men."

I've seen this with young women today, and I get very upset over it. The women and children get fed different from the father. Also, my mom tries to do it even to this day. I see my mom serving my father better or tending to him better than anybody else. She makes sure that my brother Ruben and the men get a fair share of the food, but I don't see my mother worrying too much about the females. If there is enough for them, fine, and if there's not, she'll say, "Well, they can make potatoes."

That time when I was pregnant and only had oatmeal and potatoes, I began to take eggs and chickens from the grower. I began to steal.

The grower asked, "Are there any animals around like *tejones*?" I think that's a racoon, the one that cuts a chicken's head off.

I said, "I don't know," but then the family found out. It was during the winter months when there's a lot of ice and it's real cold, and I was just so hungry.

That time everybody was eating little, but there were other times when there was a little money, and even then my mother-in-law made sure that the men were fed first. That was always the case. Always. If there was a little piece of meat, the men would eat it. She'd say, "They have to eat better than we do because they're the ones that go out there and try to find food." But I remember that often there was money for beer.

My first Christmas, when things were so bad, I cried for a Christmas tree. I knew there was no way I could get a real Christmas tree this time, so I said, "Well, I'll make one." So I went out and cut a tumbleweed and decorated the tumbleweed with lots of cotton from the fields.

I waited until I was real sick [in labor] before they took me to the little hospital in Post, Texas. There was a lot of discrimination at that time, so I was the only one allowed in. They made Andrés wait outside in the cold because he was Mexican. He had to stand on the steps even though it was winter. Then the doctor wouldn't let anybody touch me or give me anything for pain because he said, "I know you can have a normal childbirth, and I want you to experience what the pain is like. That way, next time you'll think when you want a child." It was very painful, and I just stayed there until I had Eva. I was out of the hospital the next day, and as soon as I got home with the baby, my mother-in-law moved to a different house, so I had to wash on a scrub board right away.

It was winter, and there was no heat, no light, and only an outhouse to go to the bathroom. In fact, where Eva was born, we didn't have a house for people, it was a shed for animals. It was made out of tin, the roof and everything. We'd chop wood and put it in a big tub outside and light it. Then Andrés would make sure the wood had quit smoking before he brought it in. He wouldn't turn the wood on during the day, it was just during the night. I'd go under the blankets and make a little tent in the bed so that Eva would be warm, and I tried to keep her close to my body. Eva was God's child, just like other children. Somebody should have cared.

There was really no one to help me out with the baby. They just said there were certain foods I wasn't supposed to eat, like, "Don't eat hot stuff because then your milk will taste like pepper."

My mother-in-law and Andrés decided what to name Eva. They didn't tell me they were naming her after Andrés's old girlfriend, Evangelina, but I knew. Only Johnny I got to name. Christy was named because of another of Andrés's girlfriends. It's nice to name your own kids. I always had such a big list of names. Marena was one of my names because *mar* means sea and *arena* means sand, but they thought I was crazy. I did sew Eva's clothes. I made everything for her. I crocheted and sewed little shirts, even the diapers.

After the weather was warmer, I was back working in onion fields. We'd take the tops off the onions and make little hills of them. They'd dry for a couple of days, and then we'd go back and put them in sacks. I had a little tomato crate for Eva that I fixed with blankets and a pillow. I tied a rope from me to the crate, and then as I crawled along the fields, I pulled her behind me. I thought it would be a good idea to keep her happy. If I nursed while I was hot, she'd get sick, so I cooled down a bit first. Then I'd sit and nurse her under the big *calites,* weeds, and put her in the shade.

My mom and dad had gone out to Ohio to work as migrants, but my daddy ended up working in a company. Mom found out that I was having a very difficult situation because I wrote her a letter. So my father worked it out, and the company offered Andrés a job, and we moved to Ohio for a few months.

Mom had a baby and too many kids of her own to act excited about my Eva, but she treated her with kindness. I've seen my mom get real excited with other grandchildren, the ones that have been born and stayed by her side, but with my kids, she was never attached. I did notice that my mom and dad would kind of come and look at the baby. Dad would say, "Wow, she's ugly," but I guess he was playing. Mom told me that she was an awfully small and skinny baby and tried to help me nurse her. One time she fed me all kinds of cereals so maybe I'd get more milk in my breasts.

When we were in Ohio, the farmer's wife who convinced my mom to get married by church talked Mom into convincing us to get married by church. It was after we already had Eva and was just *cumpliendo,* fulfilling, it was something we owed God so we weren't in sin. I had to do it because God wasn't happy, but I didn't expect Andrés to treat me better. And I didn't understand what I was doing to my future.

After we moved back to Brownsville, I miscarried a baby. Altogether, I had several miscarriages, and I got pretty sick with one of them. I stayed sick for eighteen days that time, and, finally, Andrés's family took me across the river, across the border to Mexico to a doctor in his office. He put me asleep, and I guess he scraped me inside. I was very, very sick. If I hadn't gone to see him, I'd have died because I was bleeding. My aunt, the one that took me, she said the baby had putrefied inside me, there was pus and blood. It was like when an egg gets rotten inside.

In those days, women didn't go see doctors, especially poor families never did. The women just had midwives. I never saw any worry about my mom when she was having babies, and I never did pay attention to my periods. I did get a lot of morning sickness. That was one sign.

I remember one time I was pregnant, and I didn't know I was pregnant. I was sick and tired and sleepy. My husband's family, they thought I wanted to be lazy. They'd say, "Well, it's not good to be laying down. You have to walk around, and you have to do housework, and if you're coming down with a cold, that will help it to get better fast." Nobody would ever say, "We'll take you to the doctor," or, "What's the matter?" And I didn't have any transportation so I could go to a clinic. Nobody wanted to waste any time on me, so I just kept getting sicker and sicker, and my stomach would hurt, and they thought I had a virus.

Then, finally, one afternoon, I felt like I wanted to go to the bathroom, but I couldn't. At that time we had a regular flush toilet. My mother-in-law said, "Sometimes it helps if you sit down in a warm tub of water." So I tried that, and I noticed that when I got up it was all bloody. I thought it must be my period, but I kept going back and forth to the bathroom, trying to go, but I couldn't. Finally, I felt something heavy, big, coming out, like it opened my vagina, and then it fell into the water. It was full of blood, like a piece of meat.

I thought, God, I wonder if this is a baby, so I took it out and wrapped it up. I didn't know whether to show them or to throw it away or what to do. Then I thought, no, I'd better not tell them. I'll just put it in the garbage. That time, I already had Eva and Tommy and the twins, but I think it was before Gloria. I didn't feel the family would take what I said as important, even about a miscarriage. Nobody ever asked me anything. I couldn't give my opinion or make any decisions.

Before that, when Eva was just walking around and Tommy was already born and I was expecting the twins, Andrés and I lived alone in a one-room shack. It was a tiny room with a little table and a kerosene stove to cook in on one side, no water, no plumbing, no electricity, no nothing, just a bed and a baby bed.

Sometimes Andrés would bring fifty cents home, but that didn't buy hardly nothing. I remember you could get like an avocado, tortillas, and a tomato with it. Avocados with tortillas and onions and one pickle and tomatoes makes a meal. Even if you don't have any cooking oil, you can eat anyway. Of course, beans have always been the cheapest and best source of food for us. When you didn't have any beans, that's pretty bad, when you can't get any beans, potatoes, or rice. That time, when Andrés didn't have work, we had nothing at all, not even a can of tomatoes, not a potato, nothing.

I was standing on a chair, trying to divide the kitchen from the bedroom by hanging a blanket, when my sister-in-law and sister Norma came to visit me. For some reason, I turned and looked down at little Eva. She was on top of the bed. I told my sister-in-law, "Oh, look at that beautiful color." Eva's cheeks were a rosy color, and we just laughed.

Then Eva got down off the bed and was playing with something like a ball, and it rolled under the bed. I saw her lay down and try to get it. Then she just laid there, with her hands stretched out in front of her, and her body began to like jump.

When my sister and sister-in-law saw her, they screamed. They turned her over, and her eyes were turned backward and lots of foam was coming from her mouth. I jumped down from the chair and was all scared. I panicked and grabbed the baby from their arms and ran outside with her.

There was a young man living close to us, and I called him, "Come, quick! Come!"

He jumped the fence, and I said, "Please, help me give her air."

So he hit her on the back, and he threw her up and down to bring her back. I was so pregnant with the twins, I couldn't do it. And it brought her back, made her conscious.

Later on, that evening, her dad had gone to find something to eat, 'cause there was nothing, and this neighbor lady came over, and she looked at Eva and said, "*Mal de ojo,*" the evil eye. Then she cured Eva with an egg, rubbing it on Eva in the form of a cross, and when she broke the egg, it had two eyes [yolks] instead of one. The lady looked at me and said, "You're going to have twins." That was the first time I heard someone say I was going to have twins, and I never did know for sure until I had them.

Anyway, I was very upset. I guess it was about eight o'clock when Andrés came home, and it was already too late to buy things like tortillas or maybe an avocado. I just cried and cried. I didn't know what to do, I felt so helpless, so unable to do anything.

During the night, I thought, I have to do something. So, in the morning, I told God, "God, I promise you that if Andrés gets a job and brings home some money for food, I'm going to walk down the railroad tracks barefooted from here to where you're at on the cross in Our Lady of Guadalupe." It was at least a mile down those tracks. I try to make my promises to God hard on me, and that wasn't the first time I'd done that either.

I said, "I'm going to close my eyes while I make this sacrifice, and I'm not going to open my eyes until I touch your feet and kiss them. I'll have someone accompany me to guide me on the way."

But still we didn't have anything to eat, and it was real cold, and I didn't have any kerosene for the stove. The kids and me were just sitting inside, all covered with blankets. They were crying. I was crying. I didn't know what to do. I just couldn't go ask Mom and Dad for nothing. My dad was not the type to say, "Well, here's a dollar, go buy yourself some food."

But Ana lived close by, and she came by and said, "*Por qué está tan frío?* Why is it so cold? Oh, my God, don't tell me you don't have any fuel." She meant kerosene.

So she went and got Don José. He never married her but he lived with her. He was as old as Pablo is, so I guess it was something like my situation now. She took care of him without being close, without the sex of husband and wife. So Don José got me a little glass container with kerosene that you put on the stove. They brought me one of those, and Ana brought me a *taquito,* a whole big casserole, like a two quart casserole, full of beans and rice and corn tortillas. The rice, I think it had some meat in it. It was so good! My kids ate like the hungry hog we have here in our backyard.

I cried and I looked at Ana, and I thought, she's done so much for us. She's such a good woman.

Then later that day, Andrés came home, and he had bread, food, and he told me, "I got a job."

So, on the third day, I got up really early in the morning. Andrés had already gone to work. I said, "Now, I have to keep my promise to God." I'd already talked to my sister and my sister-in-law both so they could take care of my kids, and I borrowed my sister-in-law's little girl, Blanca, so that she could hold my hand and be my guide.

I said, "My eyes will be closed, so when you see the train, you're going to have to pull me to the side because I can't see it, and we'll have to wait until the train goes away. But I'm hoping that the train won't come at this time. We're going to walk all the way down the railroad tracks until we get to the road, then when we get to the road, you need to lead me to the church."

So we started walking, but, my God, I thought it would take about half an hour, but it took about four hours because the tracks were full of stickers, burrs. There's a plant that has a lot of little *cadillos,* like rose thorns, and they got all over my bare feet and legs. As I walked, I was bleeding and crying, and I kept trying to pull them out. Every step I took, I'd step on some.

And Blanca was trying to help me. "Oh, *Tía,* you're stepping on some."

"*Mi'ja, mi'ja,* which way do I go so I won't step on them?"

"They're all over, *Tía.*" There was nothing I could do, they were all over.

Then, when I finally got to the church, I remembered the priest who had run me out when I was little because I didn't have shoes, and now I was barefooted again. But there was a new priest so I was OK.

Once I was in the church, it was easy. I crawled on my knees from the church door to the altar, then I kissed Christ's feet and opened my eyes and told him, "I don't think I'm going to do something like this for you anymore. It's too hard." I thought, next time I'm going to promise something easier 'cause I almost wasn't able to make it. I was young, and I had energy, which had helped, but by then I was very tired.

Ever since I was little, my mom made vows and was lighting candles and praying at home. And when something bad happens to the family, she gets upset, but then she turns around and makes vows and prays. I also believe in promises. I've done them my whole life, and I still do them.

Dear Almighty God!

If there is to be justice and Mercy for this poor people, let it be now!

I beg of you my almighty Lord of Love, please help Carlos and Lucía. I beg you, hear my plea, oh God of heaven and earth. Why must they suffer so much? Please help Lucía cross the border safely and please help her make it all the way safely to Onarga. Cover her and her children so the diabolic immigration officers don't see them.

For this favor I promise you I will not eat meat for one full year, from this day July 31, 1983 to July 31, 1984. I solemnly swear by the anguish and heartbreak over the sufferings of my brothers and sisters and especially the little ones and this sorrow I deeply feel, to keep and fulfill my promise so help me my God.

> Sweared, signed and sealed by me,
> under oath of faith in my God,
> María Elena Lucas
> Diary, July 31, 1983

The bigger I got with the pregnancy, the one when I walked down the railroad tracks, the more people said, "Gosh, those are going to be twins," because my stomach was separated, sort of like two. But I wasn't that big, so I didn't believe them. I was still very young, maybe seventeen or eighteen.

Three days before Tommy's first birthday, when Eva was about two years old, I was laying down in bed sound asleep, and, all of a sudden, I felt something like when you tie a knot and pull both ends to tighten it, something like that. I even heard a pop. It was my water bag that tore. I got up real quick, and there was a lot of water. I went and cleaned myself up and cleaned the mess in there, and Tommy was wet, so I changed him.

I washed Tommy's diaper, and when I went outside to hang the diaper on the clothesline, I had a real bad, strong pain. I couldn't move. On the steps coming back to the house, I had another one that was real bad. My mother-in-law woke my brother-in-law up, and he drove me to the midwife's house.

The midwife was Doña Elena. I told her, "I think I'm going to have a baby now."

She looked at me and said, "Oh no, you don't look like you're going to deliver yet."

"Yeah, I think I am."

So she opened the door, and she says, "OK, step in."

I was standing there when I had another pain. I said, "I need to go to the rest room." I went to the rest room, and I had the pain and I sat, and, all of a sudden, the pain got worse and worse and worse, and it started to be born right in the toilet bowl!

I held the baby's head and started walking and crying, "It's coming! It's coming!"

All Doña Elena could do was throw newspapers and stuff on top of the bed. By the time I put my feet on the bed, Christy was born. She was so tiny, she looked just like a little monkey, a newborn monkey.

After Christy was born, the midwife says, "Oh my God, I think you're going to have another one."

"Really?"

"Yeah."

"They were right."

Then I'd get little pains but not big pains, and a long time went by. Finally, the midwife told me to push, and I started pushing. But the midwife discovered that the baby's feet were coming first, and I had a terrible time.

It took me two and a half hours for my little boy to be born, and by the time he was born, I couldn't hear and I couldn't see anymore. They'd put alcohol on my face and slap me 'cause all I wanted to do was go to sleep. Every time I'd try to open my eyes, all I saw was a lot of light, very, very white. It was just a beautiful sleep, just the kind of sleep where I felt very rested, like every part of my body was, oh gosh, it was beautiful. When they slapped me, it didn't hurt. I could just hear their voices very, very far away.

I was bleeding, but I didn't care. I didn't want to listen to anything, and I didn't feel anything, and I just wanted to sleep. So they had a terrible time. The midwife had to go in there with her fingers and pull him out.

He was born black, and he was very tiny. But they hit him on his little butt and made him cry. For that I was grateful, because I didn't know whether he was going to die or not.

Afterward, the Department of Children and Family Services tried to take them to the hospital because they said they were going to die on me.

I cried and I said, "No, you don't. If my babies die, well, I did my best, but I'm not going to let you take my babies." I guess I thought I wasn't going to see them again, and they were taking them away forever. I was very young, and I didn't understand.

The department people couldn't reassure me that they weren't going to keep them. They never convinced me, so I never accepted. Then they said, "OK, if the children die, it's your fault."

"No, they're not going to die."

"How do you know? They can't even eat or open their eyes or open their mouths."

"Well, I'll feed them anyway."

I used cotton and a dropper to feed them. I'd open their mouths and just put milk in there, and you could hear the hard gulp, but I'd still stick it in. Finally, about a month and a half later, they started to move and to be bigger, and I could nurse them from my breast.

But every time Tommy saw me pick up the twins to nurse them, he'd start to bawl. So I'd sit down, and with one leg I'd pat Tommy's butt and rock him with my foot and give him his bottle and pat him on the shoulder. Then I'd put a pillow across my stomach, and I'd give one breast to one kid and the other one to the other. Then Eva would see me feeding all three, and she'd just go crazy. She'd open up the doors where I had the soap and the Ajax and the sugar and everything else, and everything would go on the floor. The three little ones would be crying as I'd try to feed them, and I'd see Eva throwing the sugar all over and smearing it with her hands, and I'd cry along with the kids. Finally, as Tommy would sleep, I'd rest my leg and try to feed the babies as much as possible. But they'd only take about a half an ounce every three hours. And there were times when we didn't have nothing to eat. There were times when there was nothing at all.

It was hard. My shoulders, they were killing me, and I couldn't keep up with anything, but as the twins grew older, I'd set them on my lap to nurse. It didn't look too good, but they were satisfied.

It was all washing diapers with the twins and Tommy. Eva was being potty-trained, but still she had accidents, and the one-year-old and the twins, they all had diapers. My mom and the other women believed that if you left diapers on the clothes line after certain hours that something like the evening dew would get into them and create diarrhea in the baby, make the baby's stomach bad. I didn't pay too much attention to that belief, but my mother-in-law made sure I was aware of it. Sometimes I forgot and left them out, then the next morning, when I'd go to get them, she'd say, "Those *pañales* have been dewed, so if you use them the baby's going to get sick." And I'd have to wash them all over again.

But I was always careful to separate their things, like this breast belonged to Christy and this one belonged to Johnny. 'Cause I always had more milk in one than the other, and Johnny seemed to eat more than Christy. He was always the first for everything. I kept their diapers separate and their bottles separate; I also helped myself by having bottles.

Now that I'm older, I see a young woman with lots of kids like that, and I say, "Oh, my God, how can she do it?" But, I went through the same thing. I didn't even have a washing machine until I went to Arlington, Texas, and worked there in the factory where they make planes, after all seven kids were born. Then I was able to save money and buy a washer and a dryer, and it was a big celebration when I got them. It was something special.

I think having baby twins like that, it was especially hard on Eva and Tommy 'cause they were still so little. I had so many people to take care of, Andrés's family and all—they didn't get much attention. Lots of things probably hurt Tommy—Tommy, the one who finally couldn't take it.

CHAPTER NINE

Caretaker of the Extended Family

Andrés's mom was almost always with us during those years. She made all the decisions. As the kids got older, I did get to go to the fabric store to make the kids' clothes and to make my clothes, and after she decided what we could eat, I could buy groceries. And sometimes she'd take off for a short period of time, and during that short time, it was like I had a big, long rest.

After I got married, little by little, I started taking brothers and sisters to live with me. First, my brother José went with me when we moved to Arlington. Andrés didn't object. It was my mother-in-law who didn't like it; she didn't like my brother José or Alfredo. But I had all my brother-in-laws come over and their wives and their kids and had them eat with us most of the time, and I'd have to babysit and take care of them. On the weekends, I never could go no place because I had my kids, and my mother-in-law would be with me, and everybody would bring all their children, so we could babysit. And I was constantly cooking.

Also, my brothers and I wouldn't eat the same as the others did. Let's say everybody else eats first, and there was no food left for my brothers and me. I'd go and try to take a piece of meat to cook, but my mother-in-law would say, "No. There's potatoes in there. Let's leave the meat for tomorrow so we can fix it." There have been so many times I've been hungry, all through the years.

Altogether, as the time went on, I took seven of my brothers and sisters, five boys and two girls. They were really no trouble. They helped me. In a way, they kept me company. We loved each other a lot and were very close. They didn't stay all together, but they lived with me at several different times while they were growing up. It's just that my mom, she had so many. And I was very happy that they were there because there were always more of Andrés's family with me than my brothers or my family.

Taking care of everybody took all of my energies. I had no rest. My brothers and sisters, they saw how much harder it was for me, so they helped to babysit. Sometimes they'd get tired of it and go back home to Mom, then come back to me.

I even took my daddy for several months at a time. This was later. My mom would tell me, "Well, take your daddy for awhile." I would and he'd stay for a couple of months. I guess that gave Mom a break. I always tried to help them. I'd get clothes, whatever I could get my hands on, old ironing boards, irons, toasters, anything I could collect to send to Mom so she could sell it and have some extra food.

But my mother-in-law really ruled me. For years and years, she would sleep between Andrés and me. Whenever she wanted me to sleep on the floor, not in bed with Andrés, I'd do it, but it hurt because I couldn't figure out why Andrés allowed it. I'd think, this is my husband and we have children, but he doesn't have the will or the strength to tell his mom to let us sleep together.

Especially when I was pregnant, she wouldn't let him sleep with me, but she also made me sleep on the floor when he caught a cold or had a headache or an earache or if his molars were hurting.

And I didn't think it was alright. To me it just became such an awful thing. I was so hurt, it made me sick towards him, but Andrés would tell me, "Like my mother says, goes. If you don't like it, you know what's good for you." Meaning he would give me a beating. And that happened not only with his mother, but also with his siters. They were much older, so I learned to keep quiet, not to get into any questions, any trouble, or start arguing about anything. But I just lost any good feelings I had toward Andrés.

I believed in promises and sacrificing. I wouldn't have sex at all with the kids' father during the Lent season, but it wasn't difficult to do because we didn't have too much going on anyway. Nobody knew it, but I'd stay away from contact with him.

But I still had other pregnancies and miscarriages. Gloria was born with a midwife, but Héctor was born in the hospital. I had complications with him, and he had a heart murmur. Then, when I was going to have Oscar, I went to the hospital and told them that I was real sick. They said, "Yeah, yeah, everybody feels this way when they're going to have a baby."

I told them, "But I'm going to have the baby now."

"Yeah, we know. We'll get things ready." So they took off and left me alone in a little room with one of my sister-in-laws. She just went crazy, she didn't know what to do, and I delivered Oscar myself. By the time the hospital people got back, I already had Oscar.

With all the babies and all those relatives, it was hard to give my kids enough attention. But I really loved them, they meant everything to me, and I tried to sing to them when I could.

A los niños de la tierra
Cuando lloran de dolor
Baja un Angel del Cielo
y les canta con amor.

Dios está aquí
Dios está allá
Dios está aquí
Dios está allá

A los niños de la tierra
Cuando cantan con amor
Se abren las puertas del cielo

Dios está aquí
Dios está allá
Dios está aquí
Dios está allá

[To the children of the earth
When they cry from pain
An angel of heaven goes down
And sings to them with love.

God is here
God is there
God is here
God is there

To the children of the earth
When they sing with love
The doors of heaven open.

God is here
God is there
God is here
God is there]

For all those years, it was like I was a maid to Andrés's family, and I
perturbed them so much. For example, I loved to stay outside at night,
and they thought it was very weird that I wanted to sleep outside. I loved
to look at the stars and the moon, and I'm just fascinated by sounds at
night. These little things would bother them a lot, that I'd pay attention
to a cricket or an owl or a bird. I'd stop everything to listen to a bird, and
I'd tell them things like, "Do you understand what he's saying?"

They'd say, "Oh, you're crazy."

They didn't like the idea of me sitting down to draw—it was childish.
They didn't like writing, because I didn't show them what I was writing.
They didn't understand English, most of them, so I mostly wrote in
English. They didn't like me studying plants and that I was always very
amused by things that just didn't catch their attention at all. I was just a
kid and they were mature in so many different ways than I was. I was just
not acceptable in the way I talked and the way I thought. But, I tell you
one thing, for everything they needed, they called me.

When Eva and Tommy were little and the twins were born, but just
babies, they told me they were taking me to another *curandero*. They said
they wanted to help me because they thought I was not right, not normal.

We traveled a long way, from Brownsville to Waco, Texas. The guy
was named Johnny Rodríguez, and he looked like an old Mexican man,
about Pablo's age, and his eyes were real blue. Several sister-in-laws went
in first, then my mother-in-law, and then they said it was my turn.

I said, "I don't think I need to go."

And they said, "Yes, you do, and it will do you good." So, finally, I
went in with a sister-in-law, then she left me there with him.

And he said, "This is to help the bad spirits go away and good spirits
to come in and to help for good luck." He wanted to whip my body and
pray over me and inject me in my neck, my main artery. He said that
would be good for me.

And I told him, "No, I don't want you to do that to me!" And I
fought and wouldn't let him.

I went out crying, and my in-laws were very upset. They said they had come a long way to help me out with the bad spirits. And I had to hold everything inside me.

After Eva was born and I was pregnant again, but before I had any of the other kids, Andrés and I were staying in his sister's house, because we had nothing. It was a very small house with two rooms. One of the rooms was the kitchen, there was a door in the center, and one side we had a tiny bed. So Eva slept in that bed, and Andrés and I slept on the floor beside her.

One night, I was sleeping on the inside between the bed and Andrés when, suddenly, I was being touched all over. I opened my eyes, and I see this person, and I started screaming, and nobody woke up. Nobody woke up at all. I kept screaming and jumped away from the man, and the man started saying, "Shhh, shhh, shut up." There was the smell of liquor.

Then I realized it was my brother-in-law who'd been touching me, but I couldn't quit screaming because I was so shook up. So my brother-in-law jumped up and hurried into the other room where we couldn't see him.

Finally, I woke Andrés up, and I told him what had happened. He was very upset, and he said, "Let's go." So I put the baby into a little buggy we had at that time, and I picked up a few items, and we started going towards downtown Brownsville. The police were there because somebody had just broken into the store, and I started telling one of the officers what happened. He called another officer, and he was telling him what had happened, and the other officer laughed. He had a real sarcastic grin on his face, and he said to the first police officer, "Yeah, you know who she's talking about. It's the same guy," and they went on and on.

I realized that they knew Andrés's brother-in-law and knew what kind of person he was, but it was like they were enjoying what happened to me, it was like they were getting off on that, so I was real hurt.

Then they said, "You can't do anything about it. If you want to do anything about it you have to go to court and put a complaint."

We went back to my sister-in-law's house and Andrés grabbed my brother-in-law and said, "Why did you do that?"

His brother-in-law said, "That's not true! I didn't do anything." He never quit saying he didn't do anything.

So Andrés woke his sister and told her, and she says, "I can't believe that. Are you telling the truth?"

And I said, "Yes, he did it."

After that we went to my aunt's house. I had a very, very poor aunt in town, and I told them what had happened, and so we finally went to bed. It happened about two o'clock in the morning, and the next day, at the same time, I had a miscarriage. I got so sick with the miscarriage that one of my uncles took me to the hospital, and I had to have something done.

When I was still in the hospital, after I had gone through everything with the miscarriage, the family came over to investigate me, to see what had happened. I told them that I didn't want to talk about it. Andrés's sister, the wife of the man who did it, and another sister-in-law said, "We have consulted with a lawyer, and the lawyer said that if you don't have any witnesses, there is nothing that can be done. And we also went to talk to the priest, María Elena, and the priest says that there is no way that a man would do that kind of thing to a woman unless the woman provoked him."

I started crying, and I told them, "I swear to God that I didn't do anything. I never suspected anything from that man. He had never said anything or I had never noticed." But I was just a very young kid, so I was dumb, ignorant. Maybe if he did have anything on his mind, I didn't pick it up, which I should have because I could notice men's malicious ways, but I just never did that time.

The thing that gets to me is, why didn't Andrés wake up? Why didn't his sister wake up? It took them a long time. Some people have said that maybe my brother-in-law gave them something to knock them out.

After that I promised to God that I was never again going to talk to them, to my sister-in-law or to him, and for eleven years, I never did. A little after the eleven years were up, that sister-in-law came to look for us and to beg me, to say, "Please, I beg you, María Elena. I want you to be part of the family again." Because I talked to everybody else, and I saw the family, except that whenever she would come over or we saw them coming, I would leave. And Andrés respected that.

For a long time after he attacked me, I couldn't really go to sleep, thinking about it. It was in my head. It was terrible to go to sleep.

CHAPTER TEN

Opportunity and Betrayal

After we moved to Arlington, Texas, and weren't doing migrant work, I worked as a maid cleaning houses for Anglo ladies. That's how I started working outside the family. One lady was real hard on me, but her husband was kind. Several times, when they were going to eat, I overheard him say to his wife, "Do you suppose we should ask her if she's hungry?" And his wife would say, "No, no." He went fishing and tried to give me some of what he caught, but she ran out and stopped him. One time she found out that I was just pregnant with one of the kids, and she decided to have me move the big furniture all over her house, like she wanted to hurt me. The more I went to work with them, the more I felt humiliated by this woman.

I was very, very shy then, and this was my first time working outside of the family, so I tried very hard to please them. So before Christmas, I thought I'd buy them a gift, so I went down to the store and I bought her some drinking glasses that I thought were really pretty.

So I took them to them, and after Christmas, when I went back cleaning, they had all these wrappings and everything from a big party, glasses here and glasses there. But when I went to the garbage, there was my gift. She'd thrown my gift in the garbage. I was so hurt. I think that was the last time I went to work for them.

Most of the time, I gave my money to Andrés, and he managed it, but at one time, I started to save two, three, five dollars from every time I got paid, and, believe it or not, I saved enough money over several years to use as the down payment for our home we bought in Arlington. I saved over a thousand dollars.

Also, I went to work in the cafeteria in an airplane plant for the Missiles and Space Division. The cafeteria was an entirely different company from the big company. All the people from the company would come and eat in the cafeteria. I began by just working in the kitchen, but I kept getting promoted until I was a hostess in the conference room for very important people. Some of them got to know me, and one man said to me, "You should be working in the main plant, training for something that will pay you better than here."

I said, "Yes, I would love that."

They told me who to see to get a job from, but the cafeteria workers were not for nothing allowed to cross the boundary between the cafeteria and the plant. Finally, I had to work out a whole, sneaky plan. I changed my clothes in the bathroom, made my cafeteria badge look like it was from the plant, and then I got through the guards speaking Spanish and looking like the other Mexican workers. And when my cafeteria boss found out, he said, "This is a great step forward for you."

At first it was hard in the factory. I worked in a unit with one hundred and fifty guys, and the guys tried to get me out of there. They'd say jokes and have pictures to get me upset. They didn't like me around because they thought they couldn't have freedom of speech if I could overhear them.

So one day I got upset, and I said, "Hey, listen. I don't care what you say. I've got a job to do, and if you want to joke, if you want to say dirty stuff, if you want to put naked ladies in the gear and tool boxes, it's not going to do nothing to me because I've got my job, and you're not going to make me quit my job if you keep on doing those things."

So after that I was accepted, and I was almost one of the guys. It was fun. There were a lot of Latino and Anglo and black guys, we were all like brothers and sisters. But they didn't like it because after I learned the work, our bosses started to get me to train newcomers. I guess that was an insult to the men. But I kept at it.

I kept working, and I was making good money, real good money, and with that money, I was able to pay for my home. I got a washer and dryer and a refrigerator and a toaster, good things. It was good while it lasted.

The home we bought was not the best home in the world, but my brother, I, and my kids worked real hard on it. Lots of dogs and cats had been in the place at one time, and it was really bad when we got it, all torn down, but we made lots of improvements. There was one improvement we could never make, which was the plumbing. They told me that to fix it would cost thousands of dollars. So I was always having problems with that.

I don't mean to brag, but I landscaped my yard, and it was beautiful. I planted the trees when they were tiny, and my kids and I christened every tree after one of them. I told them, "This is your tree, and so it's yours forever. You take care of it. You have to water it and make sure it doesn't die." So every one of my kids had a tree. There was also one big tree in the back of the house.

At first there was no grass, and the ground was real hard. We worked for one year with a pick breaking up the ground, but Andrés was never into any of that. Then, after the ground was broke up, we used José's old pickup and brought sand and loads and loads of cow manure at fifty cents a load.

I worked so hard, but I turned that yard into a beautiful garden. Every ten feet around the fence, I put a climbing red rose, and all around the house I had lots of different kinds of mint and herbs so that I'd get the fragrance inside the house, and I planted lots of different kinds of flowers, like petunias, around each tree. It was beautiful. And I was so organized then, super-organized, and I kept the kids' beds so clean.

But Andrés's mom was upset about me working with men. When I was working the cafeteria, it was all women and the only men were the ones that carried the heavy trays and two cooks and a guy that did heavy mopping and moving around equipment. The rest were ladies, so I was criticized and put down for getting a job in Missiles and Space. She'd want to know, "What time did you get off?" If I was a little later, she'd say things like, "Well, it's about time," or "I was beginning to worry about you." In fact, when I first got the job, a lot of the family made fun and laughed, saying things like, "You got a job there? They must be crazy!"

Also, transportation to and from work was always a major problem for me. Somehow, I always had a hard time getting a car for myself, and then, at night, I'd have so much housework to do, usually I didn't get to bed until about 1:30. But I did it.

Finally, they were going to have big layoffs, but because I had taken extra training in school, the company made me an offer, and it was real good. They wanted me to work in Australia for five years, and they would take care of everything and give Andrés a good job there, too. I wouldn't have to pay rent, transportation, education for the kids, and I'd have a very good job for myself. Then, at the end of five years, I could renew it.

But when he heard that, Andrés got real jealous and upset and said I was crazy. Everything I did was crazy to him. He refused, and, instead, he said, "Let's move up to Colorado." It was like an order. He had an uncle in Leadville, Colorado, so we moved, but then it was so terribly cold in Colorado that we returned to Texas. And, of course, I'd lost my opportunity.

After that, I worked in all sorts of jobs. I worked for Cattleman's Steakhouse, cleaning tables, washing dishes and busing tables. Almost more jobs than I can remember. For a while, I made cloth flowers at home, like for weddings. I baked and decorated cakes to sell to bring in a little money. I just tried to make money in every way I could. We were able to stay in our house, but, still, I wasn't really happy. I mean, Andrés and me, we just weren't going to make it.

I remember when I gave up hope for my marriage. It was around the middle of it, about eight years before I left him. I just lost any feelings for him. I couldn't bear for him to touch me anymore. It was him hitting and hurting me, the way he treated me and the way he just let everybody take over. As long as I didn't protest or argue, everything was alright. He treated me nice. But if I started complaining about his family to him or if I said, "What's wrong with you? You should be more considerate," that would trigger his anger, and, finally, he'd get up and say, "Either you shut your mouth and forget it or I'll slap you and shut you up."

There were times when he beat me up pretty bad. Sometimes I guess over stupid things, and, finally, one time he beat me real bad when it was somebody's birthday, and a lot of members of Andrés's family decided to go dancing. I really didn't want to go because I didn't like to go out with him anymore. I think that time, when we went dancing, Andrés set me up. Sort of like in [one of my poems], when the woman's been hurt and is being stalked:

> ... Three days have passed, she barely breathes
> The flies are breeding in her chest
> Then, on the third full moon
> The Lion finds its prey ...

(undated)

About a week before it happened, we'd gone to Meadowbrook Park in Arlington, and some guys were there. His family knew these guys, but I didn't know them. Someone said, "This is my brother Andrés, and this is his wife."

So we just greeted each other, and that was it. The next time I saw these guys was when we were at that dance for the birthday. These guys came in and again we greeted them and that was it. We didn't dance, we didn't see each other, I didn't even know where they sat.

Andrés and I were dancing, and he wanted to kiss me all over, down my arm, and I told him, "No, no, no, please don't."

Andrés got very upset and started calling me *puta* [whore]. Then, looking around at the other men, he said, "Which one do you like?"

I became very upset, and I told him, "I want to go home. Please."

Anyway, he kind of calmed down, but I was very unhappy. I was very uncomfortable because he was acting all drunk. Then, instead of going home, he insisted that we go to his sister's house. So we were at his sister's house, and she and Andrés kept telling me, "Come on, take another beer. Don't be spoiled, drink like we say."

I kept saying, "No thank you, I don't want to." I didn't know how to drink anyway.

Then they got out a bottle of wine, and I don't think I'd ever taken a bottle of wine. We were all at the table, and his sister kept saying, "Come on, take a glass."

I said, "I'm not sure I like that." So she served it, and I tasted it, and it didn't taste bad, like beer—it tasted sweet.

She said, in a nice way, "Come on, take it. I'm going to see how brave you are."

Well, I didn't know they were setting me up. I didn't know it was planned, so I drank the glass of wine, and, right away every time I drank some, she'd pour more in. I'd say, "No, that's enough." I don't know how many times she poured, and I kept on sipping and drinking, and pretty soon, I was pretty out of it. I can only remember that they said we were going home, and they said, "We'll let so-and-so take them home." One of the guys that we'd met at the park and seen at the dance was there, but I hadn't seen him, I didn't know who was there.

So they helped me get into the car, and that guy was driving, the one from the dance, and they put me in the front seat next to him, and Andrés went into the back seat. Somehow, on the road, the guy must have started trying to touch me or something. All I know is there was a big red light, and I was beaten up very, very terribly by Andrés. I don't know where the guy went. I don't remember if he ran or what happened. According to the story that they told me later, he jumped out of the car and ran. I remember that Andrés started driving.

I guess what Andrés and his sister did was try to find out how easy I was or how I would respond to that guy, so they set it up with him that he should try something with me, but I guess, when Andrés saw that the guy was reaching for me, he couldn't take it or he was just finding an excuse to beat me up. This all came out later.

I don't even remember how Andrés got me outside of the car, but he kicked me and kicked me and every time he kicked me, I'd turn over one way, then he'd kick me, and I'd turn over the other way, like a rag doll. And he bit me, like I was disfigured.

He put me on the floor of the back seat in the car again and started driving, and he said, "I'm going to kill you, I'm going to kill you, I'm going to kill you."

I thought, if he's going to kill me, I don't want to die that way. I thought, if I don't get out of the car, he really will kill me. He was driving real fast, and I opened the door and flew over. I don't know how many times I flew over. I just rolled and rolled along the side of the road. This happened in front of a big fruit stand, and the people there dragged me inside the fruit stand and called the police.

My brother José went after that guy in the car with a gun. He found him and told him, "You better tell me the truth because if you don't, you're not getting out of here alive."

The guy told him, "Listen, it's not my fault. I don't have anything to do with it. Andrés and his sister wanted to find out whether she would respond, and that's the reason they got her drunk, to see how far she'd go. They asked me to try something with her and see if she was going to respond."

My brother was very upset. I don't know what all he said to Andrés, but Andrés came to me in the hospital a few days later. He came and knelt by the side of my bed, and he said, "Please forgive me. I was crazy, stupid. I'll never do this to you again as long as I live, for the rest of my life. I'm sorry, please forgive me."

I think I said, "I can forgive you, but I don't know about God. You did it, and I'm not sure God can forgive you for it." I also told him, "And

I want to tell you something, Andrés. I don't love you anymore, and I'll never love you again, and the first chance I get, I'm going to leave you. I'm going to get away from here. It doesn't matter what you do anymore, I don't feel anything for you." So that was it. I didn't.

From that day in the hospital on, Andrés treated me different. He never hit me again, and his mom realized that something was very wrong and tried to bring me back to him. She'd say, "Why don't you all go to the movies? Why don't you go to the park? Go to the lake. If you want to I'll babysit, you two can go."

But I'd just become dead to him. I'd say, "Well, thank you very much," to his mom, "but I've got work to do and don't want to go." I'd make up a whole bunch of excuses so I wouldn't go out with him. It was like I was dead. I didn't smile at him. I was like a mummy, a zombie. Like something mechanical. I just kept everything inside, and I didn't share anything anymore.

One day I was very depressed, and every time I was depressed, I'd go and open my trunk and look at my poems. I had lots of diaries and poems and paintings, but looking at them would just add to my despair. So, finally, I just grabbed a lot of stuff, looked at it, tore into pieces, and burned it up. I had things that went back to my childhood. I just burned them up. The only thing I saved was "The White Crack in the Sky." Everything else I destroyed.

Then, finally, Mom told me she was going to take a bunch of kids and go up north to do farm work for the summer, without Dad. I thought, this is an opportunity for me to get away. I asked her, "Can I bring my kids and come too?"

She said, "Well, if Andrés will let you."

So I had to ask him if it was alright, but he had no idea what I was really planning on doing. Nobody did. I wanted to get out, but I had no idea how things were going to work. He said yes, so I took the seven kids and left, then went back to him for awhile the next winter, and, as soon as it was time to work in the fields again that spring, I left him again, this time for good.

When I finally went back to the house again, after they knew I'd left him, my in-laws had destroyed a whole lot of things, lots of drawings and flowers and things I'd saved. I could only find a trunk with some of my clothing and some pictures. They even took ornamental work that Tommy had done. Andrés controlled the house for years, and they kept letting it get in worse and worse shape. Then Eva heard they were going to sell it and not tell me, and she told me to get a lawyer. Finally, it was put in my name. So years later I went back to sell the house.

> ... Oh God, I can see my kids running all over this place. I can remember some very unforgettable things that happened, it seems like only yesterday. ... These are the last few days I shall stay in this house, the Gilbert Circle house in Arlington, Texas, where I lived, loved, and woed, and like Samson, blinded, pushed the pillars till they broke and the walls came tumbling down. ... (Diary, February 21, 1984)

The money from the house went to pay some debts, and I bought a plot of land near Brownsville. And, suddenly, it seemed like the whole family needed to borrow. Then it was gone.

PART TWO

Committed and Female within the Farm Worker Movement

CHAPTER ELEVEN

On Her Own: Life as a Single Parent

For part of the summers after I left Andrés, the kids and I stayed in the canneries in Ohio working. The housing was real small cabins that belonged to Libby's. They had a bed and a wooden table with a little stove and a stick to hang your clothes on, although, with my seven kids, we had a little bigger cabin with bunk beds that we put together to make two full beds, and a cot, which was where I slept. So my kids all slept in beds. Then we had one wooden table and a stove, one door and one window.

It was crowded and the rest rooms were all outside. One thing I disliked very much was you couldn't have any privacy in the rest room. Everything was open. So, if you had your monthly time, it was terrible.

There were local people working in the cannery and migrants and we were all very tired. After you had slept for about three hours, they'd come and get you up again and say, "María Elena, they need you." You had to be available all the time and that's how come I worked usually sixteen hours a day. I was very thin; I had the constant worry about not having enough money and not being able to watch my kids.

Also, in the different places we'd be, I'd try to earn extra money by making Mexican food to sell to the people, especially to the men who didn't have wives to take care of them. Like I'd make *tamales,* but I wouldn't sell them by the dozen, I'd sell them to the sugar beet haulers.

I made them a fair size so that they would have enough. And sometimes it was tortillas with meat and potatoes and sometimes refried beans with Mexican sausage and all sorts of stuff. That's how I met Fernando Cuevas, long before he became an organizer. We'd just say hello when he came by with the truck and I gave the guys coffee and tried to sell them food. Fernando, he remembers the "Free coffee, sir?"

When I was at the cannery, they made me a supervisor. I don't want to brag about it, but I think I was very good. I loved people and they loved me, and I never had any problems with people. My boss, he loved me, he wouldn't butt in for nothing. There were complaints by other bosses about why they'd see people outside during working hours. It was because I'd give the ladies a chance to go eat with their husbands, but the women would make up their time. I'd say, "Let her go take lunch now so she can eat with her husband and then you take her lunch hour." So everybody was happy in my lines.

But when I was working in the cannery, there was nobody to take care of my kids, so even though I had a cabin, they were running free. And, like I said, I usually worked sixteen hours a day. I tried to tell my kids, "Please stay home. Just play in the camp." But it's not easy to keep kids away from the street when you're working, and they don't have anybody to tell them. They were going to school while school was open, but then school was out so the kids were free. And there was nobody to watch them.

Then the kids started going to what people called a "joint." They had billiards and pool and playing machines in there. From what I gather, the owners weren't supposed to allow any children under age in there, but they did and some of my kids would go to it. When I found out, I started getting after the kids. But they wouldn't listen to me.

So one day a friend of mine came into where I was working in the cannery and said, "María Elena, your kids are at that joint and I came to tell you because that is not a good place. There's drugs and a whole bunch of things going on in there, and if you're not careful, your kids are going to end up very, very bad."

I got out of work and went up there just to see, and sure enough, they were there. When they saw me they ran, but I managed to get one of them, and I gave him a spanking on his butt. I didn't bruise him or anything, but somebody seemed to think it was terrible. I was alone with my kids there, and it was very hard. With seven kids, it was bad.

Then somebody reported me to the authorities for giving my son that spanking, and the authorities came looking for me. They went to the office of the company and they called the company managers. They made me look like dirt in front of my boss and everybody else. But my supervisor, he didn't stay to hear what they said. He says, "I'm not going to listen because I know María Elena. I'm not going with you." He stayed away but the rest of the people that managed Libby's came, and I was terribly ashamed and humiliated.

Also, the discussion was right in front of the children. The authorities were really attacking me, saying, "You're doing wrong. You're not treating your kids like you should! You shouldn't have spanked them." While they were doing that, all I could do was cry.

I asked the lady that was talking, "Have you ever been a migrant or a farm worker?"

"Well, no."

"You don't know what you're talking about, lady. Listen, if anything happens to my kids, I'm going to hold you responsible."

They just gave me such a funny look because they thought, well, we're the ones who care. We're the ones that are doing something about her problem. Look what this crazy woman is telling us.

I thought, this is not right, right in front of the kids. They are going to feel like, well, Mom is wrong.

Sure enough, I went back to work and I sent my kids home, and the next morning when I got off work, they were gone. The two youngest ran away. They were eight and nine. For one week I went looking for them all over the farms, and it had rained a lot and the water was about knee high. I've never been so scared in my life. I was crying, I was like crazy. I thought any minute I would find my kids drowned or killed.

Right away after the little kids left, I went back to the authorities and said, "This is your fault. If anything happens to my kids, I'm going to hold you responsible."

They were looking for my kids all over until finally I got a call from Texas that they were already back there. The two little kids had hitchhiked with another boy, and they were so excited because they had been in the arch in St. Louis, Missouri.

After that happened, I thought, "We're never going to come back here again." And I didn't. So I never came back even though I kept getting letters from the company asking me to.

At that time, there was talk that farm workers were organizing, and I was listening to all this talk about the farm workers getting together. I guess it was just beginning. I thought, this is going to help. But I wasn't coming back there anyway.

When I first left Andrés, and I found out I could make it on my own, I said, "My God, I'm so happy now." The pressure was gone and even though I was working very hard, still I felt good. I felt free.

But I had a lot of problems with the kids and with my father. My daddy, he was very upset with me. He said that I got married and that I should stay in my marriage. He says, "Well, your mother was always able to cope with everything, and I'm never going to forgive you." And, in a way, I agree with him. I will never forgive myself. But the only reason I say that is because of my children. It hurt them very bad. But I know it was wrong to marry my husband in the first place. Still, when you divorce or separate, it breaks the home and hurts some kids. It especially hurt Tommy.

Years later, when my former mother-in-law was about to die, my kids kept telling me, "Our grandmother wants to see you before she dies. Believe us, she has nothing against you. Please go see our grandmother." So I did and she was very happy to see me. She said that she wanted me to know that she loved me and that I was like a daughter to her. I felt sorry for her. She was real old and real beat, and at that point people don't want to hold grudges against each other but just prepare to go to rest. But Tommy always held a grudge.

The first summer I left Andrés to work up north, the summer before I left him for good, I noticed a man people called Don Pablo. I was working in the juice department at Libby's in Leipzig, Ohio, and when I went into the personnel office, Don Pablo was arguing with Tom.

Tom was the guy in charge of the migrant people, and he spoke real good Spanish. Pablo was in there arguing with him about how Tom had brought all these people up there and had promised to give each family a certain amount of money for food at the time of arrival. Then Tom had told them they'd have to wait for the money until Monday when the offices would open, but Pablo was fighting with Tom for the people. He says, "You promised. You said that you'd have the money ready for the people. These people don't have food. These people need a place, and you're going to put them up, and you're going to give them money for food like you promised."

I admired Pablo for that. In his way, he's always been kindhearted, and he's always helped people in need. He's been a good man. He's got his bad qualities, but he's got lots of good virtues. When I saw that, I thought, wow, he's standing up to Tom and defending his rights, and I thought that it was good.

Tom was sweating and pulling his hair and saying, "Look, Don Pablo, I know, but what can I do? I don't have the money, and the office is closed, and I'm the only one here."

Pablo said, "I don't care. You find a way," and so on, and later, Tom did get them everything they wanted.

But I wasn't interested in men. I was just out there alone working. I had no intentions of getting involved with men. In fact, I didn't want to look at men's faces. With seven kids, I was lonely, but I didn't really think I needed a male's company. And I entertained myself a lot with my kids and the ladies in the migrant camp. They were good friends, and that made me feel not too lonely. Still, I never went to movies or dancing or nothing at all. I'd just go buy groceries and wash and, once in a while, take the kids to church in the morning.

The next summer, after I'd left Andrés for good, I was working at Libby's again, and Don Pablo was also there. Pablo's about twenty-three years older than me. I was a supervisor again, and Pablo was working where the juice is bottled and sealed.

They were supposed to have safety guards on the machines, but they didn't, and where Pablo was working, all the bottles crashed, and super-hot juice went all over his clothing. And nobody was at first aid, not the nurses, not the emergency squad, nobody. As a supervisor I was supposed to have been trained for first aid, but I hadn't yet. Still, the people came and took me out to treat Pablo, and it was my job to do it.

I didn't know what to do, so I took all the medicine in the medicine cabinet, and I smeared everything all over his chest. I used petroleum jelly, I used sprays, and I used everything I could think of that would help.

I also knew I was supposed to make a report, and I noticed that his pants were full of juice. So I said, "I'm sorry, but I have to ask you an embarrassing question. If I don't give a full report and you make an insurance claim, but we haven't done it right, you're the one who is going to suffer."

I was shaking. It was so hard to make that kind of question. It was the first time in my life that I talked that way to a stranger, but I said, "For your sake I'm asking, did you burn down below?"

He went real fast, "No, no," like he was shocked or something that I had the courage to say that.

"Are you sure?"

"Yes!" he says again very fast.

"OK."

I guess, because he was so grateful that I had taken care of him, from then on, every chance he got, he was just watching me and offering to buy me coffee. He got jealous if I took coffee from others, especially if they were Anglos, and I heard his friends teasing him, saying, "Hey, Don Pablo," and motioning to me.

Then he started following me. "María Elena, would you like a ride?"

"No, thank you."

And one day, he says, "You know what? I feel like turning you over my lap and spanking you."

I said, "Stupid! What do you think you are? Who gave you the right to think that way? Get out of my sight! Don't ever bother me again. I don't want to have anything to do with you. I don't like you!"

I thought, how dare he say such a thing? But he kept on following me. One day he came over and said, "Well, I'd like to offer my pickup to you because I see you walk to go to wash your clothes and to go to buy your groceries, and if you'd like to, I'll take you or you can use the keys."

I said, "No, thank you." But he kept asking.

After that he began to be buddies with my brother, Alfredo, who was planning on getting married. I was the one who was making the wedding arrangements, and Don Pablo talked to my brother and said, "Alfredo, I want to be the *padrino,* the godfather, and I'm willing to buy the wedding cake and all the food."

That was a very attractive offer—who was going to turn down help for the most expensive items for a wedding? So my brother said, "Sure, thank you very much." So from then on, we had to get together about the wedding cake and all that.

Also, a few days later, I got food stamps. This was the first time I ever had food stamps, and I really needed them, but I didn't want nobody to know my business. If others found out that you got more food stamps then they did, they'd say, "Why did you get more?" A lot of gossip.

So I thought, well, I'm going to ask Pablo to take me to change my food stamps to groceries. I sent one of the kids after him, and he came flying. So I went with him in the truck, but Pablo took the long way so I'd be with him longer. We talked and talked, and then I sent him a big bowl of Mexican soup to thank him. And right away, he sent me a big beautiful glass dish full of fruit and covered with Saran Wrap and a bow.

Then I began to think he was real nice, and the closer he got to my brother, and with the wedding arrangements and all, the more I talked with him, the more we became friends.

By then my son Tommy had crashed up my station wagon that I needed to drive us back to Texas. Pablo told me he knew someone who would fix it very cheap, but he went to the guy without my knowledge and said, "Tell her you'll fix it for very little money, and I'll make up the difference to you, but don't get around to doing it. Make her stay here longer." So time kept passing without my station wagon getting fixed.

When Alfredo got married, Pablo and I danced together and sort of got more involved, but nothing serious yet. Pablo treated me very nice and was very well mannered, and I began to feel he had a lot of goodness in him. Then everybody started leaving. Mom was gone, everyone was gone, and I was real worried. I kept wondering, what's happening? I need my car, and I want to go.

Then we had the fiesta of the sixteenth of September, and that's when Pablo told me he liked me, and I thought, this is a good man I can love. I might even stay with him. And our time together began.

He said that he would like for me to stay with him, and I told him that I would like that too, but I needed to know if it was a short-time thing with me or if it was going to be forever.

He said, "I want us to be together. We can do what you want. We can move away or we can stay here."

"What about my kids? I have seven kids. I'm not going to drop them."

"We'll take them with us." So I agreed, and I started going out with him. Then he said, "We can't stay in the camp. Where should we go? How about that little town my friends talk about, Onarga, Illinois?"

A lady who was a friend of Pablo, she and her husband and daughters were from Onarga, and they always talked about it. They told us how beautiful it was in the summer, with all the blooming trees and the shrub nurseries, and how there was work in the fields all year round.

I knew I couldn't go back to Texas, so I said, "Why don't we flip a coin? If it's heads we go to Onarga, tails we stay here."

So we got a quarter, flipped it up in the air, and when it landed, it said, "To Onarga." That's how come we ended up in Onarga.

I guess the oldest kids were very upset about what was happening, but nobody was as upset as Tommy. When Tommy saw how fond I became of Pablo and how we treated each other, it hurt him very bad. I've heard from a lot of people that I shouldn't blame myself, but I do, I do. I think I hurt Tommy a lot, and I think divorce does a lot of damage to the kids. They said that Tommy was already involved with a lot of things even though he was fifteen. Even Héctor, as wild as he is and with all his problems, has never come to the point that Tommy reached.

Andrés came to the camp during this time, before I went to Onarga, and we had a terrible fight, but when he went back to Texas, Eva and Tommy went with him. So only the five little ones stayed with Pablo and me.

Pablo was from Mexico and has always has been bitter about the way he's been treated in the United States. His folks in Mexico are considered not rich, but medium. His daddy had a grocery store, and he's got a brother with a sewing factory. But Pablo was very stubborn when he was growing up and wanted to come to the United States to join the army. But when he came in 1943 and tried to join the service, they put him into jail! Then he joined up for railroad work and was taken all the way to Pennsylvania in freight car. All they gave the men to eat was baloney and cheese, and a lot of them got sick.

Still, Pablo stayed in the United States and got married here. He and his wife had four kids, but they separated. But Pablo lives with a constant conflict inside. He says that if he'd stayed in Mexico, he wouldn't be in these conditions.

When we first got together, I expected to get married to him. I wasn't divorced yet, but I was separated, and he told me he was divorced. Then I found out that he wasn't divorced either. He wouldn't talk about it, so as time went by, I began to open up the issue. It was so important to me to be married to him. At that time, I felt like the whole world was watching and condemning me, especially my family. I knew my family would never accept me if I was not married.

Looking back, if there was anything good about our first years together, it was because I made it good. Pablo has always been the same person. He was kind to me, he treated me nice, but he expected a lot and I gave a lot to him. So that was one reason we could get along better in the beginning. But he's always been the *ratón de junco*. It's a saying here, the person who keeps the junk yard is a rat. Wherever we go, no matter how much work I do, Pablo and I live in a mess.

When we got together, Pablo had some letters and things that belonged to a woman. He said they belonged to his cousin, but, finally, I put two and two together and realized it was not a cousin. I said, "Please tell me. Who is this woman, and what are these things, and why won't you get rid of them?"

He said, "Well, it was a woman that I lived with before."

Then, all of a sudden, this woman shows up in Onarga. She started working at the same place I did, and she started talking to me, trying to convince me to let him go. Trying to tell me he was no good, that I was going to be sorry. But at the very end, I found out they had a piece of property that they owned together, and she wanted it put in her name. She told me, "I don't care about him. You can keep him. I want the property." I didn't want to believe what she said about him, but I noticed that while she was there, Pablo was showing off. Like, "This is who I dropped, and this is what I gained." Like he was *muy macho*.

I didn't like Pablo showing off like that. When I first got together with Pablo there was an Anglo guy that was fixing Pablo's truck. He was a grower, but he also ran a gas station in town, and he'd known Pablo a long time. He called Pablo over away from me and started talking to him. Later Pablo told me that the Anglo guy had asked, "Where did you get that girl? I've heard that señoritas are really good." Like in bed, he meant.

Then, later, that guy came personally up to me and says, "Excuse me, but I was talking to Pablo and I asked him how he met you, and he said that you got some more sisters. Do you think there is any more for me?" I couldn't believe it. I'll never forget it. It was like picking cotton, he's just going to pick one out.

And I remember other talk like that. See, Mexicans and Anglos weren't allowed to get together, but when the men went to the taverns, sometimes Mexicans and Anglos drank together. The grower would sometimes drink with the crew leader, and they would make it a big joke. They'd say, "Hey, I've heard that the Mexicans are the best. If you want your first sex to start out on the right track, go out with a Mexican señorita." So I always tried to protect and warn my daughters about the growers' sons.

I did love Pablo a lot back then, and I still care for him, but not like

I used to before. For a long time, I thought that he would ask me to marry him, before I finally gave up. Now that's over. He's never going to ask me to marry him, and in some ways, I'm kind of glad it never happened. Now I just feel sorry for him. He's so old. Mostly, I just take care of him. He has some problems and we live like brother and sister.

But I felt terrible guilt and pain about our being together. I'd been married in the church, and now I was living with another man. I tried to get lost so the family wouldn't know. But my shame came to me in my dreams.

> I walked into a house, I think it was my mother's. I saw the Virgin of San Juan in a picture. I stood in amazement because her eyes were burned.
>
> "Mother, what's wrong with the Virgin? Why are her eyes burned?"
>
> The Virgin keeps looking at me very sad, she can hardly look at me, and she says, "My daughter, your mother burned them as a promise so that you would return to your house, and because of you I am suffering, and you are living in sin and I am punished for that. You should leave him and not live with him until you are married by the church." (Diary, June 24, 1976)

I'd committed myself to Pablo, so I felt I couldn't leave him, but I also felt such anguish to cause God such pain. And Pablo and I've had problems, personal problems, almost from the beginning. But I wanted love so much, I just wanted kindness and companionship so much that for a long time I was willing to let the rest go away. Pablo and I lived more like a father and daughter, or a brother and sister, than a husband and wife. I loved him, but I still wanted to be hugged and wanted by someone, to feel like a woman. But those problems, they made Pablo bitter, and he blamed them on me. And I want more. Sometimes I say to Pablo, "Let me go. It's like you have a plate of food, but you won't eat, and you won't let anyone else eat either."

Then he gets mad and says it's my fault. He'll say, "I'm leaving, I'll go so that way you will be free. You can go to the taverns and drink and go with men. That's what you want." And we have terrible fights.

But I loved him so much in the beginning.

Today as I looked into his eyes,
    he looked at mine
We both reached far into each other's heart
What we give each other with our eyes
    is beyond man's imagination.
I take his senses one by one
    and united with mine,
I take him on a journey into another world,
    deep inside my body, my heart, my soul and turn him
wild . . .
    and stop time . . .
Just by looking at each other's eyes.

Seconds later,
    a century has gone by.

                                        (January 13, 1990)

A Ti

A ti
te quise, por todo el tiempo que no había querido.
A ti
te quise, por tantos años que sola y triste había vivido.
A ti,
a ti te debo lo que nunca había tenido:
Tu amor,
que hoy, con el tiempo y poco a poco he perdido.

[You
I loved, for all the time that I had not loved.
You
I loved, for all the years I lived alone and sad.
To you
I owe what I never had:
Your love,
that now with time,
little by little, I have lost.]

                                        (undated)

Dear God,
    . . . last night, in the darkness and intimacy that witnessed my an-
guish . . . I turned to you for your love and understanding . . . I promised you that Pablo would not touch my most intimate self which he

had been able to obtain without any effort of his own but selfishly and conveniently accepted.

This my God is meant to teach him that I am a creature made by you, like you, and demand to be treated like you.

Perhaps my promise will make me lose him and perhaps we won't be alive to come to an understanding by the time my promise is up, which is from today, October 20, 1984 to January 1, 1986, but I already feel your strength, your will power, your support, my God. So it is promised by me and written to confirm my promise to you.

Your daughter with faith, María Elena Lucas

October 20, 1984

. . . Oh God, I wish I was back home. I miss Pablo and Eduardo and our little place and all the plants and the baby chicks and the sea, Mexico. . . . I miss sleeping out there under the stars . . . And, my God, I need a companion. Someone that I can reach, someone that I can touch and can touch me back and can kiss me . . . and will love me. (Diary, June 13, 1988)

The Hardships of the North

> . . . It's true, Illinois is beautiful. Beautiful trees and flower farms and all kinds of vegetables. But behind every flower, fruit, or vegetable, I see a human being, doing stoop labor, taking cuttings from shrubs or trees, out in the bitter cold and snowy fields of winter.
>
> —Winter, 1991

We came to Onarga on November 2, 1974, when the wind was blowing and it was snowing. Pablo and I went to work in the big nurseries, like the other Mexican workers. During the wintertime we were between eighteen and twenty women working outside most of the time. We'd start at seven or eight in the morning and work out in the fields in the snow in below-freezing temperatures. We'd try to wear heavy coats and everything, and we'd really hurry to move our bodies 'cause our feet and our hands felt like ice. But the more we'd move, with all our garments on, we'd sweat inside because of the activity. Then if we'd stop for a little while, we'd get so cold from the sweat freezing, and our hair and our eye drops [tears] would freeze.

Sometimes our boss would stay out there with us for a little bit, but then she'd go back to the pickup and leave us alone in the fields. Sometimes when she'd be sitting in the warm pickup, watching us from the cab, one of the women would say, "We're too cold, Sally. Let us in the back of the pickup for a little while."

Sometimes she'd say, "OK, just for a little while." There was a canvas over the back of the pickup, so we'd go in there and huddle close together.

165

After a while, she'd say, "Out now. I can't let you stay too long." So we'd go back again and really hurry up so our bodies wouldn't get so cold. It was stoop labor too. We'd take cuttings of red dogwood and yellow dogwood and poplars, corkscrew willow, and other trees. We'd make piles of them, then bring them into the shed. We'd get a fifteen-minute break at 9:30, then go back to the fields till lunchtime. After lunchtime, we'd work in the shed, which was freezing cold too. They had a heater, but it wasn't any good, so we'd get so cold, we could hardly move our hands. We'd cut the cuttings into a certain size, and we'd package them and store them in a corner.

The wintertimes are horrible to work in. I hate the cold so much because it's not the weather I grew up with. You have to keep moving to keep from freezing, and I can tell you that the people that come from the south really dread it, and the people that were born and raised in Mexico are afraid of the weather.

And the workers don't know what we're doing with the chemicals. I myself was spraying chemicals, and at first, I wasn't even curious enough to worry. The chemicals came in something that looked like a butane gas tank. It was hooked onto the water system, and it would go through the water hose. Then we'd disconnect the hose from the chemical tank, let clean water run through it, then drink what we thought was clean water and use it to wash our faces. And many times I got the chemicals on my feet and my arms, and sometimes it would sprinkle on my head and face.

Then I saw what was happening to Don Lupito. I think he'd got the chemicals in his boot, and it was like his foot was rotting away. They told him he had leprosy, but I began to think it was the pesticides or chemicals. Then I met another María. She was all swelled up real bad. She went to a migrant clinic and they gave her medicine to relieve the itching.

And it was sad to see the women being mistreated. I don't like to say the words, but our boss, she'd say, "You Mexican bitch, come on, get to work. Move it." Like that. I complained about that once to one of the owners, and he said, "Hey, if you want to keep your job, keep your mouth shut and bear with it." I needed the job, I needed it bad, and I had to put up with it, just like the rest.

It was mostly illegals who did [winter work]. White women, others, didn't want that job. They'd also hire kids real young—fourteen and fifteen years old—as long as they were illegal. Sometimes even thirteen-year-old, real tender, young kids. I've seen boys come in and take a job and stay there and grow into young men.

Pablo saw a real bad accident while we were working there. An undocumented boy from Mexico, just fifteen, was standing on some boards, working with a machine. His mom, my friend, was working down below him in the conveyor. The boy, Trino, was working up there when one of the boards fell in, and both his legs went in the machine. He managed to pull one leg out, but the other got jerked in, and he started crying, "Help! Please stop the machine," but at first no one understood.

When they finally realized what had happened, his leg had been taken. His poor mom fainted, and they had to call welders to get him out. Pablo said he saw like a stick in the machine, but it was the boy's leg and his bones with the shoe. Years went by and he was still trying to get compensation. Because he was a kid and undocumented, there was a whole bunch of red tape.

Once I took another job that a friend got me, in a factory-type place. Because they asked her to find somebody, it meant they wanted a Spanish person. Otherwise they'd have asked a white woman to find somebody.

So I was really happy that I had a job, and I was working on a machine with a saw that took three to operate. But a girl accidentally dropped a whole bunch of wood on my finger. My foreman saw what happened, and he took me right to the first-aid station, but the woman in charge came over and was very upset and said, "Already you got yourself injured?"

Then about two weeks later, another accident happened, and I had to go to first aid. This time the woman looked at me and says, "Hey, listen, if you want to keep your job, we can't afford to have you complaining. You better not get hurt so often." So I knew better. Keep your mouth shut if you want your job.

Later, when Pablo and I were trying to help with the Mexicans working around here, sometimes we'd go from farm to farm to check on the conditions in the winter. In 1979 we had a terrible storm in here. Nobody was supposed to be out on the roads that time, but Pablo said, "Our pickup will make it."

So we got out and found a little house way isolated and alone. When we got there we just stopped and we looked. Everything was so quiet, and, all of a sudden, there was a guy banging on the window.

I said, "Pablo, there's people in there." Anyway, we got out and Pablo started shoveling, and, God, those people didn't have any food, fuel, nothing. They could have died in there. There were about nine undocumented Mexicans, and their lights had gone out, their water had been frozen, and they were all surrounded by snow. They couldn't get out, and they had no heat and were freezing. I don't know where their boss was, but he certainly wasn't worried about them. So we left food, and Pablo went back with supplies so they'd be warm.

Once when Pablo and I were out in the winter, checking on people who might be stranded on the farms in the snow, we got in terrible trouble. Our pickup broke down way out in the country when it was really freezing. We were really cold by the time we got it to a gas station that was way out away from town. It was already late and the gas station guy said he'd fix it in the morning.

We didn't have any money with us but Pablo had a payroll check from one of the nurseries, so we asked the gas station guy if we could just sit locked in the truck in the garage overnight so we wouldn't freeze. But he said no, then he closed and shut us out.

We went to a restaurant next door to the gas station and asked if we could sit in there for the night. They said no too, that they were closing, and they kicked us out. When we went outside we saw a phone booth out in the snow, so we decided to call the police and beg for help. Then, when we got to the phone booth, the phone had been ripped out. It was gone! I was so cold, and I just stood in the phone booth and screamed and cried. Then I just bent down in the phone booth and thought I was going to die.

But Pablo fought with me. He grabbed me and tried to pull me out with him. I just kept crying and telling him to go for help, that I'd wait in the phone booth, but he kept screaming that I had to keep moving and come with him, that I'd die in the phone booth. I fought him, but he finally forced me to start walking down the road with him. He kept pounding me and moving my arms to keep them from freezing as we walked.

It seems like we walked for about five miles in the dark when we finally came to a fancy motel. We went into the restaurant and ordered coffee.

When we could finally talk, Pablo asked for a room and told the motel clerk we'd pay for it with his payroll check, but the guy said he wouldn't take it. Can you believe that? It was like we were dying. Then we started begging, asking if we couldn't sit in the restaurant for the night drinking coffee. They kept saying no.

Finally, we asked them if we could call the police, and we called the police and asked them if we could spend the night in jail. The policeman who answered said, "I'm going to come out to you." When he got there, he questioned Pablo a lot to see if Pablo really did work at the nursery, then he finally said to the motel guy, "Listen, I'll vouch for their check, you can give them a room." But the motel guy still said no. I couldn't believe it! Then the policeman got real disgusted and said, "Listen, I'll pay for this room myself. I'm not going to let them freeze."

Lots of people up north treated Mexicans bad like that, in some ways like we'd been treated in Texas. I had to ask for food stamps again for awhile, and it was so hard. You hear people say, "Yeah, they live on the food stamps. Yeah, they're on welfare. Dumb people, lazy people." I didn't want to be called that. The man that was down there in the office, my God, he put on such a terrible face, like it was coming out of his pocket. I noticed one of the clerks in the grocery store, she'd hand the money to the white people, but she'd throw the Mexicans' change on the counter.

Mexicans weren't considered like people, and I think it still happens. I was told many times, "You're not human," or, "These people are used to that." I've heard that people did not think of Mexicans as human beings. "The Lord gave us these people to toil the land."

We always had trouble finding a place to live. Everywhere we'd try to rent a house, they'd say no. We were living in a tiny little house that was falling down, when we found out that the owner was trying to get rid of a bigger place next door. Just single men were there, and the house was very bad. So he said he'd sell us that house on contract, and at least we had a place to stay.

But it was a hard house to be in. The plumbing didn't work, there wasn't a place to bathe. It was just a miracle that we could keep clean, and I couldn't keep the house clean. The light, the electricity was so dangerous, and the whole house was covered with newspapers, not wallpaper. I used to lay in bed and read the walls. And Pablo's always being messy and not wanting to spend money, and I didn't have water to clean up from him.

I remember once a Mr. Brown came. He owns a newspaper. He and I were sitting down in the living room, and I had a lot of roaches. Mr.

Brown was bald and he used to wear a little black cap, which he took off. And while we were talking, I just froze. A roach was crawling up his head, all over the top. I thought, what if he scratches! It just walked around and went down and up again, right over his bald head. Then when he put his cap on, it was gone!

After he left, I told Pablo, "If you don't get me some medicine for the roaches I'm going to be gone. I'm going to move out of here, and I won't come back." So he got me some poison, but it hardly helped.

It also really hurt me when people said we were dirty. Once we had a meeting with the mayor and went to his house to talk with him. The woman who had arranged the meeting with him, Mrs. Hurtado, was a very clean, spotless lady. They dressed well and were one of the oldest Mexican families that migrated to Onarga and were pretty well off. They'd been there longer, their property was theirs, and they'd had two jobs so they could earn a little more money. But the rest of the community was in a pretty bad shape. Two other families and us were probably in the worst shape. When you're right in town and don't have plumbing, it just makes you terrible, especially in the wintertime. And so we had that meeting and were talking and the mayor didn't know who I was. And he started saying, "Those people . . . " he named the two other families and said, "and the Ortegas, they're just hogs." We were the only Ortegas. It just was so painful. He went on and said, "I've always had such admiration for you, Mrs. Hurtado, and for some of you people who really keep your places clean."

Mrs. Hurtado looked at me and turned color, she could see that I was hurting terribly. I said to him, "Yes, you're right about some people. They're pretty dirty, but, see, it isn't their fault because they don't earn enough to have water or things to clean with. If we all got together, maybe we could help those people change their lives so they could live more decent." I couldn't tell him I was one of them. I couldn't tell him he was talking about me.

All the time, I kept trying to write things, and for awhile I had a tape recorder and I made little skits. Like I acted out the different voices in a *mercado,* and I taped a little play. It was about a girl from the mountains in Mexico who was hired to clean by a rich lady in the city. It's all in Spanish with just two voices. The girl is praying to Our Lady of Refugio, then Our Lady answers and tells her to try to change the conditions.

And I'd dream my songs, like my *carpintero* song. In my dream I saw an old man who looked like Pablo, but in another country. He was barefooted and in rags, his pants were torn, and he was blind. He was by a bakery and smelled bread, and I saw him go in there and take the bread and run. In my dreams he'd run and fall and get up again, and he gave bread crumbs to the birds and to the children. Then, when he went into the church, I realized he was holy. Even though he was blind and had stolen the bread, he could see God and hear the angels sing.

We did have a really beautiful, old, carved glass window in our door. Some people came by and asked to buy it, but we said no. It was the only beautiful thing we had. Then one day, we came back home, and it was broken, all smashed up, and I got so disgusted. After that, we just had to put plastic up, which didn't help in the winter, especially when we didn't have heat.

One winter, when only Oscar was with us, we went without gas for heat because some other people had used our house without paying the bills, and the heat was cut off and we couldn't afford to get it on again. It was so horrible. It also happened with another family. I cried with the cold, and I really was terribly sick. It seemed to me it was bronchitis. We kept coming from inside to the van and turning the motor and we'd go riding around warming up. We'd go visiting, but everybody's so crowded in the winter. One family had about twenty-nine people, all sleeping in the living room and everywhere. I went to my daughter Christy's house, and she had all her husband's family too, and it was pretty bad.

I got a cough and I couldn't get rid of the cough, and my chest was like I was being choked. We used up all our blankets, and at that time, Oscar would sleep with us when it was too cold, and we'd try to keep warm in bed together. I'd just cry and say, "I can't sleep, it's so cold." I kept praying someone would give me an electric blanket.

Sometimes, we'd bring hot wood coals into the house and put them in the living room, but they would smoke and burned the floor, then we had a hole from the fire in the middle of the living room. It's not good to bring burning wood inside the house. I worried about fire and the wires in our house because it was so cold and the building was in bad shape. I tried to keep all my papers handy by the door, in case of emergency, so I could run out with a box of vital papers. I thought about fire a lot, and I thought about being asleep and being caught in a fire, but then I thought about freezing. I thought, I'd rather burn than freeze, so I had a choice there. But I didn't know if I could stand the cold another winter. I can accept dying any way except freezing.

> . . . Cold is dark,
> Cold is lonesome,
> Cold is blue,
> Cold is her.
>
> When the sun shines,
> Hear her sing.
> When the spring comes,
> See her smile.
>
> When the moon shines,
> Watch her pray.
> Back comes winter,
> And despair . . .

"It's very cold and it's raining too,"
(December 2, 1989)

CHAPTER THIRTEEN

Everything Shall Come to Pass: The Loss of Children

My kids, they had a really hard time in the Onarga schools, with all the harassment that was going on. They would be beat up after they'd come out of school, they'd be called Spics. And kids would say, "Go back, to where you belong."

What happened was that the mean kids wouldn't usually bother the quiet little Mexican children who would just keep their mouths shut at the remarks, but my kids didn't keep their mouths shut. Therefore, it got real bad, and it was like even some of the teachers didn't want them in school. One time, one of the teachers even said to Gloria or Christy, "If it's real bad, you're old enough that you could get out of school and go work and help your parents. You wouldn't be breaking the law because you're of age to make that decision."

I was really upset, to the point that I started fighting back. Once I had a problem with Johnny, my son. Johnny is such a kind and good person. But Pablo usually takes a beer at lunchtime, every time he eats, and sometimes I would too. At this time, Johnny was home from school for lunch, and he was old enough, so he says, "Mom, can I have a beer?"

So we ate and then he took a beer. He went back to school but was about three minutes late, so he had to go to the office. When he talked to the secretary, they smelled beer. They kicked him out of school and made such a big fuss and called me. They said, "Did you know that your son was drinking?"

I said, "No, he wasn't drinking. He just took one beer with lunch."
And the members of the school board called me for a meeting, and they
just looked at me like we were the scum of the earth. They said, "Your
son's drinking is against our rules," and this and that.

I said, "It is our custom, sometimes, at lunchtime to take a beer. We
allowed him to drink one beer."

"But he's a minor, and we don't do that."

"Well, my husband comes from Mexico, and he drinks a beer every
time at lunchtime. We don't see anything wrong with it."

"Well, you're in the United States. And have you heard of the saying,
'If you live like the Romans, you do like the Romans'?"

I looked at the woman who said that, and I said, "No, but I'm
learning."

"Well, that's the way you have to live in here. You can't live with
Mexico rules. You're in the United States, and you have to do what we
do. Your son is going to be expelled for the rest of the year."

And while they were talking to me, they weren't even listening. They
were passing the papers like the agenda around. I felt out of place. I felt
dumb. I felt terrible. I wanted to stand up and say, "Piss on you," and get
all of my kids out, but I didn't do that. I just thought, the day will come
when this will all change. But Johnny was so heartbroken because he's
such a good kid.

When my kids started dropping out of school, it was a heartbreak
because I had worked so hard and put my hopes up so high trying to get
them educated, knowing I didn't get educated and seeing the kind of [life]
I was living through. I had thought maybe it would be better for my kids
because it seemed to me that sometimes education was the way out.

Eva got married in Texas when she was about fifteen or sixteen, and
Tommy just took off. He seemed so mad and upset about everything. He
fought with us all, and it was like I lost him, but I kept praying for all of
them. Johnny was still here, and they beat him up so many times after
school. He'd come home all beat up, and he didn't want anybody to tell
me what happened, but eventually, the word would get back to me, and
I'd cry and be very upset. I'd complain to the school teachers and they'd
say they had nothing to do with it outside the school grounds.

I'd say, "It's not outside the school grounds, it only outside the school
door."

So they called me a troublemaker and said, "If you have any more questions, any more problems, go to the school board when there's a meeting. Talk to them."

I would always beg my kids not to fight back. "But, Mom, they hit us." People ridiculed them so much. Christy, she didn't take too much of it. She quit right away. Christy has always been more vulnerable, more sensitive, so she married one of the Mexican field workers. But Gloria and Johnny were fighters. I kept crying all the time and worrying and going back and forth to school and also arguing with Johnny.

Johnny was a very decent kid and very knowledgeable, very intelligent. Finally, Johnny said to me, "Look, Mom. All this bullshit is going to stop. It's too much. I'm leaving now. There is no way I can stay in school and put up with all that bull. They can all go to heaven and make a U-turn."

He quit and started running from one town to another around the area, and I didn't know where he was. Then he'd come back a few days later looking like garbage, all dirty and torn up. He'd been looking for jobs. Every time he'd come home, I'd start crying and begging him to go back to school, and the whole thing would start all over again.

Finally, he said, "Look, Mom. Please." He's so gentle. He'd say, "Look, Mom, please, trust me. I'm not into anything, Mom. Really, I'm alright." And he joined the service. To me that was such a blow because I didn't want any of my kids to ever join the military force because I don't believe in that, but I had no choice but to accept it. I thought that instead of him going off like Tommy and my losing him, maybe the military will be good for him. Maybe it will keep him busy, keep him doing something. And Johnny did build a good life. He's very disciplined and organized, he's kind and he's got a good family.

They were hurt in so many ways. Gloria had been a cheerleader in Texas, so she had all the experience and a lot of talent. When she was a little girl, her group had won first place in the whole state. So she was very excited about cheerleading beginning, and she said, "Mama, I want to try out. Will you buy me the outfit?"

I said, "I certainly will."

So she did, and the minute that the girls saw that she was trying to write her name down on the list, they began to harass her. I don't think there had been any little Mexican kids for the try outs before. I remember her coming home crying and very upset and telling me that it didn't seem that she'd be able to do it because everybody was putting her down. They didn't want her to participate because she was Mexican. She felt like even the teacher who was training them was prejudiced and was against Gloria doing it.

I didn't really break until one day after school. Gloria was walking by a brick or concrete building, and a group of girls came in a car and started squashing her between the wall and the car. Gloria came home crying, and I told her, "I'm going to disguise myself and go in someone else's car and wait outside the school grounds, and when they come out and start harassing you, I'm going to step out, and I'm going to go after them."

Sure enough, the next day I was waiting there, disguised, sitting low in a seat with a hat pulled over my face. Nobody paid any attention to the car I was in. Then Gloria came out of school, and they started calling her names and throwing her the finger. Gloria knew I was out there and got red in the face. And when one of the girls did that, I jumped out of the car, ran up to the girl, grabbed her arm, and pulled her up to my face and said, "Don't you ever, ever dare to do that again. I'm going to make you pay for this dearly. I'm going to sue the school, and I'm going to sue your mom and dad for discrimination."

Several teachers were out there watching, and I turned and looked at them and said, "You're going to pay for this because you allowed this to happen. I'm going to go to the school board, and I'm going to sue the school board, and I'm going to sue the city of Onarga. I'm going to sue everybody here because I can't take it anymore! I'm sick and tired of you all!"

The first thing the next morning, the principal of the school called me to the office and said, "I'm very sorry. I had no idea this was going on."

I was shaking and crying and told him, "You had no idea, no idea what's going on? Well, you better start paying attention, mister, because I'm very sick of all of this. I'm not going to feel sorry for anybody. None of you. I'm going to talk to a lawyer, sue the school board and sue you. And did you know your daughter is one of them, sir?"

He looked like he was going to faint. "My daughter? It can't be possible, Mrs. Ortega. My daughter is a good Christian, she's a volunteer worker."

I said, "Maybe she is a good girl, and maybe it's the rest of the girls that make her act that way, but I'm telling you, this is the last time. I want you to tell all those school kids, every one of them, what's happening. Go to every room and tell every one of them that whoever turns against my kids again, strikes against my kids, I'm suing their parents." So I turned around and left, and he just sat there staring at me.

A few hours later he called me back. They had a meeting and called all those kids into the room, and they called Gloria and had every one of those kids apologize and make friends with her and promise that they would never do it again. Then I said to the principal, "I demand you call all these parents, and I want to have a meeting with them tomorrow at two o'clock. I want to talk to them. No excuses. Either they show up or they are in trouble." Gloria's eyes got real big, like oh, Mom! Oh, Mom!

Right before I left, the principal said to me, "I swear to you, Mrs. Ortega, that before twenty-four hours are up, the whole thing is going to be taken care of." That was the last time they harassed my kids. But, one by one, my kids dropped out, and Gloria got married when she was sixteen. I was so heartbroken, I thought maybe she had a chance to be a teacher.

But on November 27, 1981, something happened that probably changed me forever. I lost Tommy. . . . It seemed like everything began to go wrong for Tommy when his father and I separated, and he wouldn't come with me—he hated it here. I could understand how he got so bitter, when you see your parents dating different people, and then your mom seeing someone else. Tommy didn't want to have anything to do with me after I went with Pablo, so he decided to live on his own. And I understand Tommy began to get into problems, and his father didn't want to help him with them and they fought. I don't know if he stole anything, but there was too much partying around, drugs, speeding tickets, and he was put into jail several times. Also, he found out he was sterile.

One time when I was in Texas Tommy had been drinking, and he and my daughter Gloria had a big fight, and Tommy really beat Gloria up. Gloria came to me all bloody and said, "Mom, help me."

I was very upset and went looking for Tommy. When I found him, we started to fight. I ended up saying, "Maybe that's why you can't have kids, 'cause you don't deserve any if you're going to treat them bad and beat them up."

Tommy was very upset, and he made fun of my religion, and yelled, "Get out of here!"

After that, every time I went to Texas, I tried to find him because I wanted to ask him to forgive me and try to have him make up with Gloria, but I could never find him. Then, one evening, two years after I'd last seen him, Tommy called me.

When I answered the telephone and realized it was Tommy, I was very, very happy. It was a total surprise to me. He said, "I just wanted to call you and tell you that I hope you can forgive me and that everything's alright. And that I'm sorry that I insulted you."

I said, "Tommy, I love you. Let bygones be bygones. Just forget what happened." I was so happy. "And I want you to forgive me for insulting you."

He said, "Oh, Mom, don't say anything. It's alright."

Then he said, "I also want you to answer one question that I have to ask you."

"What is it, Tommy?"

"I want to know if before you left my father you were ever unfaithful to him."

I told him, "No, I wasn't. I didn't go with Pablo until after I left your father, Tommy. I never went out with anyone when I was with him."

He says, "OK, that's all I wanted to know."

Then we started talking, and I told him that I was organizing the other farm workers, and he said he was happy for me. I also told him I was composing a song, and he said, "Would you sing it to me?" So I sang him that song. Then he said, "I also called you because I wanted you to know I'm taking a long trip."

"Where are you going, Tommy?"

"Well, you'll find out when I get there." He was so calm.

I said, "Tell me, I want to know."

And he says, "No, I don't want to tell nobody. You'll find out when I get there."

"You promise? Will I hear from you?"

"Oh, yeah. Yeah."

A couple of days later, I got a phone call in the morning. I think it was from their father, and he told me Tommy was dead, that he'd been dead since the day before. From a gun, a rifle that had been sawed off. Tommy was dead.

I went into shock. It was like I was there, but I wasn't there. I remember and I don't remember what happened next, but we left right away for Texas.

They say it was suicide, that he left notes, but I never saw them. They said he shot himself in front of a church, and I just can't believe Tommy would do that. Also, all his identification was missing.

I wanted all of Tommy's clothes, but the police wouldn't give me anything, it was too bloody. But I went to his apartment, and I told everybody to just leave me alone, and I went through everything he had. It just amounted to a few things, a bundle of clothing and a few objects and that was all. I thought, wow, this is what life is all about. We're just a bundle of rags. That's all we leave behind, a few things, nothing more. You can have lots of property and everything, but you're nothing when you're dead. You have a baby, and you just don't know if that baby is going to make it or not. I tell Gloria, "Enjoy your kids and be good to them because you never know if you are going to have them from one minute to the next."

I cried and broke down real bad; his father had to take tranquilizers and shots, and they wanted to do that for me too, but I said, "No, I don't want nothing. I want my senses to be in a whole mind, fully aware of what is going on. I don't want to be numb." Mostly, I tried to hold up because of my other kids. When a person dies in a normal way, a heart attack or an accident, it's one thing, but to take your life is the worst kind.

I felt real guilty because of the divorce and how that seemed to ruin Tommy, but I felt like my other kids had to see that I was not giving up on life. I just had to do it that way. I was dying inside, but I was standing up and holding onto dear God. I think I've been a very strong woman.

Johnny and Tommy were close to each other because they were about the same age, and I knew it was hurting Johnny terribly, in an ugly way, but all my kids struggled to get through it. That's why I didn't even want an aspirin, because I wanted to be sure I wasn't going to lose another kid or nothing was going to happen. And my kids were all very worried that something was going to happen to me.

I tried to say, "We all have to stand and stick together. We have to face this together," and that's exactly what we did.

I grieved for Tommy for so many years. During the first while I wanted so bad to find out what really happened. I kept saying, "Please, God, please. I want to know what happened to my son. I want to see him one more time. I want him to tell me why he done this. In a dream, God, please, bring me Tommy in a dream."

Finally, I dreamed Tommy. It was like he was in a picture frame, a big, life-size picture frame. I was looking at him, and he was crying, just tears floating all over his face, and I felt so sad. Then it was like that picture was erased and another came out, with the same Tommy, but a different picture. This time he was just staring, in a deep thought, no expression or nothing, just staring far away. I thought, what's he thinking? What's happening? Then that one went away, and the next one came, and it was him again. This time Tommy said, "Mom, don't cry anymore, OK? Believe me. I'm happy. Believe me, I'm alright. Now I understand why everything happened, and I'm alright, Mom. Don't cry for me anymore." And that was the last time I dreamed the grown-up Tommy. I've dreamed about him when he was a little kid, a little boy, but not like that again. But over and over, memories of Tommy returned to me.

. . . On this day Oct. 21, 1983 . . . I met a young man named José Romo . . . José Romo looked almost identical to Tommy my son and even one of José's little boys looked just like my Tommy when he was a little boy too. This has been the happiest moment in my life. It was like as if Tommy had come back to see me and comfort me. José Romo delivered a message from the Lord to me and I understood it. There is no doubt in my heart of what God wants of me, there is no doubt in my heart of how He speaks to me.

Blessed be José Romo, his wife and his children for ever. Blessed be José Romo's descendants for the Lord my father has spoken through him . . . (Diary, October 21, 1983)

Dear Friend of my Silent Thoughts,

. . . I'm cold and I can't write too good cause my hands are stiff. It's a gray day, just like my feelings.

I've finally paid my promise to my Mother Mary Guadalupe in Mexico City, thank God. I had no idea it was going to be so hard to drag on my knees from the very first stair outside of the Cathedral to the front of the altar where our Lady of Guadalupe reigns. After so much pain I was very thankful it was finally over. As I handed over the large and heavy bundle of fresh flowers to the altar man, I felt a great relief. Then as I dropped the tiny golden body symbol of my wish, I felt I was letting go of Tommy forever. It was sad and very painful to feel this kind of burying forever. So it was, and so shall it be, that everything shall come to pass . . . (Diary, January 21, 1984)

CHAPTER FOURTEEN

A Sacred Call to Action

Viva La Causa! . . . I'll make Union out of these kids if there can't be union
yet.
> Ha, Ha, Ha, Jesus taught the children right!
> Mom and Daddy learned to fight!

—Diary, July 1983

As terrible as the loss of Tommy was, I'd already been doing important
work when it happened, and after his death, I had to go back to my work.
As the kids were growing up, I'd always had a sense of being lost, of not
knowing what direction I had to go. But I also was aware that something
was calling me, something that didn't let me rest. I remember the time I
went to the Baptist Church on an Easter Sunday, and I had a strong
feeling of calling from the Lord. I couldn't identify it, but I felt I was out
of place everywhere.

It was not until my early years in Onarga, when I started going
through all those terrible things together with the other migrant people,
that I knew that God was calling me in some very special way. When we
went through the wintertime and hunger and discrimination and everything altogether, I began to see people not like I would see my kids, my
children, but different, and to see myself, not just like their friend, but I
began to see myself like God was telling me something. I don't even know
how to describe it. I began to see it like my obligation, my duty, like I
was their sister, but more than their sister, like I had to do something on
behalf of God.

And I began to see people not just like my friends or my sisters, I saw people like a suffering Christ. It seemed like Jesus, like the passion, like when he had been crucified. It was like I was seeing the crucifixion of God or Christ through their sufferings.

It wasn't just like this group of people here are having problems with the grower and we're going to fight, it was more a sacred thing. I don't know why I developed that feeling, but I remember exactly when it started. We were working out there together in the fields in the snow, and I was looking at the women and the men, and, somehow, I began to change. It was just like God was there, it was God I was seeing, and something was terribly wrong. I was very moved that I had to do something about it. I still feel that way. If I see something wrong, I say, "This is not what God wants. This is not the way it has to be." I get into a lot of trouble for feeling that way, but, oh God, I loved those people in Onarga.

It was like there was something holy between us. Sometimes we'd be out in the fields working on a beautiful day, and I'd look up and the sun is working, the bees are flying, some children are crying, others are laughing. I'd be with Gloria Chiquita and Comadre Lencha and Lucía, and people'd be picking tomatoes and putting them on their shoulders. I'd stop and look at them and say, "Don't you feel something? Don't you think it's just so beautiful, like God is here?" And sometimes Gloria Chiquita would look up too and say, "Ah, yes, María Elena, it's beautiful!"

And my dreams were telling me things. Like in my dreams, I've seen colors that are so beautiful beyond anybody's imagination, too beautiful to describe. Sometimes I try to give myself a logical explanation. I say, "Well, it could be the images of the daytime that at night spark a different kind of light image into your dreams." And in my dreams, I've been able to see a different kind of plant life, flowers with beautiful color and an aroma, a fragrance, that I've never smelled before. Maybe it's because I'm asleep, and there are a lot of flowers in the nighttime that expel fragrance, like the *huele de noche*. Or maybe it's like when you're hungry and go to sleep, and you dream of food and you can taste it and smell it.

In one dream, I was in the back of Our Lady of Guadalupe Church, the church we built later, and I was very depressed because the only things I owned were a crucifix and a little purse with one dime and one grocery store trading stamp, but I'd even lost the purse. Also, there were three women sitting in front of me. Their faces had a lot of pimples and were terribly painted with a lot of makeup, like masks for Halloween, and they were looking at me and were laughing and talking about me.

I thought, here I am, penniless. I don't have anything to give the collection. Then I started telling God, "God, I want to give, but this crucifix is all I have, so I'll give it to you." So when they passed the basket for the offering, I put it in the basket, and when I did, gold tears started coming down from the saints, and gold started pouring down from the pillars of the church. Then Our Lady came to life and started motioning me to come forward. And a man who was standing there, dressed in robes, like a bishop or the pope, motioned for me to come forward also.

Then Our Lady started making like the sign of the holy cross, and the man said, "Do you know what that means? A miracle. This is a miracle. She wants you to look in the baptismal fountain."

So she came down and stood by one side of the fountain, and the man stood on the other side. And I looked in there, and it was water, the kind of water that is holy water to baptize. Then it wasn't water anymore, it was the sky. It was the universe, heaven. Beautiful! With colors I'd never seen before. And I looked deeper into it, and it was light, but not all light, also a face.

Then I heard a voice; I think it was God who talked to me. And the voice said, "María Elena, all I ask from you is that you see that your children abide by my law."

I didn't really understand what it meant, but, looking back, I think it happened at the time when we were trying to get a dance troop and a church going in Onarga, and we were going through so much opposition. I guess I thought the voice meant more than just my kids, maybe it meant, "This is your job. It's your mission." Also, God's law meant more than just rules.

About that time, in the summer of 1975, we had an idea. We thought, "Why don't we get Panchita to teach the kids to dance, and we'll celebrate the bicentennial that way?" The bicentennial was coming the next summer.

When we'd lived in Mexico, I'd seen the Mexican ballet, and in school, I'd even participated once or twice in the Mexican Parade, the Charros Days, doing dances, but I didn't really know much about it. But we got about twenty young girls and boys together, most of them weren't citizens, and these kids practiced and practiced. We made up a beautiful group, and I spent a lot of money making Mexican dancing outfits for them. They were all excited, and a friend and I kept sewing day and night. We organized a Mexican Folk Ballet and called it "Guanajuato."

Then we really came together. We had meetings and we started dancing here and there. We planned fundraisers, and I guess the more the kids danced, the more prestige they got and the better they looked. I was always with them and telling them to have good posture and to smile and for the girls to act coquettish and the guys to be real aggressive, like with Mexican folk dances.

I remember our happiest time. It was on the Fourth of July, 1976, the first fiesta we put on for the people of Onarga, the ones who were so against us. I remember that they'd never seen anything like it before. We stole everybody's show. We were in the limelight, if that's how you say it. We were the main attraction.

They had a hotdog stand and a barbecued chicken thing and several games, but when we put on our presentation, it became the biggest thing of the day. From then on, every Fourth of July, they invited us. They saw us dancing in there, and it inspired awe. That time we also used skits about the American Revolution and the Mexican Revolution and poetry, patriotic poems about Mexico and the Mexican Revolution. That was for our own Mexican community, but mostly it was dancing.

Everybody was saying, "Gosh, we didn't know they could do that. That's beautiful! And those costumes. Where did you get this? What do you call that?" They wanted to know where we came from. I said, "Well, we're just farm workers, that's all." So the Fourth of July was my greatest time.

In some ways, this was the start of my organizing, even though I didn't know the word then. Also, there was a small grocery store in Onarga who treated the Mexican community bad, and one day, when they did something to us, I just reached my limit.

By that time, we had been doing like a census. We had been counting people, and we knew we were about fifty-eight families and three hundred or so single guys, so we were about five hundred people. And I'd been keeping track of the type of foods we bought. So I said to the grocery store manager, "We buy your groceries, but you treat us like this. I'm going to work with the rest of the community, and we're not going to buy from you until you treat us better." I didn't know we were boycotting, but that's what we were doing. And we got them to change how they had been treating us.

But, anyway, after we started getting invitations for the dance group to go around the area, that's when I met Olgha. Wonderful Olgha. Olgha is God's gift to the people. It was like when Jesus was organizing, and He called upon all these people and organized them to carry on his work. That's the way I see her. Olgha Sierra Sandman, she's the director of the Illinois Farm Worker Ministry. I met her at a fundraiser in Hoopeston, Illinois, in 1976. In a way, Olgha came to me almost like the Virgin comes to Rosamaría in my play. Olgha brought me the same kind of message, like a message from God.

In the play, Rosamaría has the Virgin of Guadalupe come to her, almost the same way Olgha came to me. When Rosamaría is attacked by the people carrying the signs of her suffering, she falls and cries to God. Then a woman comes from behind. This is Mother Mary. She's dressed as a farm worker. She wears her blue cape, but underneath she wears old pants and a shirt, old tennis shoes. She's got a scarf and a basket next to her, and she's carrying something red in her hands. Two angels wait for her where she entered so everybody can tell who she is. But Rosamaría does not see the angels. Then Mother Mary says,

> Rosamaría. Rosamaría. Don't cry anymore,
> please, Rosamaría.
> Look, search for the man
> whom they call César Chávez.
> You will find him
> where the sun sets
> and the beast falls,
> where a black eagle flies in my flag.
> In the fields
> where they sing "De Colores."
> There, reigning you shall find
> Justice, Peace, God, and César Chávez.
>
> Fly, fly black eagle,
> and when you return in these fields,
> "De Colores" you shall sing.

(1983)

The Virgin then turns around in her cape. The back of the cape says, "The National Farm Worker Ministry."

But the first time I heard of Olgha was at a fundraiser, and I thought, oh, she's probably one of them. She is probably just going to give me a hard time. But when Olgha makes up her mind about something she sticks with it, and she wanted to meet me, so, finally, I said OK. And, God, when I met Olgha, I knew it right away. I looked at her eyes when she was talking, and I knew she was a person who was true. There was nothing misleading. I knew that in a way, I'd found what I had to do.

I think that Olgha taught me everything. She took the time to talk. Every time I get together with Olgha, it never fails, she's always telling me something different. It's not that she's trying to organize me any-more—it's just how Olgha is—but all the time, I'm learning. In the begin-ning, I think that was the purpose, to teach me everything she could, and I've always felt thirsty and hungry for her kind of knowledge.

Olgha also helped me understand where organizing came from. I read a paper Olgha handed out to me, and it said that Moses was an organizer. I looked at it and thought, my God, that is true. I remembered that my father used to tell us beautiful stories about Moses. He said that Moses was a leader and that he opened the water. He said that Moses used to care for people, that the people were being persecuted and that Moses tried to lead them to a better land. And when I was a child, whenever we would go up north and there was so many migrant farm workers on the road, somehow I connected Moses with the whole thing.

And Olgha taught me about the labor law. I'll never forget that. It's in my diary.

> . . . I made a dreadful discovery. I read the National Labor Relations Act that was passed in 1935. It stated that "All people have the right to organize for collective bargaining except for the farmworkers." All of a sudden, for the first time in my life, I realized what I really was, due to the law, a farmworker in bondage, a legal slave as inconspicu-ous as an earth worm. I laughed and laughed and laughed, and then I cried as I never did before. I felt bitter and resentful. No wonder I've never been able to eat or live decently . . . (Diary, April 9, 1983)

I also learned from Olgha how to stand and talk. Since I was very young, I could stand and sing and talk to people, but they were my people in my time in my poverty level. Olgha taught me something different. I think that Olgha made me feel that I was worth something. I learned from her that I had the ability, even if I didn't have the education, and I took her as an example. Later, as we got organized, I taught the same thing to Gloria Chiquita, then Gloria my daughter.

So Olgha started helping us try to organize the people, and she offered the Illinois Migrant Ministry to assist us. She said she could help us get a big community vegetable garden, that she could get us hoes and seeds and speak on our behalf to get us land. See, the nurseries had much land they weren't using. So we went to one of the nurseries and asked if we, the whole group of us, could use some of the land to grow food.

The nursery finally gave us a dump area on a hill, and they said we had to clean it if we wanted a garden. It was very difficult to clear away all those old motors and tractor attachments and old refrigerators, but we cleared an area in there and made it real good for gardening, and we planted.

And Olgha was very excited about our dancing group, so we started talking with her about the Latin American Association we had formed. We'd started the association to share things like emergency money, but by the time we met Olgha, we didn't even want to be any part of it anymore. Uppity people had gotten on the board, and it wasn't helping the people who needed it.

So Olgha said, "Well, you could form another association." And right there, Comadre Lencha and a whole bunch of women, maybe eleven persons, said, "Let's have an election." So we formed the Sociedad Cívica Mexicana, and for awhile it turned out real good. We began to apply for funds to do this and to do that. Then Olgha began to take me out and introduce me into the farm worker movement, and in 1982 I ended up going to Avon, Florida, for a meeting, and I was super-impressed because there was people from several church denominations there, the National Farm Worker Ministry.

I was just very touched by it. I thought, God, this is a great example of teaching people that it doesn't matter what religious background you come from or poverty level or social level, that you can work together. But when I got home, I had trouble expressing that to the people. I kept getting the names all mixed up. But it was the women who helped me learn, not the men at all. Men always put me down, kept me from getting educated, but the women taught me.

Sometime during all of this, I met César Chávez for the first time, probably in 1978. It was at a fundraiser in Chicago, and I sang. Then I had my picture taken with César, then Pablo did, and Héctor did. Olgha told me César was doing good things, and I was happy about that. After it was over I realized the fundraiser was for him.

And during that time, our dance group, the Mexican Guanajuato Folk Ballet, began to turn into Teatro Campesino.[1] We put on the dances but also skits and poems too. We began to get calls from Chicago, all over the state, to picket lines, conferences, and meetings. We even came to Texas to perform for the United Farm Workers Convention. We performed to raise funds for the union and for scholarships for Latino and low-income children. We did it for elderly people from nursing homes and for school kids and for fiestas in the migrant camps. We went out there to the migrants, to entertain them and to bring happiness to their lives.

I had a dream, and I could see the whole thing. I bought the kids' hats, the scarves, the earrings, their boots, everything that went with their outfits. It took all I had, but I did it because I was angry about what we were going through. I thought, I'm going to teach these gringos that our culture is beautiful and that we're not animals. And I think I accomplished that. And I thought, if I can teach the girls to have enough confidence in themselves, they will eventually take it over. I'd never seen a play but had been in skits, so I wrote lots for it—skits and melodramas, poems and songs and dances.

"Somos Campesinos"

. . . Somos campesinos,
trabajando tierras,
le damos la vida a la Nación.

Nuestras penas
sufrimos sin clemencia
    en esta tierra,
que Dios hizo con amor,
    con amor,
le damos vida al campo,
    regando sangre y llanto
bajo el ardiente sol.

---

1. In 1965, Louis Valdez formed a small acting company called El Teatro Campesino which was designed to inspire California farm workers to join César Chávez and the United Farm Workers. Eventually, the company served as a model for post-1960s activist Chicano/ Chicana theater throughout the country.

[. . . We are farmworkers,
working on the land,
we give life to the nation.

Our hardships we suffer without mercy
on this earth that God made with love,
with love we give life to the field,
watering blood and tears
below the burning sun.]

(Song and Drama, November 1, 1983)

When we first started doing the Teatro Campesino and I started doing public speaking, I just had to depend on God. I kept saying, "I don't have the vocabulary. I don't have what it takes to talk to people." But I prayed and prayed, and I knew I had to do it because nobody else was going to, and I knew that God would help me. I'd see large crowds of people, and I'd say, "*Dios mio*," and I'd hold on to Olgha for dear life, but she was like my teacher. So how she taught me, I knew how to teach the rest. I felt the same strength that she was giving me.

When Teatro Campesino came to perform, first I'd look out to see what kind of audience we had, to see if it was elderly, young, middle-aged, teenagers, kids or all mixed together, because you had to get the audience in the right kind of mood. So I'd say questions like, "Have you ever been a farm worker in your life? If so, raise your hand. How many farm workers do we have in the audience?" So if a majority of them raised their hand, like in Chicago, then I'd go in a playful way, "¿Qué tanta raza tenemos aquí de México?" How many people do we have from Mexico? "Hey, how about Guanajuato? How about Durango?" That way I'd find out whether our audience was Tejano, Mexican-Americans, or Mexican.

First we talked and joked a little bit, and if the audience was mostly from Mexico, I'd say, "Well, you've got a whole bunch of wetbacks in here ready to perform Mexican style." If our audience was middle-class but they used to be farm workers, I'd do it another way. If they were college kids I knew that most of them were studying about La Causa and would have some knowledge. If they were church people I'd try to use Christian or spiritual ideas. And if they were growers, I'd really hit hard. I'd say, "How many of you have ever gone out there and seen what's really happening? Have you thought about being pregnant or on your period out there in the snow and having to make a hole to go to the bathroom?"

What I wanted to do was raise the consciousness among all the people and even make them cry when they heard about our struggle. Sometimes when they asked real profound questions, I'd cry with the answer. But I didn't just want to make everybody sad, I also wanted to make them happy. So, in the end, we'd make sure everybody was happy and very motivated and ready to do something and excited, like, "Wow, look what they're doing!"

The last number would be Gloria, my daughter, doing a tribute to America with the fire batons, and little Verónica [Gloria Chiquita's daughter] was part of that too. It was very extraordinary for a child her age to have lost stage fright and perform in her own special way. People'd say, "Look at the little farm worker girl. Look at her abilities. Look at how articulate she is." And we'd have five or six kids in the show, and you'd see them dancing and performing. The poorest kids around. I loved it and the results were good. Just by myself, I raised thousands of dollars.

Once, in Naperville, Illinois, there was a conference with several state senators, and I was invited to be a keynote speaker. Olgha would tell me, "This is the kind of audience we're going to have," and, "María Elena, it would be good if you touched on the boycott or this or that, and remember we're trying to pass a law and be sure to bring up these points." Then I'd just commend myself to God and say, "Be my voice," and sometimes I'd look at people, and they'd be crying.

CHAPTER FIFTEEN

To Live on Our Feet: Organizing the People

Forjada bajo el Sol

Un quejido se escucha en la labor
Del cansancio de un pobre pizcador
Un suspiro profundo y sonador
De la gracia de Dios al trobador.

Soy criatura forjada bajo el sol
con amor y dolor
Mi sonrisa humilde y mi color
son patente del Creador.

Padre nuestro, mi Cristo piscador
bautizado en mi pila con sudor
He aquí un bocado de mi arroz
es la hostia que como en la labor.

De mi cuerpo vive el pecador
Ay ay ay que dolor
Y mi sangre se beben en tu honor
Ay perdónalos Señor.

Cae el Sol y llora el Angelus
pues ya es hora de dejar de trabajar
me reclama con voz de obscuridad
ya Dios padre quiere descansar.

Cuando salga de este
surco vo'a cambiar
Vo'a correr vo'a llorar
y de aquí en adelante lucharé
con coraje vo' a luchar
Por Justicia, por Paz, por Dignidad.

[Forged under the Sun

A moan is heard in the fields
From the fatigue of a farmworker
A deep and longing sigh
of the grace of God to the harvest picker poet.

I'm a creature forged under the sun
with love and pain
My humble smile and my color
are evidence of the Creator.

Our Father, my farmworker Christ
baptized in my fountain with sweat
Here is a bite of my rice
It's the eucharist I eat in the fields.

From my body lives the sinner,
Oh oh oh what pain
And my blood they drink in your honor
Oh, forgive them, my Lord.

The sun sets and the Angelus begins to cry,
For it's time to quit working
She calls unto me in the voice of darkness
God Our Father wants to rest now.

When I get out of this row
I'm going to change
I'm going to run, I'm going to cry
And from now on, I'm going to fight
With anger I'm going to fight
For Justice, for Peace, for Dignity.]

—Song, June 16, 1987

I tried terribly to organize the people, with everything I did. Even with the stories I'd tell the children and that I still tell my grandkids. I'd say that during the daytime there's a big guardian angel with golden hair and blue eyes that watches over us. The golden hair stands for the sun, and the blue eyes stands for the sky, and she's dressed with a white gown and beautiful white wings, which are the clouds. Then I tell them that when darkness comes she turns into a beautiful, beautiful dark angel with white hair that is shiny, like the moon, and black eagle wings. At night, she turns into a United Farm Worker's Eagle and guards over children.

Before the teatro campesino got so involved and before I was so close to Olgha, I thought, maybe a priest would help us fight all this injustice. At that time, we had to go to Gilman for a Catholic church, and then the mass would be in English. And also, when I watched the men, I thought, maybe a church would give us someplace besides taverns to be in.

So we just started talking to people, and everybody was agreeing a church and a priest was a very good idea. That's when we did the census, to see how many we were. So Pablo and I started inviting people over. I started baking cookies; that's the way I attracted people, because our people love to eat. And we started fixing tostadas and taquitos and tamales and having meetings. We went to talk to the priest in Gilman and said, "If you can get us a Spanish-speaking priest, we'll get a place to meet." Then we invited him to the Fiesta of Our Lady of Guadalupe, and he invited two other priests.

Those priests told us to go talk to the bishop. So we went and were nervous but we told them that we thought a church would really change our lives. They approved it and told us to raise about three thousand dollars as a down payment on an old abandoned Protestant church in Onarga for our building. So we all pitched in our money, everybody, and we made several dances, and sold tacos and whatever, and came up with the money.

But then we ran into trouble with the Anglos in Onarga. They didn't want our church. They said the town had a legal clause, that Onarga already had too many churches, and another church was not allowed. One person said that there had never been a Catholic church in Onarga, and there never was going to be one either.

But the bishop hired a lawyer and fought for us, and one of the Anglos in Onarga said to the rest of the people, "Why should we be so greedy? The empty church is just sitting there. These people want a place to praise the Lord. Maybe that's the best thing that can happen to the community." So then it was agreed that we could have our church.

Once we had the church, everybody started working. We washed floors and scrubbed, polished and painted, and I sewed the curtains to

Our Lady of Guadalupe. They're still hanging there in the Mexican colors—red, white, and green. Our Lady of Guadalupe is in the center.

A priest came and we had our church and were so happy, but he turned out to be a conservative priest. He didn't want to, how do you say it, rock the boat. He just wanted religion, he didn't want to do anything about how we were being treated.

In the beginning, the dance group practiced in the basement of the church, but the more I got close to Olgha and the more I started speaking out about the injustice, the more uncomfortable the priest got with my work. Finally, he ordered me to stop, and it turned into something really terrible. I guess he was terrified about my speaking out, that the growers would come down on him and hurt everybody.

The struggle with him went on and on, because I wouldn't stop my speaking, and finally he made me get in front of the cross and said, "Do you believe in God?"

I said, "Yes, of course I do."

"Then you are condemned because you're not obeying me. There's going to be trouble, and you're going to cause it. And I'm going to see that you are run out because you're going against your priest."

I said, "Padre, don't say this to us. It's them, the ones with the money, that are hurting us."

"No, it's you. You're the one who's going to leave everybody without a job. There's going to be blood, don't you understand?" It was so terrible. I couldn't believe it, from a priest. We'd had such hopes and he let us so far down. But there were other priests, good ones from Chicago, like Father Charlie Kyle, and they'd come down to be with us when we needed them.

What I started saying shocked the people all around the state. I think I was called to the churches in practically every small rural area because especially the women, the wives of the growers, wanted to see me personally and find out what was going on. Sometimes I'd go into a small community church, and everybody would be so tense. It would seem like everybody had a rifle in their hands and was ready to go to war. But when I finished talking to them, some of them would cry and say, "We didn't know." They'd come and hug us and say, "We're glad that we heard it from you." It seemed like each place I left, I left a sister behind.

But one time I was in a church meeting, and this woman came up and said, "I want you to know there are Ku Klux Klan members in this

194   Forged under the Sun / Forjada bajo el sol

community, and I've been told to tell you to lay off because they're going to pay you a visit."

I said, "What do you mean?"

She said, "They're very upset with what you're doing."

I didn't know what the Klan was, so I said, "Well, tell them if they want to pay me a visit, fine. I'd be glad to talk with them." I wasn't scared until afterwards when I found out about the Klan. I learned they were from Paxton, Illinois, and belonged to one of the churches.

Finally, Olgha helped us work it out so we became part of the United Farm Workers with César Chávez. Pablo and I had a little bit of land that we gave, and the Illinois Farm Worker Ministry donated a trailer, and we started the first Farm Worker Service Center in the Midwest. On October 25, 1981, César Chávez came from California, and we had a wonderful ceremony to dedicate it. We had a mass and a rally and hundreds of people. We had banners that said, "Viva César Chávez," "Boycott Purina Pet Foods,"[1] and all sorts of things. César spoke in Spanish and English, and it was wonderful.

Then César gave the microphone to me, and I said, "Brothers and sisters, we have rights and we must fight for those rights, and we need to let people know what kind of lives we live, what is happening." Then I said, "It is better to die on your feet and not to live on your knees for the rest of your life."[2] It was the biggest moment of my life, like climbing Mount Everest and sticking the flag with the black eagle on top of it.

The women had cooked tamales all night and during the day, so after the rally, everyone ate, and we had music and danced. So, in that way, Pablo and I became organizers for the United Farm Workers.

After the inauguration I went to California for training. It was not until then that I really sat and talked to César. To me, he just spoke like another campesino, but by then I really knew about his work, and I didn't see him as just an ordinary man. I saw him as part god.

We did all sorts of things in the service center. It was a place for people to have meetings. Sometimes people who didn't have any place else to go would stay there. I'd try to help people fill out forms. Sometimes we had clothes to give away, or people would just come and talk to me

---

1. At that time the UFW had struck Dole Pineapple, which owned Purina Foods.
2. This is an indirect quote from the Mexican revolutionary Emiliano Zapata. See Ruiz, *Cannery Women, Cannery Lives,* 52.

about their problems. I'd take people to the hospital and pick them up. I'd take them for food stamps. People would come to get me to translate. We were just working all the time.

There were two women that I especially loved, and they were the most helpful—Gloria Chiquita and Lucía. They both had six kids and were illegal and couldn't really read or write, and neither of them spoke English, but, still, they were the ones who took the risks.

Lucía was tall, big-boned, with beautiful eyes, and she was the type of person who had a lot of determination, but Lucía's nerves were bad. One time, when Lucía left some of her kids in Mexico and came to be with her husband, she was nailed in a crate with other people in the back of a vegetable truck. It was like they were in a coffin so Immigration wouldn't catch them. They went like that all the way from San Juan, Texas, to Chicago, without water or food or having a chance to go to the bathroom. A whole bunch of people nailed in a crate. And it was winter and they didn't have coats. She was with her little brother, and his feet turned black and peeled from the cold. It was terrible. When she arrived she was so sick.

Another time she and her husband were deported with their baby girl, and they had to send the baby back alone with other people. For a long time, they didn't know if the baby made it. Then Lucía went back again to get the rest of her kids. Lucía suffered a lot and had bad nightmares. She also hurt her back while she was working in the fields, and we went back and forth, trying to get help with her medical bills. Then Lucía and her husband bought a trailer, but when they went to move in, the people had stripped everything out, the doors, the toilet, the thermostat, everything was gone. But Lucía still helped me; she was a big supporter.

And I'm so proud of Gloria Chiquita. Gloria Chiquita was tiny, with the face of the most beautiful Indian. I dream of having a beautiful big main room, with the pictures of my heroes. And I will have her picture in the center with a story beside it to show all the public. Gloria's husband was here when she first came, and she left her two oldest kids at home in Mexico with her mother-in-law, and she came suffering through the desert. It took them about eight days to get here, and when they were in the desert, they were without food or drinking water.

Then Gloria had two more kids here—one was her only girl, Verónica—and she went back to get her older kids. They were five and six when they walked through the desert. She says at night, it got very, very cold.

Gloria Chiquita is very strong. She didn't have a mom and had to start working when she was six or seven, and then she got married at about fifteen. Her father was very strict with girls. She says that one time, when she was all alone and her husband was working in the United States, her two little boys got real sick with a fever, and she only had two baby aspirin. She gave one aspirin to each of them and just kneeled down between them and prayed. And they got better. Now they're almost men.

And another time, there was a raid, when she was here and had all the children. And Immigration came after her. They asked her, "Where were you born?"

"Here."

"Do you have papers?"

"Yes, I do."

"Where are they?"

"At home in my trailer over there." She acted very strong, like she knew what she was doing, and they never came to get her. They took lots of people, but Gloria wasn't one of them. She just acted disgusted like about what they were doing.

But Gloria's got a very hard husband, a *burro* husband, and she used to be real scared of him. But I kept believing in her, and she kept getting stronger.

In our Teatro Campesino we had a play called *La Chamuscada* for Gloria Chiquita. She played a woman of the Revolution of 1910, one of the women my grandpa had told me about. La Chamuscada's father was hurt in the fighting and died in her arms, so she took his place as a fighter and became a revolutionary woman. But she was also sad because once that she was so strong, she couldn't find anyone suitable to love. We were trying to show people that we had the spirit of a guerrilla, a fighter, but, of course, we also had the philosophy of nonviolence.

But I think what I tried to show with that was what Gloria Chiquita had turned into. Gloria had been so beat down, first by her father, then by her husband. Who would have believed that Gloria could develop the courage to stand up? But with the acting, she became a braver woman. While I watched her, she really played the part as though she'd gone through the whole story, like if she'd become a fighter. And when she talked and sang, her voice was strong. I saw her develop into a very brave woman. And as time went on, and we had all sorts of problems, she'd look at me and smile and say, "We the women will overcome." I tried to teach everything I knew to Gloria Chiquita.

The women had such terrible problems, like this lady Meche. Meche was very timid, very shy, kind of beaten down, with a lot of sadness. But she was also very kind and gentle. In Mexico, she'd rented herself out for corn, then she started picking peanuts for thirty Mexican pesos. She had four kids and was just pregnant again, when her husband came here working. Then she lost touch with him, and they got poorer. It was like they were going to starve.

So she left two kids in Mexico and took the two littlest with her and came here searching for her husband up in Illinois. While she was looking for him, she had her baby, a girl. Then she found where he was, and he came back to her for a little time and got her pregnant again, but then he went away without her. So Meche had another baby, this time a boy, and after he was born, she got a tubal. But she was terribly, terribly poor.

She lived in just a couple of rooms from November to May, and part of that time there wasn't any heat and she didn't have food. I was leaving Illinois for a while, but before I went, I went to a church group for her and got her a big bag of beans and four tanks of butane gas to cook them with and said, "Meche, these have got to last the winter." But they didn't last, and when I came back her baby girl's legs were curved and her tummy was swelled from hunger.

Then Department of Family and Children's Services came out to investigate, but they didn't say who they were until I demanded to know. Then they said, "She has ninety days to get in a better situation. If not, we take the children."

"But she needs help, not to have the kids taken away."

"Well, you've been notified."

So I went to Meche and said, "This is how it is. I think they are trying to take your children away."

She says, "Oh my God, María Elena. It will kill me if they take my children."

So I said, "Pack your stuff, we're leaving." So I took her someplace else to hide her. But finally it got so bad, she just took her kids and went back to Mexico. So now they're back down there, very hungry.

That's what Family and Children's Services did, they just took away the kids, but didn't really help the parents. One girl was even a citizen, and she was living in her car with her kids, and Family and Children's just took the kids away. They said the woman was being neglectful. Lots of people tried to live in cars. There was no other place, but that's real bad during the winter.

But the people came. They came 'cause they were starving in Mexico. And because it was so bad in Central America, too. It's the only way the people saw for their kids. Families got separated and went through such anguish. Sometimes mothers almost felt like committing suicide, they got so desperate. Lots died along the way. And they lived in constant fear. And I've seen women, very husky when they go back to Mexico to get their children, but if they show up in Onarga again, they were very, very skinny and had got a bad color, a bad complexion. They had sunken eyes, and they looked very weak. This happened with the young kids too. They arrived looking very sick and broken.

People went that far north 'cause there was less chance of Immigration getting them, but I tell you, they suffered from the cold. It's not what they grew up with, and they didn't have money for warm clothes and heat. And there was less work in the winter, so winter was also the time of hunger. It's a very high price these people pay, and it's still going on, except now maybe, if anything, it's worse. After I left Onarga, life got even harder in Mexico and Central America.

When I was working for the service center, that's when I first started finding out what was going on in El Salvador, in Central America. It all started with this young kid who was about thirteen or fourteen from Salvador, but we didn't know that's where he came from. His name was José Mendiola.

A minister and his daughter and family were going over a bridge out in the country in Illinois. And the daughter, she said, "Dad! There's somebody under the bridge."

So they stopped and went down and found this boy curled up on the ground and burning up with fever. They took him home and cared for him for a few days, and they'd heard about the service center so they brought him to me. They said, "Can you take him in?"

I looked at him, and he was so young and frightened. I said, "Yeah, we'll take him and see what we can do for him."

So I started taking care of José , helping him get stronger. And I kept noticing that he didn't seem like he was a Mexican. He said he was from Mexico, and I said, "Which part of Mexico?"

And he'd said, "I'm from Acapulco." Then I asked him about the area, and he said things all contrary to what it was really like. So I knew he was not telling the truth, but I didn't say that. And I'd ask things like, "What's your mama's name?" but I could tell he was so troubled, so I didn't push it. He wanted to go to Dallas where he thought he had friends who would help him.

Finally, after he'd been with us about two weeks, he seemed well enough to me to work. And so we went to work in the fields, and working together, he started telling me what happened. He said, "Really, I'm not from Mexico. I'm from El Salvador." And he started crying. He said, "I don't know how I made it this far because I really thought I'd be dead by now. But the thing is, I don't know if my mom and dad, brothers and sisters are alive. And that hurts so bad. And it's so terrible there, it makes me sick to see all those people dead, all the killing. Such horrible things."

Then I was terribly troubled, and he kept talking. He said, "One of these days, I'm going to be a priest or a minister, someone from the church because maybe if I have power in the church, that way I can help my people. Nobody else can do it, but the church still has some power. I want to help people down there, but I don't know if I'm ever going to see my mom and dad again."

I was so moved by all of it. I said, "You know what, José , wherever I go, wherever, I'm going to talk about you. I'm going to tell people all over, whenever I get the chance." Then, all of a sudden, I started singing to him, and I said, "Not only talk. I'm going to start singing about you, too." Right then and there, in the fields, I started making up my José Mendiola song. And he seemed so happy.

He stayed with us about a month, and when he had enough money to take off to Dallas, he gave me a little picture of his face. I never talked to him again, and I don't know what happened to him. But I continued to work with that song, then I translated it to English and paid a man to write out the notes, and my daughter Gloria copyrighted it for me. Later, I sang it to Dolores Huerta in La Paz, Keene, California, during UFW's twenty-fifth anniversary celebration, and Dolores had the most special look in her eyes. And she had me sing it on Radio Campesina.

José Mendiola (Danza de la Vida)

José Mendiola
tienes en tus ojos
la nobleza bella
de los campesinos

Negro Mulato
coarazón de santo
Siervo de la Tierra
Tierra del Salvador
Tierra del Salvador.

Danza, danza de la vida,
De agua, viento, sol y tierra,
nace, nace la semilla
que José Mendiola
con amor sembró
que José Mendiola
con amor sembró.

Miren, como nace el trigo
mi madre lo vuelve pan
y de los racimos de uva
mi padre hace el vino
que en la Misa dan
y de los racimos de Uva
mi padre hace el vino
que los ricos toman.

¿Por qué canta la patrona,
¿Por qué llora mi mamá?
La patrona tiene techo
y mi pobre madre
nunca lo tendra.

Huelga, huelga, campesino
por justicia y libertad
por un techo, pan y vino
pa' José Mendiola
su mamá y papá
Danza, danza de la vida
Danza de los pobres
Dios amor y paz

[José Mendiola (Ballet of Life)

José Mendiola
You have in your eyes
the noble beauty
of the farmworkers.

Black mulatto,
heart of a saint
Servant of the land
Land of the savior
Land of El Salvador

Ballet, ballet of life
of water, wind, sun and soil,
born, born is the seed
that José Mendiola
planted with love
that José Mendiola planted
with love.

Look at how the wheat is born
my mother turns it into bread
and from the clusters of grapes
my father makes the wine
that is given at Mass
and from the clusters of grapes
my father makes the wine
that the rich people drink.

Why does the farmwife sing?
Why does my mother cry?
The farmwife has a roof
And my poor mother
Shall never have one.

Strike, strike farmworker
for justice and liberty
for a roof, bread, and wine
for José Mendiola
his mother and father.

Ballet, ballet of Life
Ballet of the poor
of God, Love, and Peace.]

(Song, July 1982. Listed in Diary, May 14, 1984)

But Pablo and many of the men always gave us so many problems. Lots of the men thought I was too macho, that I came on pretty strong for a woman, that I was too militant for a female. There's a lot of guys where it sort of hurts their pride to have a woman be the one to tell them how to change things. They think the man is supposed to be the boss and have the macho image.

I'd talk to them and say, "What have you got to lose by organizing? We have to sacrifice a little bit."

Then the men would answer back, "Our jobs. We've got our jobs to lose."

I'd say, "Your job! You're worried about losing your job. I'm worried about losing my life over this. But I'm going to fight to change things." That would shake them up, and they'd look at me like I was a very macho woman.

The men would tell Pablo that by me hanging around and having meetings, I was teaching the women how to be rebellious. They'd say, "Look at her, Don Pablo. She stands up. That's not right. The man is the boss of the house."

It seems like the men, they feel that either they are the head of the thing or they don't want to mess with it. In the beginning, we figured, well, we understand. We didn't want them to lose their jobs because we didn't have the resources to take any big action. I was already blacklisted, my kids were blacklisted, and a lot of other people, farmworkers who'd begun to be active, were blacklisted from the nurseries. So we said, "OK, but don't be opposed."

But still the macho thing came up. It was all right to take clothing and food and emergency help and for me to provide social services, but when it came to, "Hey, let's get together and sign cards and start learning what César Chávez has done for the people in California," and, later, "Let's understand what FLOC means and how we can improve our condition," then the men would say, "This is a woman thing."

And when the women began to get very brave and very aggressive, they'd say, "Oh, look what María Elena is doing to our wives." They didn't like it, but they never wanted to come and learn to change. So that was a big problem.

Pablo was always accusing me of not acting like his wife. He was always saying that I was trying to put him down, that I said ugly, stupid things. It seemed like he was always trying to cause me problems.

. . . [Pablo] is so bitter and resentful. . . . He . . . cares not whether I'm in the center of a very important meeting or if I'm talking to a friend or busy doing something that needs to get done. He'll come and won't even say, "excuse me for interrupting." He'll just come and pull me away (take me away) for things he could have done himself . . . (Diary, July 10, 1983)

. . . I decided to go look for Pablo cause he hadn't come home yet, and I thought it was just too late to be selling his food, so I went [to] downtown Onarga, and . . . was in the tavern. So I walk down there, and sure enough, there he was, playing dice with money. Oh God! I could tear him limb by limb. . . . He's won't even buy me a cup of coffee if I don't ask for one, and yet he's gambling . . .

I came home and felt like I was choking with desperation. I wanted to get back at Pablo. So I called the sheriff's department in Watseka and asked if gambling was illegal and he said, "Yes, it is." So I said, "I want to report my husband. He's gambling in the tavern." (Diary, April 23, 1983)

Life can be hard for women and it's hard for men who don't try to keep their wives down. Often, in Onarga, a young man who didn't practice machismo toward his wife was teased. Other men put him down. "Joto. Te manda la vieja." *Joto* means gay, not manly. Your wife is the boss. "Ya te agacharon los cuernos." You put your horns down. It means that he has surrendered to his wife. He's been dominated. According to them, he's supposed to be like a bull, a bully. So when he puts his horns down it means the wife has put them down. They tease each other, even if the man is not married.

Oscar was such a good kid, and his friends would call him *joto*. If he asked my permission before he'd stay out late, they'd say, "Suelta las enaguas de tu mamá. No seas tan jotinche." Let go of your mom's skirts. Don't be so unmanly.

There are still many men who brag to each other, "Hombre, a mi vieja yo controlo la nota con una bola de chingasos." It's a bad word. "Y con eso tiene que hacer lo que yo digo a huevo. Y si no le meto una bola de patadas." My woman, if she doesn't do what I tell her to do, I'll kick her butt, I'll give her a good whipping.

You see, that kind of attitude is passed on to the smaller ones. The men would say these things in front of their sons, and the little girls wouldn't get to eat with their brothers at the same table. And they would have to go to bed early while their brothers could be on their bicycles and play all over the neighborhood.

I think women really live in bondage, really truly, especially the farm worker woman. I don't know too much about other women, but I imagine the poor people in the city in the slums live in bondage too. And many Anglo women also. It's hard to even realize it because you're so tied up with trying to survive. It's like it's a controlled system, we're not really free, and I don't know how long it's going to take. It seems like you have to start in your own home with your own man and your own children, then the educational system, the way the neighbors act to each other, and on and on.

One time we women were having a meeting, and a few stayed behind, and we began to discuss how uneducated the men were about sex. The women started sharing their most intimate problems. I said, "Well, maybe it's up to us to teach our men." I don't mean to put our men down, but they don't ever think about bringing the wife a rose or just hugging her or saying that she looks pretty or giving her a kiss. Believe it or not, we women had talks about how to make men more aware of our bodies, how to make them realize we are there. We said a lot of things.

I told the women to say to their husbands, "Hey, I'm tired of this. I want you to treat me different. I want respect and caring." Then one day one of the men came over to the service center, and he told me he didn't know what was going on with his wife. He said, "You know, María Elena, she's so changing. She's coming up with all these ideas, and she wants me to kiss her and do this and that. What am I supposed to do?"

I thought, this is one big breakthrough, for a man to tell me that. So I said, "Well, you see, we have programs in America that teach people that it's not just making kids. There is love and touching and caressing and just trying to please your partner. Otherwise the wife has just become an object, part of the household, like a broom in the corner or a plate in the cupboard. And women are people too."

My mom keeps telling me that it was meant that men have all of the power. She says that's the way God meant it from the beginning, that man was created in the image of God.

I say, "How do you know God is a male, Mother?"

Then she really blows.

I say, "Mom, I don't think there's any place in the Bible that says that God is a man. Besides," I say, "Who wrote the Bible anyway?" Then I answer myself, "Men, that's who. What can you expect?"

That's why I wrote my play, to try to change all this.

But we tried to do good work with the people in Onarga. And my kids helped a lot. My daughter Gloria, in just six months, she taught a teenage girl, Rosenda, how to read and to speak English. She worked with her like crazy. Then we had a test, what a terrible test! This was before the service center was actually going, but it shows how close we were to each other.

One time there was a death and some big problems with Rosenda's family on their farm in Guanajuato, Mexico, and Rosenda was needed back there, but, of course, she was illegal. So we gave her one of my daughter's papers, and I went back with her as her mother. Then while we were there, Rosenda's little sister Julia begged us to take her to Illinois with us. Her mom and dad were up there, so she wanted really bad to come, and we decided to try it.

We crossed the border OK and were in the airport near Brownsville ready to fly north to Houston, where we expected to get a ride. I went into the toilet in the airport, and when I came out, Immigration was waiting and said, "Excuse me, lady. We need to talk to you. Are you the mother of these girls?" They had Rosenda and Julia.

I said, "Yes, sir, those are my kids. What's the matter?"

They said, "We need to talk to you all." This was right about the time the plane was going to board. So they started investigating us, but Gloria had been teaching Rosenda to speak and read English, and she'd done so good, Rosenda was able to fool them. Also, Rosenda had my daughter's papers. But Julia couldn't speak English.

I kept on insisting they were both my daughters, but Immigration said, "Well, how come this one can speak English, she can understand, but the other one doesn't?" They kept saying, "This one [Rosenda] is your daughter, and she's from here, but this one isn't, is she?"

I said, "She doesn't speak English because she was raised with her grandma in Mexico. So what's wrong with that? She's still a U.S. citizen."

And Rosenda said, "Yeah, she's my sister. ¿Verdad, Mami?" She was real good, Rosenda.

Finally, they said, "We're going to put you all in different rooms, each one of you, and we're going to get to the truth, and then you'll be tried for that."

When they said that, I thought, God, if they separate the three of us, they're going to find out that Rosenda is also illegal. I thought, I can't let that happen. Rosenda had her job and her mom and dad up there in Illinois. I thought, Julia will have to stay. I can't risk the two of them.

So I said, "No, you don't have to do that, sir. You're right. This one's not my daughter. But it's just like if she was. She's the daughter of my *comadre,* and I was going to take her because she needs me."

So they said, "See there."

And Rosenda went like, "Mom!" But the minute I had a chance, I gestured to Rosenda to accept, and she understood. So they let Rosenda go on the plane, and they put Julia and me in a room for several hours.

While we were alone, I told Julia, "I'm going to give you half the money, and if anything happens and they split us up, just get on the first bus to take you home and don't worry about me."

Then they took us out and put us in the *perrera,* the green immigration van with bars. When we went outside a *chubasco,* like a hurricane, was getting started, and the weather was terribly bad. Also, there were two different immigration guys in the van, Anglos, I thought, and the guys started talking. One of them said, "You know, I'd like to take the young one."

The other guy said, "Well, the old one isn't that bad." I was listening to their talk, and I thought, oh, my God, Jesus Christ! Julia is just a girl! I never thought that this could really happen. I've heard stories, but I never thought that I would be in a situation like this. My heart started pounding, and I started talking in English to them.

I said, "You know what? I know what you're saying! Don't you even dare! If you do anything to us, you better get rid of us. Because one of my daughters just took a plane out, and when she gets up there, she's going to tell the rest of my children, the rest of her brothers and sisters, my family, what happened to us!"

One of the guys said, "The bitch talks English! The bitch understands."

And I said, "Don't touch this child because if you do you'll be in so much trouble. If we don't show up at the other point, where they're expecting us, you're going to have to answer because you're the ones who took us out of here. If you're going to touch her, you're going to have to kill me first!"

He just said, "Well, the bitch." Then they said, "Está bueno, puta." OK, whore. Also they wanted to take our money.

So they took us to the U.S. side of the bridge and said, "Now, walk across to Immigration on the other side." They gave us some papers we had to show when we got there. Then they said, "You can go."

We got away from them as fast as we could, and I called my mom. This was about two or three in the morning on the Brownsville side of the border. But at that time I wasn't that close to my family. We'd see each other once a year or every several years. I said, "Mom, I'm in a big mess. I'm stranded. Can you get someone to meet us across the border in Matamoros?"

Mom said, "Well, no *mi'ja*. Right now you're not going to get anybody up."

I said, "Please, one of my brothers, Mom?"

She said, "No."

And I cried. Such a big rain and wind storm was hitting and we had to cross the bridge to Mexico holding on to the rail because the winds were so strong. By the time we got to the other side, the phone lines were down.

When we arrived at Mexican Immigration, they started making jokes: "¿Qué pasó, muchachitas? Mira nomás como me las mandaron." It means, "What happened, little girls? Just look at the way they sent you back here. All wet and dripping."

Julia was crying, and she was real nervous and upset. I said, "Julia, Julia, contrólate. Sígueme la onda." Get a hold of yourself. Play along with me. And since we were all wet, you couldn't see that we were crying. So I started smiling and laughing, and I said to Mexican Immigration, "Yeah, that's right. They got us."

Right away one of the guys said, "¿Adónde las pescaron?" Where did you get caught?

"We were just about to board the plane."

"Aw, look at you? What happened? Did you get tired of being a maid?"

"Yeah, really."

"Yeah, I bet you thought you were going to sweep in those green bills, huh? Those green dollars."

"Yeah, that's what we planned on, but it didn't turn out that way."

"Aw, it's better if you go back to your home and don't get into stuff like this." He says, "Sigue siendo criada." Keep on being a maid.

"Yeah, that's what I'm going to do."

"Where are you going? Where do you live?"

I knew several addresses from when I lived in Mexico before, and I said the colonia Mariano, Matamoros.

"But you can't even get in there. Too much mud and rain."

"I'm just going to get to the *plazita* [little square], and I'll wait there until morning."

"OK, pásale, pásale."

Anyway, we took off, and then I saw a guy with a cab that I thought I could trust. He took us to the *plazita,* which had lots of different roads running off from it, and I had no idea which one to take.

I had remembered a friend, Elsa, and I said, "Julia, I know Elsa lives in one of these streets. We are going to have to try every one until we find her."

Julia said, "We can't even see, María Elena."

And I said, "Every time when the *relámpagos,* the lightning, strikes, we'll be able to see."

So we went wading into the water that was coming up in the colonia, and it turned out I had taken the right road. Then it was like a *vecindad,* a neighborhood, that I recognized. We were in the right spot, but I found out later that Elsa slept in the very last room. So we knocked and knocked and we called, and nobody answered. Julia and I had to sleep sitting in the water up to our chests. We just hugged each other and leaned our heads together and waited until morning, but by morning we were burning up in fever.

When Elsa came out, she says, "María Elena! What are you doing here?" We were so sick that she just put us to bed. After we had rested for a day, I went all the way back down to the farm in Guanajuato in Mexico with Julia and returned her home. It was a bad experience for her. She was all shook up, and she had lost so much weight, and I felt so sick and so bad, but it wasn't my fault, and they didn't blame me.

It was hard on Rosenda too because the plane only took her to Houston, and it turned out she had the wrong address and phone number for there. And a guy was chasing after her also, harassing her. Finally, another man helped her find out where to go.

At that time, I had no idea what was happening to Rosenda, and Rosenda had no idea what was happening to us, and for several days no one knew where we were. It was all worry and pray and worry and, finally, I came back, but I was so tired and so drained and so sick in my stomach. I had been real scared. When we were in the van with the men, my voice, it was breaking, stuttering. We'd been terrified. But, you see, all us people, we all went through so much together.

And as we did our organizing, the women in Illinois got so brave. Whenever I see them, they keep asking me, "María Elena, when are you coming back? We want to keep fighting."

I say, "I hope it will be very soon."

And they say, "Well, when you come, we're ready." I think, oh yes, we're all ready.

CHAPTER SIXTEEN

"Nosotros Venceremos"

I really loved those people. Working with them changed me forever. I could never forget it or really fit in some other place. My whole thinking was altered. We shared so much together. Part of my play is about all those things, the sadness and the happiness, we people in the fields went through together.

I tried to have the characters act like the real people I knew. In the second act, Rosamaría, her husband Miguel, their kids, and their many farmworker friends were in the field picking tomatoes. Some of them were talking and laughing and others were singing, and in the distance, you could hear the noise of an airplane.

The airplane gets louder and it comes over the farm workers, spraying them with pesticides. And everybody yells at the same time at the plane. "Hey you, we aren't worms!" and "Hey you, stop it!" "Jíjole! Ya ni la friegan!" (you really can't translate that), and "Cover your face!"

Then the narrator says, "At last the plane leaves. Everything is sprayed with pesticides, and the farm workers rub their bodies with their hands trying to clean up a little, and they go back to picking."

The next part of the play points out the problems with sanitation in the fields, and Gloria says, "I need to go to the bathroom, but I don't want to go in the ditch because I'm afraid of the snakes. How should I do it?"

The women say that they will let the men go ahead, and then will circle Gloria so the men won't see her, but the boss, the patron drives up and says, "C'mon, move it. Catch up. Not a lot of tomatoes, not a lot of money, understand? Move it."

211

After he leaves, Lucía says, "Now, Gloria, now, because it's almost time to eat and the men will come back soon." So the women circle Gloria, and the narrator says, "A human act." Then the women hear the calls of the farmworker men. It's time to eat, and some run to the ditch to wash their hands, and others break up tomatoes to wash their hands with the juice. Then all of them gather at the end of the field. They laugh and talk and offer their lunch to each other.

Finally, the narrator says, "And that's how, day after day, the beautiful season of harvesting is spent."

When we were all working together, there was always still so much work to do for everything we did, like if we were going to picket or to perform. I had to worry about Lucía's kids, if they had sweaters, caps, if they had shoes and socks, and I had to worry even about the car they were going to drive, whether the heater was working. I had to see if they had transportation money, what they were going to eat on the road. Mainly we fixed tacos and coffee at home. I had to deal with Gloria Chiquita's stubborn husband. I had to go talk to him a week before anything we did, and I'd have to practically kneel to beg him to let Gloria Chiquita go.

Sometimes it was almost funny. One of the women would say, "Well, I don't have this or I don't have that." "Well, I'll lend it to you." And things like scarfs and gloves would go around and around the circle.

But, I'll never forget those days. There has never been another group of people that I loved so much. I love those people with all my life. We went through so much misery and so much happiness together. Those are not just friends, those are real brothers and sisters to me; I'll never forget.

One time we went to picket in Kankakee, to demonstrate in front of a grocery store to get the people to boycott Red Coach lettuce. Usually there would be some church person or somebody else to accompany us as a spokesperson for the group. But this time, nobody was available, so it was a job that I had to do myself.

Gloria Chiquita and Lucía and other women and kids came with me, and we started picketing outside the grocery store. We did everything that we knew so we wouldn't break the law, but, still, a whole bunch of policemen came to harass us. But we'd had training, so the ladies were ready. They'd been trained that nobody would speak if someone came up to them. They'd just say, "She's the leader," and point to the spokesperson.

So that's what happened. The police wanted to know who was responsible, and they came up to me and said, "We want to see your papers." See, almost everybody was illegal. I was about the only citizen.

I said, "We don't have to show you our papers."

He said, "Either you show me your papers or you're all going to jail, and there will be a fifty-dollar fine for each person."

I said, "Go ahead and put us in jail." But several of the children began crying. Then several of the women started trying to walk away, and I got so worried. At least half of the children were undocumented and all the undocumented women. They could all get sent right back. And I saw everybody in jail and their whole lives going down. I thought, Jesus Christ, everybody will be deported, and what are we going to do?

Then Lucía did something very brave. I'll never forget that day. The policeman was right in front of her face, and they were all around us, and, suddenly, Lucía grabbed the United Farm Worker's flag and stuck out her arms holding it high in the air. And she lifted her head up and looked at him like, so what. I dare you. Like the Statue of Liberty!

That made me get back to the world. Then Lucía started singing "We Shall Overcome" in Spanish.

> Nosotros venceremos, nosotros venceremos,
> Nosotros venceremos ahora.
> O en mi corazón, Yo creo,
> Nosotros venceremos.

And the other women started singing with her, and I started to function. I said to the guy, "I want to talk to my lawyer."

"Huh? You have a lawyer?"

"Yes, I do, and I will not speak one word until I go talk to my lawyer."

"Well, go ahead. You have ten minutes to do that."

I ran to a phone. I finally got this good organizer, Mike Matejka. And Mike was so calm. Boy, did I learn a lot. He said, "María Elena, don't worry. Don't give out any information. Tell them that you are going to wait and talk to your lawyer and that they can go and put you all in jail. But I'll take care of everything." He was so serene, and I had faith in him.

So I calmed myself totally. I figured if Mike says to be put in jail, then that's what we'll do. Then I thought, this is going to make a great newspaper story and will help us with the boycott.

By the time I came back to talk with the policeman, the sheriff was already there, and I was very calm. The store manager had come out and he was very upset, walking up and down, and a crowd had developed. The sheriff introduced himself, and I said, "I'm María Elena Ortega, and I'm the spokesperson for all these people. Sir, we're not breaking the law, and I don't know what the problem is with the officer. We're within the right number of feet from the store, and we're not harassing anybody. We're not disturbing the traffic. All we're doing is putting our signs up so that people will know. And we did notify them about what we were going to do."

Then I said, "And I just came to tell you that I talked to my lawyer, and I'm not going to show you any papers and that you can go ahead and put us in jail. Our lawyer will help us."

But the sheriff answered, "I want to tell you that we have a union too, and I know of your struggle. We know what's happening. It was just a mistake. This is a rookie here." He looked at the policeman like the policeman was in big trouble. "We know what's going on and we're not against it. You can go back home or you can keep on your picket line as long as it's peaceful and everything's alright."

Of course, the older women, Lucía and Gloria and *mi comadre* Tencha and Rosa and all the ladies weren't really afraid, but the young girls, some of them never came back to picket or do other work. They said they were too chicken. It took me months before I could convince them to participate in the service center again.

I tried to say, "If they put us in jail for something like picketing, it's Godly, it's like baptism. It's not like we'd be breaking the law. We'll just get stronger, and the people from outside will understand that something is terribly wrong." Finally, that seemed to sink it; they were prepared to go to jail.

Sometimes there was something very special between us. When we sang "De Colores," we all looked in each other's eyes and touched each other in a very special way. When we had meetings we'd hold hands, and when we'd sing, we'd become like one. It was like when you hug and say, "I love you and I care for you and God is with us and be strong." Sometimes we'd sing "De Colores" and "We Shall Overcome" in the fields while we were working, and it was something very moving.

During this time, we worked real hard on the sanitation in the fields bill. Olgha and the others proposed an Illinois Field Sanitation Act that

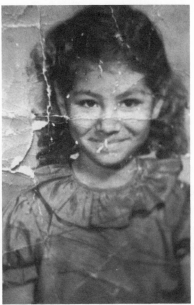

María Elena's parents, November 1944.
Her mother was nineteen years old with
two children at home (María Elena and
her brother) while her father, age
twenty-five, served in World War II.

María Elena around age six.

Roy Lucas, María Elena's paternal grandfather, near migrant housing, about 1957.

Age fifteen, with neighbor children in Texas shortly before her first marriage.

María Elena (third from left) age sixteen, with husband and in-laws, the winter her first child was born.

María Elena's father, about 1957.

Age twenty-two, with five of her seven
children, 1963.

Pablo Ortega, César Chávez, and María Elena at the Onarga United Farm Workers Service Center, Onarga, Illinois, October 25, 1981. (Photo by Kevin Bronson, *Labor Paper,* Peoria, Ill.)

María Elena speaking to farmworkers during the dedication of
the Onarga UFW Service Center. (Photo by Fran L. Buss.)

María Elena and unidentified migrant woman demonstrating
outside grocery store in Kankakee, Illinois, 1981. (Photo by
Mike Matejka.)

Back row, far right: María Elena and Pablo with members of Onarga UFW Service Center dancing group. María Elena's youngest son Oscar is in the front row. (Photographer unknown.)

Gloria "Chiquita" Carmona with Farm Labor Organizing Committee flag, around 1985. (Photo by Fran L. Buss.)

María Elena with migrant children in near migrant housing,
Onarga, Illinois, about 1981.

María Elena and her father on front porch of his house in a colonia near the Texas-Mexico border, 1988. (Photo by Fran L. Buss.)

María Elena (far right), her mother (second from right) and several of her siblings, Brownsville, Texas, 1988. (Photo by Fran L. Buss.)

María Elena's mother (standing), her aunt, and one of their comadres at a public housing project in Brownsville, Texas, 1988. (Photo by Fran L. Buss.)

María Elena and elderly family friend, shortly after María Elena's pesticide poisoning, 1988. (Photo by Fran L. Buss.)

Undocumented Guatamalan refugee woman and child in south Texas, 1988. (Photo by Fran L. Buss.)

María Elena on the land she purchased near Los Fresnos, Texas, 1988. (Photo by Fran L. Buss.)

Un Eco Navídeño

Era María, mi cara, la suya.
En su vientre, un hijo,
en mis manos, una semilla.
Nace un amanecer,
por primera vez, ve sus ojos,
"Ay--- Madre mía"----

Mama de sus cenos
la dulsura de mi miel,
y la amargura de mi vida.

Pisa la tierra,
y siente el sol que me quema
y el sudó que me tortura.

Habla, y sale un grito que estremece al mundo
y aquel que me lastima.

Queda su eco, soy yo---
y su grito sale del alma mía.
Yo soy campecina!

Copyright ® Maria Elena Lucas
Dec. 16, 1989 Friday

María Elena's 1989 Christmas greeting, "Un Eco Navídeño."

would give us toilets and clean water, and we testified for it at the state capital.

> ... Father, there is a lot of you around us. Please, I ask you humbly, let the light of your spirit provide for the farm workers and please, let the darkness of your suntanned heart show all nations you're the leader of justice in the cause of the poor Farm workers plight.
> ... [When I was ready to testify in Springfield,] ... I was really nervous and just didn't know what was going to come out of me when I would finally give my testimony ... I surely didn't want to show any signs of irritation, if in case someone irritated me. And what do I do! First thing I knew, I was irritated, and next thing I know, *¡zás!* It showed. I almost felt like saying something like, "hey don't waste your time tossing the toilet tissue back and forth, toilet tissue is not the issue, we've been using weeds and leaves for years and years, what we need are the toilets!"
> You should've seen and heard some of 'em. I can't believe it myself, really. I'm talking about real educated people, and what's worse is, these are the people that govern America? Oh God ... no wonder we're all messed up!
> You know what? We need to clean house, we need Sanitation in America! ... (Diary, April 20, 1983)

Later, we wrote a letter to the governor. Thirteen of us signed that letter. We said:

> 8-16-83
>
> Dear Honorable Governor,
> HB-1045 "The Field Sanitation Act" is now in your hands, and so is our dignity that only you with the power invest in you, Sir, can our dignity be respected and the welfare of all the people in the State of Illinois be protected, with one humane and Christian gesture from you, "your Signature" for passage.
> We know there is great opposition, but we implore you respectfully Governor, do not allow greed and ignorance to tarnish the promise of our country's principles.
> By God we were concerned enough about this dreadful unsanitary conditions in the fields to expose this reality to all of you. It took a lot of courage, at least people will check very well the food they eat now.

Please, Mr. Governor, answer us personally as this is a very personal and serious petition we're asking of you.

Thank you sincerely,

María Elena Ortega and twelve others

On the letter we drew a life-sized hand, stretched out with a vine in it, and the words, "Thank You-With All My Heart-For HB-1045, Your Farm Workers." So we tried just everything.

For a while, Olgha and I were trying to organize the mushroom workers in west Chicago, and I'd be going back and forth to have meetings with them. At night, I've have to walk about a mile and a half from where we had our meetings to where I'd catch the bus to Onarga. I was in poor black neighborhoods, and during that time, nobody ever bothered me, everybody was good. I'd use that time alone in the city at night to think, but Olgha worried about me. We had union cards signed and everything, but César said the timing was wrong. He said, "No, not yet." So we had to give up for the time being, but I kept wanting to organize, not just give out social services.

In Onarga we were always being labeled a bunch of activists or crazy or troublemakers. One time we were supposed to give out government cheese, but I wasn't going to deliver it, I wanted people to come to our trailer or attend our meetings, and the uppity people accused me of refusing them cheese. It got so bad, they called down the Mexican Consulate from Chicago.

And I became like a social worker for the day-care center and the doctors and the schools, the hospital, for everywhere, and I was always analyzing the situation. I realized that in the schools the teachers treated our children different than the others. The kids would come home very anguished, because the teachers would check their heads for lice every day, but they wouldn't check the heads of the Anglo children. I'd call meetings and I'd tell the parents everything that was going on. The teachers were invading the kids' bodies in a very cruel way.

And I worked such long hours, during the nights and on the weekends. Olgha kept telling me not to work so much, but I just didn't know how to say no to the people. I got very skinny. People from Kankakee and Hoopeston and Milford, from all over, would call for help. Sometimes I'd have thirteen or fourteen people waiting for me to do different things for them. It was just impossible.

César had told me, "It's not good to play Santa Claus to the people. It'll be neverending," and I started getting to the point where I understood what he meant. I was burning out. It's not good to have people so dependent. But it was like César was giving me a double meaning. First, he said I shouldn't just give and give to the people, to make them dependent, but then he said there weren't resources to organize them for a union, that we'd just have to go on and on with a service center. But the longer I worked, the more I wanted to organize them to fight.

We did so much and everything brought so much emotion, so much good, so much bad, so much confusion.

Dear Hope,
   . . . I have to share with you the FLOC March of Farmworkers from Ohio[1] . . . I drove all the way to Philadelphia, [and Oscar and I] were the first ones to arrive. We walked towards the marchers and when we met them, there was César Chávez, Baldemar Velásquez, Frank Ortiz, and Fernando Cuevas leading the march. We greeted them and then started the hugging and kisses of old friends and continued the march back to Vernon Park where we held a rally. So many unforgettable moments, God. The most moving moments were the Farmworker Rainbow over the Franklin Bridge, it reminded me of Judy Garland's "Somewhere over the Rainbow." Then, as I marched through the ghettos in N. Camden, New Jersey, my heart began to swell and ache, and I began to feel at home and I began to feel the bitterness and resentment that is born in that misery too. I thought for a moment and then I praised God, César, and Balde, for they chose just the right place to share and strengthen our hopes. Where else is justice born but in a manger, and this time I remembered where Jesus Christ was born, how he lived and how he died and how he still was living and marching on, probably carrying a very, very heavy cross, and headed to Campbell's Headquarters so my feet were blistered and I ached, but I carried my cross just like everyone else and marched and chanted, "Boycott Campbell's Soup!"

---

1. This was a six-hundred-mile march of about one hundred people, led by Baldemar Velásquez, from Toledo, Ohio, to the headquarters of the Campbell Company in Camden, New Jersey. Thousands of people, including César Chávez, Olgha, and María Elena, joined Baldemar and the others for a rally at Independence Hall in Philadelphia, then they all marched across the bridge to the Campbell headquarters in Camden.

I thought, "What a blessing" when the priests were washing the feet of the farmworkers, I thought, "What a privilege it must be, they deserve it so much." All I could do was cry and feel compassion and think about the hard life and sufferings we have gone through. 560 miles in one month, how many miles in so many years, crop and crop, I wondered.

. . . When we finally made it to the front of Campbell's headquarters, somebody said Let's kneel down and everybody started to kneel down . . . and so did I, but as I kneeled down, all of a sudden, I felt angered and I said, "Dammit, do we have to kneel down at them too?" And I started crying cause I felt humiliated and oppressed once again by these money scavengers. . . . . Then I felt someone touch my right arm and softly patted me like trying to comfort me, and as I turned, I saw a beautiful young lady smiling at me and as I smiled back my rage turned to peace and I realized very strongly all at once, Hey, I'm not kneeling to this company. I'm kneeling to God, Jesus Christ and his Holy Spirit! This is my final and total humble offering to prove my love and faith to God almighty in front of the Campbell Soup Company headquarters to show this company that they might have control of the wealth and agrislave system, but God has control of Justice and is our source of power, wisdom and strength, and I felt great and strong and looked up at the faces of our oppressors and said We shall overcome someday . . . (Diary, August 13, 1983)

CHAPTER SEVENTEEN

Exhaustion and Retreat

> How can I be a Christian and a warrior at the same time? How can I
> be living and feel dead at the same time?
>
> —Diary, 1983

Early one morning, we had a raid. People came running to tell me, and I rushed out to where Immigration was loading Mexicans into the van. I was crying and I started shouting at the Immigration officers, "Why do you do this? Why don't you quit this dirty job? Can't you tell how much these people suffer?" But they wouldn't listen to me.

Then I saw a black Immigration guy, and I didn't know what to do, I felt so terrible. So I went up to the black guy and said, "Hey, Brother, have compassion. Your people were slaves once. Can't you do something?" He just looked at me real strange, and his fist got real, real tight on the van.

So I went back to the women. Immigration had several of their husbands, and they were almost hysterical. I just loaded the women and a whole bunch of kids into the van and took off to hide them. Everybody was crying; there was so much suffering.

And almost every weekend there were fights and problems with the undocumented. There was a gang of young Anglo and young Mexicans who were born in the U.S. and raised in Onarga, and on weekends, they'd get together and disguise themselves, and when the undocumented workers got paid, they'd go to their apartments and hold knives on their throats and steal their money. Then, when the undocumented were out on the streets, they'd beat them up. We had lots of fights like that. Pablo and I lived about a half block away from where it would happen.

One night they stopped one of the Mexican farm workers and demanded money. The gang started pushing him around, and a big fight started. Pablo and I ran down to try to stop the beating, and several police cars showed up. One policeman threw the undocumented guy on the ground, stepped on his neck and head with his foot, and yelled to the other policeman, "Give me the rifle."

I recognized the policeman with his foot on the guy's head. Once, before the police knew who I was, I'd been in the back seat of a car that belonged to a man who knew the police real good. And while I was just sitting there, the man had exchanged beer and marijuana with the same policeman.

So I threw myself between the undocumented guy and the gun. The policeman yelled at me, "Get the hell out of here, lady!"

I looked up at him and said, "Don't you dare shoot this guy or hurt him, because if you do, I'm going to say that I saw you break the law with my own eyes. I'm going to tell everybody about it." By then a real crowd had come up.

The policeman looked at me, and, suddenly, I guess, he remembered. Then he grabbed me and said, "You shut up and get the hell out of here. If you have anything to say, go to court, but you better get out of here because we're going to put you in jail too."

"Put me in jail. I don't care. I saw what happened. Those other men started this fight. They wanted to steal this kid's money." So the police let him go. But there were many robberies and fights like that, and the police didn't usually help the Mexicans. One time one of the young men was stabbed and died in my arms. He couldn't speak and just looked at me. It was so terrible.

Things were always happening, and I just got more and more exhausted. I even started falling asleep when I was standing up. And underneath everything, I was always grieving Tommy. Also, Pablo said my work was making me into a terrible wife. And it was true. It would be midnight, and I still hadn't fixed him any food. Then Pablo did something to really hurt and humiliate me. It was so bad, I didn't even write it in my diary. We even split up for about three months.

Despite everything, we did do so much with the service center. We had a day-care center, a food co-op, a medical and dental clinic, maternity, and we gave all sorts of emergency help and the women were behind me from all over, but it still seemed to me like we were just taking charity. With all of this, we still weren't organizing to demand justice, but I almost couldn't think, I got so tired and confused.

But César didn't want me to organize Illinois. He said the UFW wasn't ready for that. They wanted me to organize the community services, but not the real thing that I wanted to do. I kept trying to communicate with them that I needed to be doing more direct organizing for the union, something more powerful than just social services, like what we were trying with the mushroom workers in Chicago.

> ... People around here don't see me as a person who's doing a job through the Union, or, as a union organizer, they see me as their own personal savior ... (Diary, November 2, 1982)

There came a point that I was so terribly exhausted from wanting to work miracles that I almost couldn't think, and besides, I was slowly learning that social services weren't going to solve our problems.

Later on, I got that directly from César himself and from Baldemar, the head of FLOC, that a service center was never going to do it, a different kind of organizing was needed. César would say, "When the people are ready themselves, they will do it. They will fight for justice." At the time, I couldn't quite understand what he was telling me, but later I realized maybe he was saying, "Go for it on your own. You don't need us to start a labor union." Maybe he was thinking, if this woman is bright enough and has enough courage, she can lead the people herself. But, for some reason, he didn't tell me that directly.

Now I know, there's no reason why there only has to be one or two labor leaders; we could have done it on our own. In some ways we were ready. The women were ready. But for some reason, César didn't say that to me, and I kept thinking that if we went on our own, if we didn't wait for the United Farm Workers, it would be like stabbing the UFW and the Migrant Ministry in the back. But now I know I was wrong.

And what I really did wrong was not talk to Olgha about it. I just so didn't want to hurt her. She came down a week before I resigned and I was going to tell her, but she was so sad because somebody else had quit that I just couldn't do it. I should have sat with Olgha and the members of the Farm Workers Ministry and discussed it. But I didn't know how to do that. I hadn't organized with FLOC yet. I didn't know how to build up a strong membership and to start fighting for labor contracts—not yet. Still, somehow Olgha and I and the other women, we could have done it together. But I didn't talk to her. Instead, I wrote my resignation letter, and on December 15, 1983, Oscar and Pablo and I left for Texas.

I tried to write the last act in my play so it would point out all the changes we need to make, so it would put everything together, and especially make men treat women better. When I left Illinois, I took the play with me, so that some day, some way, I could make people understand.

Especially during the last act, the audience, the farm workers, are supposed to get involved. See, by now the farmworker woman has been oppressed by the growers, the church, and her husband. She and the other farm workers have gone through many trials together. Then Rosamaría's husband dies from drinking, and, finally, when she can't stand it any more, the Virgin of Guadalupe appears to her. She is dressed as a farmworker woman and tells Rosamaría to go west, to César Chávez and the United Farm Workers, that Rosamaría should start working for justice.

Then act three is supposed to be like a farmworker convention. There are microphones in the audience; the actors go to those microphones to make resolutions. And the audience is supposed to get involved.

The actor playing César Chávez says, "Welcome farmworker friends to the first meeting of the United Farm Workers of America, AFL-CIO. My companion on microphone number one, would you please state your name and the name of the committee you represent?"

Farmworker Number One is Rufino Contreras. He was a martyr killed during the union campaign in California. See, God has resurrected him from the dead so he can make the important resolution: "Considering that the farmworker woman is the person most suffering, most oppressed, and the most treated like a slave in this world, we resolve that now and in the future, we, the men farmworkers, will respect, honor, be considerate of, and give freedom and love to our women farmworkers, recognizing them worldwide as 'the brave women.'"

Farmworker Number Two then says, "My general, Cesar Chavez, my name is Rosamaría de los Campos, alias, La Chavita. . . . I second the motion to approve the resolution that my friend and loving brother Rufino Contreras made because I believe in God, peace, and justice for the farmworker struggle."

The narrator says, "And the great Moses of the farm workers, with deep emotion, asks the audience for a general vote."

Cesar says, "Everyone who is against us kneel down to beg God to forgive you, and everyone who is in favor of us, rise and sing 'De Colores,' and may God bless us. Long live the United Farm Workers!" And that's the end.

When I resigned from the service center, I made up my mind that I'm not going to ever go through that again. I think the answer is in really organizing for union contracts. This is what we have to learn: We can be on welfare forever, we can receive handouts forever, there's enough clothes forever and enough compassionate people out there to be giving handouts, but that's not going to solve our problem. The problem will be solved when we deal with the growers, and they pay better wages, and we have political power.

CHAPTER EIGHTEEN

Mujeres Valientes: *Union Organizing for FLOC*

After I resigned and went back to Texas, Olgha kept the service center alive by working on the amnesty program for immigrants through it. She did so much good work, and now most of the people that I cared for so much back then are legal.

Olgha knew how much we wanted to organize Illinois, so she finally worked it so that I could come up from Texas and four of us women from Onarga could go to Ohio and learn to be organizers for FLOC in the summer of 1985. FLOC was the Midwest farm worker union, so it made sense that we become part of them, rather than the UFW in California. It was a big, big thing for us to go. Gloria Chiquita had to get permission from her stubborn husband and take her six kids with her. My daughter Gloria also had to get permission, and she took her three kids—the littlest one was still a baby—and Rosa Gaytán had two kids with her. Olgha wrote about us [in an article for the newsletter of the Illinois Farm Worker Ministry, Summer 1985, entitled "Courageous Women, Farm Worker Women"].

First we went to a campaign orientation about union organizing. It was taught by Fred Ross and Baldemar Velásquez, the head of FLOC. Then we went to Ohio to work for two months with other organizers on the campaign. We were trying to get the cucumber workers to sign union cards. If enough people signed cards, then there would be secret voting on the farm or wherever the election would be held. Then, if, I think, fifty-one percent of the people voted yes, we would represent them.

But it was a very hard summer, very hard for all of us. It was a terrible year in many ways. There were a lot of threats to the organizers and to the workers if they signed up for our union, and we were very harassed by the growers, and Baldemar—or Balde, as we called him—was under a lot of pressure. But we'd finally begun real union organizing where we could try to have a union and bargain for contracts.

Many things happened when we did this. For one thing, people who were against us tried to blackmail the women organizers. One time I had to stop at a camp and tell the people there, "I've come with your membership cards." The men were playing dice and cards when I got there. The guys that had become members were very respectful, but another guy said, "Oh, you're an organizer for FLOC." And right away, I noticed the expression on the rest of the men's faces, like they were trying to communicate a message, but I couldn't understand. Then this guy says, "I'm going to be in another town with a whole bunch of farm workers, and I bet they'd all sign their cards if you meet me there."

So I took the directions, and when I was in that place, I started to look for him. Finally, I found him in his apartment, and it turned out that he really didn't have any influence over anybody, he was just trying to get me alone.

He tried to get me to drink with him, but I told him, "Wait, I'm not wasting my time with you. What I'm doing is very serious and means a lot to me. You've got the wrong person. Don't ever do this again!" And I got out of there, but I was afraid because he could have hurt me.

Later we found out that the crew leaders were using men to try to entice the women organizers. One time a crew leader asked me to come to talk to him in a camp on a certain day. So when I arrived, the crew leader comes out of his house with a bottle of tequila and says, "Come on, how about a drink?"

It was a very hot day, but I said, "No, I'm not here to take drinks. I'm sorry, but I came to talk to you." I'd been very happy when I heard he wanted to talk to me. I'd thought, my gosh, maybe I've convinced that guy, but, instead, he pulled me into the house and practically began to stick the bottle down my throat. I kept saying, "No, wait a minute. I don't drink, and I'm not here to take a drink. I'm not even thirsty. I came here because you said you wanted to talk."

Then it turns out there's a guy in there with a tape recorder and a camera, waiting for me so he could take pictures of me drinking with the crew leader in order to make the union look bad. I got very mad. "I'm leaving!" I yelled and got out of there.

They did all sorts of things to scare us and keep us away from the workers. One time when I went into one of the camps, the crew leaders let loose their wild dogs to chase me down and get me. Another time, one of the growers followed me in his pickup, and I had to speed in my car to get away from him. I was tearing down this road, and suddenly, I came to this big expressway with a red blinking light to stop you before you pulled into the traffic. But he was coming so hard behind me, I just gave my car all the gas I had, and said, "Oh, my God! Here I go!" And I pulled into traffic and got away.

At times, we were so frightened that every day, as we'd leave to go out by ourselves, we'd look into each other's faces, and we all knew what the other one was thinking. We just wondered if this might be the last time we'd ever see each other. But we did it. We learned to add oil to the cars, to fix them, to do so much.

Of course, there were also good people, really trying to help and be part of the union. Sometimes the workers got in bad trouble with the growers for what they were doing, and people went into the rest rooms with us to sign the cards to try to keep others from knowing.

One day, when I was out in the fields organizing I saw a crop-duster airplane heading at all the people, then it began spraying right directly over them. They were just dressed with flannel shirts and handkerchiefs across their faces to protect them. I got so upset I climbed up on the roof of my car and started yelling up at the airplane. I started screaming and hollering and shouting, "Hey, don't do that! They're not animals! Don't you spray on top of the people!"

The guy in the plane must have seen me because instead of coming back, he just kept circling and circling, and, finally, he took off. The people, everybody, were so submissive, so accepting, that I started hollering at several people. "Hey, don't let the guy spray you! It's dangerous."

And one guy said, "But what can we do? They don't listen to us."

I said, "Get out of the field."

He said, "But, the *patrón,* he'll fire us."

I thought, my God, the same old story. I wonder how many will get sick. When is it going to change? There are supposed to be some sort of signs, notices, when they are going to spray. How do you make everybody understand that? You have to keep pushing and cracking it into their heads.

Finally, during the actual election, I had something really good happen with a whole family of crew leaders. I'd been working so hard to try to convince the people in that camp. I'd go to their doors, and I'd talk with them slowly, and with time, more and more people signed the cards. They'd say, "We want to sign but we're so afraid." The family who was crew leaders watched what we were doing, and I guess they slowly started believing more and more.

Then the day we were to have the elections, about fifteen minutes before the Dunlop Commission[1] was to arrive in the camp, the grower came up to me and pushed me and said, "What are you telling my people?" They always call them, "my people." "Why are you telling my people that if they don't sign the card, they aren't going to get a job with the unit next year?"

I said, "Who's been telling you that?" Then I turned to the people and said, "Did I tell you this? Is this how I'm explaining what we are after?"

And the crew leader and his wife spoke up and said, "No, that's not true. You haven't told us that."

So the owner couldn't fight about that. Then he said, "It's true, though. You sign it and you won't have a job!" And he pushed me again.

And I turned to him and said, "Don't you ever touch me like that again."

Then this girl comes forward and said, "I was the one that told the grower that."

I said, "Why did you do it? It isn't true."

"Well, I couldn't understand. I thought that's what you were saying."

"No, but how can you all expect to be part of this if you don't sign the card? If you don't vote for us, we won't be able to help you later on. We won't be able to represent you."

So the girl admitted she was wrong. At that very time, the Dunlop Commission arrived, and I shouted, "They're here! They're here!"

---

1. Baldemar Velásquez had negotiated the formation of an independent commission, chaired by Harvard professor John Dunlop. The commission drafted rules extending collective bargaining rights to Midwest farm workers for the first time, essentially acting as an Agricultural Labor Relations Board by private agreement.

So I stepped back up with some of the farm workers, and the male crew leader, he turned around and said, "María Elena, is there still time to sign the card?"

"Yes, but what about your wife?"

And his wife said, "Sign it, sign it." So at that time, they signed the cards real quick, and the woman said, "Well, our problem is that we are undocumented, and we're just now getting our papers, and don't you think Immigration will find out about our signing?"

I said, "I'm not going to tell them, and I don't think anybody else here knows except me."

And she said, "We believe you," and then the whole family signed, and we won that camp. They voted for the union.[2]

But there were other issues for us women that summer, with our own leaders who we really looked up to. Balde and his assistant were very dictatorial. I couldn't understand what was happening and why, but they were very into discipline. We women weren't supposed to talk together at night. We weren't supposed to say absolutely nothing to each other about what happened to us during our day while we were out organizing. I began to think that maybe they really didn't trust us women, and as the weeks went by, we began to whisper together at night.

We'd leave to go out by ourselves to work at 1:00 in the afternoon, then we had to be back by 11:00 at night, and during the mornings, we'd have "post mortem" meetings where we were supposed to report how we'd done the previous day. And Balde was very hard on all of us, not just the women.

FLOC made it like everything had to be a test of courage, we had to be real tough people and take whatever came. The first two weeks we went out to the fields and to the camps in pairs, but then they made us each go by ourself alone. We women tried to say we didn't feel good about that, but they wouldn't listen. I was OK by myself, but I was real worried about the younger women. What if they had car trouble? What if men got them alone? Gloria Chiquita didn't even speak English. And the young women would be up all night with their kids, then the leaders were hard on them during the day.

It seemed so strange to talk all the time about the need to discipline. We were all adults. We were all working for something good. Gloria,

2. FLOC won with over 60 percent of the vote and signed nearly five thousand new members over a two-year period.

Gloria Chiquita, and Rosa wouldn't have gone through all that with their kids if they didn't believe in what we were doing. I finally challenged Balde on some of that, and he didn't take it good. Things were real tense between Balde and me at the end of the summer.

> 8:45 on Friday Oct 18, 1985 we picked up Lucía Carmona, Rosa, and Gloria (my daughter), and we drove all the way to East Bay Camp for the Illinois Farmworker Ministry Retreat. . . . It was raining, not hard, but incessantly all the way. It was noontime when we got there. As we walked through the woody, beautiful trail that led to the dining hall where we were to meet with the rest of the people, we saw Baldemar and his wife and children crossing the old wooden bridge . . .
>
> Gloria and I [both said], "Look, there goes Baldemar and his family . . . *Ay, Diosito, el nombre sea de Dios* . . ." (Diary, October 22, 1985)

I still don't understand some things. All the years that I've been involved, I can't understand why it's so strict, so controlled. There have been a lot of unhappy organizers who say, "It's too dictative, not democratic." There are ways they punish people who go against them.

> . . . But within the decision makers "Discipline" is lord! It's mechanical, emotionless, cold, hateful, oppressing, enslaving, humiliating, intimidating, mind-destroying, cult-oriented, and threatening . . . (Diary, October 22, 1985)

And they especially didn't seem to pay attention to the women. At first, I couldn't quite understand that was what was happening, but over the years, I really began to see it. The first time I really started feeling put down in the union because I was a woman was that summer. It's not that I expected to get any special treatment different from the rest of the people, but I also didn't expect to be put down in little ways that amount to a whole lot.

> Dear Mother of Jesus,
> As far as I know, we've yet a long way before we women receive any credit or recognition for anything we do. I'm surprised your

name and the few others in the Bible are even mentioned, I mean women. One of the most distinguished and prestigious women in our time, who I am honored to know, is Mrs. Olgha Sierra Sandman, and I hope she goes down in the Future Testament of the Bible . . . [Yesterday] Olgha and I spent hours talking about this summer. Mother of Jesus, I pray to you that you help me sort out all that in my heart still hurts because of what I went through as a Farmworker Organizer for FLOC . . . (Diary, September 9, 1985)

But our campaign in 1985 was successful. And at our Constitutional Convention at the end of the summer, I was elected third vice president of FLOC, and Gloria Chiquita was also elected a vice president. And even while I felt really bad about the discipline, I also really looked up to Balde for all the good he was doing.

The Mission of John and Jesus

When Jesus (Baldemar Velásquez) finished instructing his 12 apostles (The National Farmworker Ministry) he went on to continue teaching the people in many other cities (asking them to support the Farmworker struggle and to boycott Campbell Soups because of the injustices we the Farmworkers were suffering).

John was in jail when he heard of what Jesus was doing (I was in Brownsville, Texas, living in a small mobile trailer without plumbing, water, light or cooking fuel, stranded and jobless . . .).

Jesus (Baldemar) said, Go now and tell John (María Elena) what you have seen and heard (that Campbell Soup Co. has signed an agreement with us). Tell John (Gloria Chiquita from Onarga, Ill. who has six children and lives in deplorable conditions imprisoned in a cell—a shack in rambles)

That the blind can see (God's light is upon us,
    our faith and dedication has been rewarded).
That the lame can walk (because we have toiled without rest).
That the leprous are healed and the deaf can hear (and that there are
    thousands of farmworker who were in tears and are now
    rejoicing) . . . (October 19, 1985, Matthew 11, Verses 1–8)

Then in February, 1986, we won our contract with Campbell Soup Company, after all those years of working at it. Winning the Campbell contract seemed like a great victory for the people, and I admired Balde for sticking with it.

God knows, Balde has done such great, great work. And he has very good ideas, like he said if we just keep giving charity to the people, it's like subsidizing the companies. That's when I gained the experience and the real understanding about what organizing for a union really was like, how to get a labor contract, not just to give social services.

For years, I kept begging Balde to let me go organize the nursery workers in Illinois, but over and over he kept telling me it wasn't the right time, that they didn't have the resources. He'd lead me on, "Maybe, maybe soon, María Elena," but then, again, the same reasons. It was almost like the same thing as with César, but now I knew how to organize. Olgha also kept saying, "Balde, send María Elena down here to organize the farm workers." But the answer was always the same.

Balde wants to cover the whole Midwest, but they don't have the resources, they don't have the personnel, they don't have the funds, they don't have the time. But it seems like he won't let other people do it. See, I was very well known in Illinois, and Balde does not like that kind of competition. I've seen it with other people.

Finally, in 1986, I came up from Texas to go to an IACOMA Conference.[3] It was at a beautiful retreat center, and they gave me a private room with my own shower and a desk and everything, and I guess I should have said, "Oh, thank you," but I didn't. Then I realized that everybody else was sharing rooms and bathrooms and I realized they were doing something special for me.

I'd just sit at the desk by myself, and I kept thinking and praying about how much I wanted to be in Illinois organizing the nursery workers. Balde kept saying, "We have to wait, María Elena. We're not ready."

Suddenly, I thought, why do we just have to have one or two labor leaders? I could also be a labor leader. It was like God put the idea there. It came at the moment I was praying. Then Olgha and Mary Ann Poskin came into my room, and I said, "Why do we women have to depend on

---

3. IACOMA, standing for the Illinois Inter-Agency Committee on Migrant Affairs is a " . . . Committee of state agencies and not-for-profit organizations dedicated to providing services and advocacy on behalf of migrant and seasonal farmworkers and their families in Illinois." [Quoted in "IACOMA Statement of Mission and Purpose."] María Elena and State Congressman Lane Evans were primary speakers at its annual conference at Mayslake Franciscan Retreat Center in Oak Brook, Illinois, in April of 1986. [Information from personal correspondence with Olgha Sierra Sandman.]

men to do things and take the lead? I could be a labor leader. I could organize Illinois."

They looked at me like, wow, what a beautiful thought! It seemed to me like they were thrilled. And they said, "Well, María Elena, César Chávez said that when the people are ready, they themselves are the ones that will do it. Maybe this is what he meant would happen." We shared at that moment the same hope. I just knew I could have their support.

I thought, heck, I'm probably not as intelligent as Balde, and I didn't go to school like he did, but I know enough about it and I have enough love and dedication that I think I could make it work. I even figured out inside of me how I would approach Balde.

But I never told Balde about my plans. I was waiting until I was ready, because if he refused then I'd have to say, "Well, Balde, I love you, and I'll always be with you, but I'm going to go forward on my own. We won't be rivals, but I'm making this decision."

CHAPTER NINETEEN

Retrenchment in Texas

It had taken so much work to get my life just a little organized in Texas. See, after I resigned from the service center at the end of 1983 and before and after I went back to organize during the summer of 1985, Oscar, Pablo, and I just struggled to survive from day to day in Texas. Then Oscar decided to stay in Arlington to go to school, and for a while, Pablo and I stayed with my mom, then Pablo started buying and selling fruit and vegetables, and that's pretty much how we lived for years. During all that time, it was like I had my organizer's life and my life in Texas, and I kept trying to figure out a way to make them work together, but I couldn't seem to accomplish it.

At one time, Pablo and I were also in Arlington, Texas, for a while, and both of us took a temporary job with a company that was supposed to go into factories and clean up after disasters, like an earthquake or hurricane or great big fire. They hire a bunch of people from around the area and work them temporarily until that job is done. It was just minimum wages, and they worked us very hard, and they made you sign papers that you wouldn't hold them responsible for different abuses.

It was terribly hot, terribly dangerous work. They worked you like in movies I've seen about prison. It was awful. There were Anglos, blacks, and Mexicans working there. People fell and were hurt, they called people names, and there was much sexual harassment of the women. The supervisors walked around like they were Immigration themselves. Finally, one day I saw something so bad it made me mad enough to start to organize, although I knew the work would be gone in just a few weeks.

There was this black kid who turned out to be underage. Somehow they found out he was young, and they called him and said, "Get your ass out of here. You don't have a job."

The kid said, "OK, but if you're going to fire me, I want the money you owe me in back wages." He'd traveled a long way for this job, so he really needed it.

You know what they did when he said that? These three big guys picked him up off the floor, swung him back and forth, and they went, "One, two, three," and threw him out the door onto the street. I followed him out and tried to figure out all sorts of angles to help him, but there wasn't anything I could do. So that's when I started planning.

I gathered a group of women, Mexican and black women, and started talking to them about standing up for our rights. The black women responded, but I didn't feel any support from the Mexicans. They were all saying, "Yeah, it's a good idea, but I'm undocumented, and so I can't afford to try."

So I started documenting abuses, but I couldn't figure out how to change things until one day I came up with a scheme. I went to one of the supervisors, a white woman named Nancy, and told her I was a UFW organizer that was taking a little break from organizing and writing a story about women's working conditions in different places and that I'd like to interview her about what it was like to have to push people. And I did have in mind writing something like that.

Well, this was right before lunchtime, and right after lunchtime the bosses called me. They said, "María Elena, Nancy was telling us about the job that you're doing."

"Well, yes, but actually, I just want to interview Nancy."

"We'd like to know more about it." So I made up all sorts of things, saying that I was investigating women's work conditions. They said, "Do you really work for the United Farm Workers?"

"Yes, sir. I'm a union organizer. You can call the Illinois Migrant Ministry. I haven't checked in for a couple of weeks, and they probably wonder how I'm doing."

Well, after that things really changed tremendously. They didn't mistreat the women. No more signs of abuse. And as time went on, even some of the undocumented Mexican women began to go along with some of my ideas, and a couple of times we had a lot of laughs while we worked there.

Then, when the job was over, we went back to Brownsville. I started getting much closer to all the Central Americans who were coming and also the migrants and all the undocumented Mexicans down here. More and more people were crossing the border, and they had so many problems. We started taking them in, and we'd feed them whatever we had. One young guy, Eduardo, stayed with us for a long time. He was undocumented and had been working here for some chicken growers who kept all their chickens in this huge building. They made Eduardo stay in there all the time and sleep on the floor with all the chickens, and the only thing he got to eat were chickens that had died. Eduardo said he didn't care how poor Pablo and I were. At least we shared what we ate with him. We treated him like he was human.

Pablo always wants to be out buying and selling fruit and vegetables, so we decided to try to start a fruit stand. But nobody's ever been willing to give us credit. I had a little land left from selling my house, and I tried to put up my land as collateral, but when I went to a bank and told them I was a farm worker and they found out that someone had taken their kid to the doctor and put it on my account, the bank said, "No way."

So I went to work in a school cafeteria, but I really didn't like it. I missed being outdoors and working with plants. After I'd worked there for about eight months, I went back to the banker and said, "Now I've been working for eight months, and I have things for collateral. I want to make a big fruit stand."

The banker said, "We'll wait until you do your income tax." So after that, I went again, and the banker said, "No, I'm sorry. You still don't earn enough."

"You think I'd let myself lose the land I'm putting up for collateral? That land is the only thing I have for my kids. I'll pay you back."

"No, I'm sorry."

Finally, Pablo and I got a little money together from different places and started one on our own. Then I went back to the banker and said, "I just want you to go check our fruit stand out. See if you didn't make a mistake."

The banker said, "You have a lot of nerve. You're really serious about this, aren't you?"

"Yeah, and one of these days, you'll really see what I can accomplish."

Time went on and we had all sorts of family complications, good and bad. Mom and Dad stopped living together. I think it just was totally unbearable to stay with Dad anymore, but they didn't get a divorce, and Mom still helps take care of him and calls him her husband. It was convenient the way it happened. My daddy moved away, saying he was going to build a house for Mom in one of the *colonias,* and then he moved there permanently because he wanted to take care of the lumber so it wouldn't be stolen. And my mom said, "I'll stay here until you finish the house." But I guess each one knew it was better to do it that way than to totally split up. It was like my dad was giving Mom a break, and she was glad to take it.

My kids Johnny and Christy got good jobs in Texas and settled down with their families. Then Gloria took her GED in Illinois and started junior college. She did it even though her husband was against it, and she had three baby girls. And Oscar got married and had two baby boys, and they named the oldest Tommy. When Oscar saw Gloria start junior college, he decided to do it too. So Gloria and Oscar and his wife, Sulema, lived together in two different rooms of the same old motel and shared their babysitting and went to classes together. Then, when Eva saw how good it was working, she and her second husband, Gus, and five kids moved into another room, and she started going to school too. I was so proud of all of them, with ten kids they did it!

But Pablo and I were so poor, and Héctor and his wife and his two baby boys lived with us in a tiny trailer. You wouldn't believe how bad it was. It was just a shack. It makes my [small camping] trailer look good. Sometimes we all wouldn't have any place to stay. We'd sleep at my sister Mary Jane's or even in the car at my mom's. Then Héctor's wife left him and the babies. She wanted me to raise them, but I told her I just couldn't, not with Pablo and everything, so Héctor got them. Héctor's wild, but at least he's kept his kids.

And the fruit stand grew, and, finally, we decided to sell it and try to build a new one by my five acres where we were supposed to have irrigation water. We planned to build a new, big fruit stand there and grow our own plants and vegetables. Oh, I had ideas, such wonderful, great ideas. It was going to support us and be a home for my children and be a center for me to organize. 'Cause I didn't stop dreaming about organizing, not for a minute. And I stayed being third vice president for the union.

Also, I thought my plans were blessed. Because before we bought the land, while we were still searching for it, Pablo and I went to the church in San Juan, Texas. Every time we go to church, we kneel down at the entrance, and we don't walk but go on our knees all the way to the altar where Our Lady of San Juan is at. Most people do that. It's a respectful way to approach her. Because Pablo has a problem with his knee, I let him go ahead of me so I can keep an eye on him. I wait until he reaches the altar before I start my *peregrinación,* my pilgrimage.

This time, as I watched him go down the aisle, at the very center of the church a little girl came over and took his hand. I didn't hear what she said to him, but I know that he turned and looked at her. She led him down to the altar, and then I didn't see her anymore.

I always close my eyes when I work my way on my knees down to the virgin. I guess it's just a sign of respect. And the same thing happened to me. This little girl came, and when I felt her hand, I opened my eyes, and she said, "May I help you?"

I said, "Oh, yeah. Thank you very much. What's your name?"

She answered, "María de Monserrat." And that's the name of the virgin of the mothers, of women. She is venerated by all the midwives because she helps the mothers that are bringing birth and the people helping the midwives. It's a belief I've known for many, many years because she was one of my mom's virgins at home.

Right away, when the little girl said that, I thought, oh gosh, what a beautiful thing this little girl is doing. If I ever have my own property, I'm going to name it after this child, Our Lady of Monserrat.

So this little girl took me down to the altar, and I said, "Thank you very much." I didn't get a chance to talk to her, and I didn't see her again. She must have gone. I wanted to give her a *limosna* or something to buy candies.

When I got up, I said, "Pablo, wasn't that something?" Pablo said, "Yeah," and, of course, his eyes were watery. We get very emotional. It was very meaningful to us. Then I said, "Whenever we get a place, let's name it La Villa de Monserrat."

So I was paying a little bit each month on these five acres that were supposed to have irrigation water, and, oh God, we worked so hard and made so many plans. With some of the money from selling the fruit stand, we dug a U-shaped road into the land, and we put down cement for Pablo's new fruit stand. We were going to start building a little house, but a lot of our money was stolen, and then, one by one, family needed to borrow the rest.

I did plant tiny fan palms all along our U-shaped drive. After they'd grown just a while, if you were very quiet, you could hear the wind blowing in them, and they'd almost talk to me, like my grandma had taught me. And I wrote out all sorts of designs, labeling where every tree would go, where every plant would be. Because even though the money was gone, I didn't give up my plans for the land.

At first I thought we could turn the front into a great flea market where people could come to sell, and I designed an open theater to be part of it. I thought we could rent spaces to the people who wanted to sell, then on weekends we'd give performances on the stage. We'd have another Teatro Campesino about all the issues down here in Texas. People would come from all over to sell, and we'd raise their, how do you say it, consciousness at the same time. And sometime I'd build my house and my place to organize out of. I thought people would pay me back the money they owed me, and I at least could get started. I kept dreaming that when I got it set up, then I could live in it in the winter and organize in Illinois in the summer.

I wanted La Villa de Monserrat to not just be a service center where we fill out forms for food stamps and all that, but also an organizing place for refugees and just farm workers. Certainly, I wanted to connect to the United Farm Workers, but I wasn't sure they'd want me after I'd quit the center in Onarga. And Pablo was against everything.

It didn't happen. I worked and worked, but I couldn't make it happen. See, the people who sold us the land cheated us out of water. They made a breach of contract. It says in the contract that within sixty days they would install the irrigation line and valves. When they didn't do it, I went to a place like legal aid, and they said, "Yeah, this contract has been violated. They should have done that," and they filed a complaint, but nothing ever happened.

We had planted so much, fields of watermelons, corn, trees, and Pablo and I had to get up at four or five each morning and carry buckets of water to try to save the plants. It was such a heartbreak.

For a time after we sold our fruit stand, we didn't have nothing. We just slept from house to house or in the cars. Later, we ended up living in a really broken-down camping trailer, just a shack like on the border. It didn't have plumbing or electricity, and whenever it rained, we didn't even have an outhouse. I slept outside on an old mattress when it wasn't raining, but for a while, we just survived.

Time went on and we kept just trying to get along, and I kept trying to figure out how I could do everything for us and organize also. Then, finally, in February of 1988, it worked out so FLOC hired me again. They wanted me to work with the people in the Valley during the winter and spring, then go organize in Ohio for the summer. And I was so glad to be able to do it. That way, Pablo could pretty much stay in Texas where he wanted to be, and I could spend a lot of time with him, but I could also be doing my work in the summer, sometime, maybe, in Illinois. I'd finally figured this all out when the poisoning happened.

Yellow Rain

I remember waking up the morning that it happened and just laying there in our little shack. It was beautiful outside, and I was looking around at everything and thinking how pretty the world is, but I also felt so bad 'cause I still didn't even have a place to live. We hadn't got this camping trailer yet, but Pablo was on his way to pick it up, and I kept thinking, hold on, you're going to get a place to live. You're going to have something. It was March 3, 1988.

Then, about 10:30 AM, Héctor and I left our land in my old car and were on our way to see a priest to give him some union papers from FLOC. I was driving 'cause Héctor didn't have a license, and the windows were down to about four inches from the bottom. As we passed the road called Resaca Retreat Drive, Héctor yelled, "Ah, ¡watchále, mamá! Look out!"

So I turned my head and looked out the window, and at that moment I saw a plane coming right towards us, and I heard its motor, then the next instant it was like, how can I describe it? It was yellow, and it was like when the wind is blowing real strong and it kicks up the dirt and blows it around in a cloud and it's whirling. It was like a sudden rain storm hits with very large raindrops, and you can't see anything through the windshield. Immediately, there was this heavy thick cloud of powder that hit everything outside and inside the car, including us. My face was looking directly at it. I couldn't see anything in front of me and slammed on my brakes, and the car swung off the road to the right.

Then, right away, we both started coughing and choking, and we opened our doors and got out. We were covered in yellow. The plane had been crop-dusting pesticides, and it hit us directly. We were choking and coughing and trying to shake the dust off our bodies. I looked at Héctor and his hair was yellow, and my nostrils and eyes and my mouth and throat were burning. I vomited in front of my car on the grass, and Héctor was bending over in the other side of the car.

I saw the yellow plane way across the field, and I started to yell at the plane, "God bless! Look what you did!" But then I couldn't yell anymore. I told my son, "Let's get out of here, *mi'jo*." I vomitted again and by then the plane was coming back, but he was flying kind of high. I noticed he circled about two times, maybe three, before he flew back. Then he went to the other direction, so I'm sure that he had to see me. We were on a big public highway going down between two open fields. He had to see us. Anybody could have been coming down that road. Since our car was so old, maybe he just thought we were a couple of illegals.

Then I began to feel my mouth swell like I had big, big lips, and my stomach was so nauseated. I asked Héctor, "¿Cómo te sientes, *mi'jo*?"

Héctor answered, "Bien gacho."

I told him, "Yo también."

Then I said, "*Mi'jo,* this is bad, *mi'jo*. I'm going to stop and call the UFW in San Juan and ask what to do."

I drove the rest of the way to Los Fresnos, and when I got out of the car, I was still coughing. Then I got to the pay phone, and I didn't even have a quarter. I think I used the Sprint card from FLOC. When I got the San Juan Service Center, Juanita Valdez Cox told me to call the Department of Agriculture and they would advise me of what to do. Juanita also told me to go see a doctor as soon as possible, and she gave me the name of Doctor Margaret Díaz of Brownsville.

I called and I told [an inspector] what had happened to us and how I was feeling sick and nauseated. When I explained where we were, she said, "You should go to the doctor now." I said, "No, I'll wait for you." Because at that point I didn't realize how bad it was, not at all.

So she said, "We're leaving right now, and we'll be there as soon as possible."

But it turned out to be about a forty-five minute drive, coming pretty fast, and so it took her a long time to get there. By the time she did, I was feeling very sick to my stomach. It was burning inside, and I was already dizzy.

As soon as she got there, she took some tests and pictures of my car, and right away we left in both cars to the place where we'd been sprayed. I showed her where it happened, and she said, "This is all I want to know. You go on to the doctor, real quick. She's in Brownsville, and she knows about cases like this." So I agreed to see this doctor. But Brownsville was about thirty minutes away.

So Héctor and I drove off, [but] I had to stop by the side of the road 'cause I felt real bad. I told Héctor, "Can you drive, *mi'jo*?"

"Yeah, Mom, I'll drive."

"Ay, *mi'jo*, I hope you don't get stopped by the police."

We didn't talk much after that until we were in Brownsville, when Héctor said, "Mom, I'm going to Grandma's house to pick up Uncle Rubén so he can drive the car 'cause I don't feel good. I feel bien gacho." Héctor was vomiting too by then, and I was already going into sweats. As soon as we got to Mom's house, my mouth was very foamy and I had a lot of slime.

My brother Rubén and Héctor helped me into the car. Héctor never got as bad sick as I did, but he needed treatment too. The next thing I knew I was in the doctor's office. I remember noticing my son Héctor's hair again. It was yellow.

By then I was very dizzy, *volada de la cabeza,* and my eyes were very blurry and burning, and I could feel burning inside my *garganta,* my throat, and my stomach. And I had a lot of pain. I was also short of breath, and I had the sweats, and my skin was all irritated, and I couldn't concentrate good. Then I remember somebody saying, "This is Dr. Margaret Díaz."

Right away she started working on me, and I heard her say, "She needs to get scrubbed right now." But I think she gave me a shot first.

Next I remember being bathed and scrubbed in a shower and laying down in a bed in one of the doctor's rooms. I remember she was looking into my eyes, and I think I heard her say that my heart was going down and my pulse and my blood pressure. Then I couldn't see anything any more, and I lost them.

Sometimes I'd come to, and then I'd vomit black stuff, not regular, and my saliva started to turn to foam, like meringue. They kept giving me something to bring out the slime, and it was real thick and heavy. And every time I'd come to, they would give me a towel, and I was vomiting black.

I remember the doctor looking at me and saying, "I don't like it. Her eyes are dilated, and she doesn't respond to light." Then I went to sleep or got knocked out again, and all I could see was that it was real pitch dark, and I felt that I was traveling on a long road. I could see a light very far in the distance, and the light was coming towards me, and I was going towards the light. I remember being in very deep thought, wondering very intensely, but I was trying to reach the light. I was just very anxious to get there, but I couldn't reach it.

And every time I was trying to get there, I'd wake up again, and the doctor was injecting me. But I couldn't hear anymore, I don't know what they were saying, and I just seen her face. Oh, she was so pretty, like an angel. She's the most beautiful doctor in the world, I think. Every time I opened my eyes, she was there. Her face I remember very well, because she kept calling me back from where I was going.

Finally, I said, "How long have I been here?"

"Over four hours."

Then Dr. Díaz said, "I've got to put her in intensive care. I don't like the way she's not responding."

I don't know how I got to the hospital, but my family was with me. A machine with wires was attached to my chest, and I had oxygen in my nostrils and needles in my veins giving me some clear liquid, and I remember seeing my daddy. He kissed me on the forehead.

They told me my heart stopped three times during the whole thing, but I don't remember being afraid. And I felt kind of bad afterwards because I thought, my God, I didn't think of my kids. How could I not think of my kids? After all, I'd want to at least see them for the last time. But, no, I didn't think about Pablo, I didn't think about my mom, dad, sisters—the doctor's face and the light are what I remember. I was released from intensive care two days later and went to stay with Mom.

I hardly had any sleep since last night. My chest began to get very tight. My voice has changed, and I'm very congested. My head is spinning, it's like I'm half here and half somewhere else . . .

As I'm on my way to go vote I'm sweating and feeling very weak and tired. Pablo is driving the car 'cause I have too many problems right now to dare drive. I feel like just going right back to bed, but I don't want to miss voting.

I guess I better write down everything that's happened to me lately 'cause the way I feel I'm really worried. (Diary, March 8, 1988)

Today was a pretty bad day for me. All day I've been feeling like I'm running a temperature. I've hurted in my left side. It feels like my heart but I don't know for sure. I've also felt dizzy, much more than yesterday. On and off I've had a headache, mostly my *nuca* hurts. I've been congested all day long, and it's been hard to concentrate on things. I've kept to myself most of the day.

This morning I talked to . . . the investigator for Attorney Ed Stapleton here in Brownsville [in order to sue the crop duster for medical costs and damages; María Elena had gotten the lawyer's name through the San Juan United Farm Workers Service Center]. (Diary, March 14, 1988)

Just a few minutes ago I went to the rest room . . . and I noticed blood. Pure blood and too much for just a simple rash or anything else. This blood came from inside my body . . . (Diary, March 15, 1988)

. . . There at the American Legion Hall we had the County [Presidential] convention. The names Jesse Jackson, Al Gore, Mike Dukakis filled the Hall and the Hall was full of us people.
. . . we all voted for Mr. Ed Stapleton to be Delegate and I to be alternate for the 17–18 June State Convention in Houston.

When the resolutions committee was taking resolutions, I jumped at the opportunity and asked Ed Stapleton if there was still time to submit a resolution. . . . So I wrote one, and it was more or less like this:

> I María Elena Lucas, a farmworker, propose that we
> resolve to support the UFW AFL–CIO campaign against deadly
> chemicals that are dangerous to our country, our food, our
> environment and Human beings.
> I furthermore propose that we resolve to support the
> studies of this deadly and dangerous chemicals conducted by
> the UFW AFL–CIO Doctor Marian Moses.

I stayed till I heard from the resolutions committee. I was thrilled when I heard my resolution had been accepted. I was informed that it was reworded though, but I thought, who cares how they write it! As long as it delivers the message we want.

On With the Union!!

I was beginning to feel so happy 'cause I've been feeling good today. I mean considering that my last problem was not too bad. . . . I started noticing that I was getting a lot of pimplelike lumps. They started in my forehead and temples and then yesterday I had them all over my head. There's hundreds of them all over my head. (Diary, March 19, 1988)

My daughter Gloria and others thought my poisoning might have been attempted murder. It had been tried like that with other people, but I said, "No, Gloria. It could have happened to anyone. It could have happened to a whole school bus full of kids."

Whoever had been sprayed, it would have been very difficult for that person, unless that person was in contact with an organization like the UFW, which can help. But most likely, it would have just been another case of pesticide poisoning. So many of these people, the undocumented and even citizens, they have a lack of knowledge of chemicals and pesticides. If it had been an illegal alien—there's been cases where it's happened—I think it's like when you don't have insurance. You're just like María Elena without insurance, without no nothing. I was just very lucky because Dr. Margaret Díaz was with me, and she sent me to the hospital, and she made them take me.

It would have been difficult to go to the hospital by myself. If I'd just gone and said, "I've been poisoned with pesticides, and I want to be checked," they might have required some kind of insurance and might not have helped me. I probably would have died. Lots of people, when they get sprayed, they just do or don't die, without any help, and I know people that can never work again. Nobody worries too much when they think it's just a bunch of wetbacks.

And I keep thinking in my heart, maybe God was sending me a message. It was just one more thing that I had to feel and go through so I could do this work. But it wouldn't be because I already didn't feel enough, because I already cared. But to go through it and see how it feels, that's another thing. Still, I don't know why God makes me suffer. I get angry, and I say, "Why do I have to go through so much? Why do I have to feel such pain?"

I was so sick sometimes I felt like I was going to die, like I wasn't going to make it, and I've been very disabled. But I had to keep fighting. Like I had to be willing to die for La Causa, but I had to be willing to fight to live for it too. In that sort of way, it reminds me of a song I wrote once that I called "Plegaria Campesina." It means "Farm Worker's Prayer" or "Farm Worker's Pleading." You sing it to the melody of "Taps."

> Si he de morir,
> Si he de morir,
> Por Justicia,
> Por huelgista, y el derecho de vivir,
> Moriré,
> Moriré,
> Pero nunca mi bandera la águila negra soltaré.
> Quiero vivir,
> Quiero vivir,
> Quiero vivir.
> Viviré,
> Viviré,
> Y del campo un racimo de uvas frescas pizcaré.
> Y a Diosito,
> Mi testigo,
> Con un grito,
> Con coraje llamaré y este fruto que es mi sangre ofreceré.
> Cantaré,
> Cantaré,
> Con un canto campesino que es mi llanto de tristeza y sufrir.
> Mi plegaria campesina cantaré.

> [If I should die,
> If I should die,
> For Justice,
> For being a striker
> And for the right to live,
> I shall die,
> I shall die,
> But never my flag, the black eagle, I shall let go.
> I want to live,
> I want to live,

I want to live.
I shall live,
I shall live,
And from the fields a fresh clump of grapes I shall pick,
And unto God, my witness, with a cry of anger I shall call,
And this fruit that is my blood I shall offer.
I shall sing,
I shall sing,
With a farm worker's song that will be my cry of sadness
and suffering.
My farm-working plea I shall sing.]

CHAPTER TWENTY-ONE

The 1988 Campaign: Commitment, Disappointment, and Resignation

Dr. Díaz said I could never go in the fields again. Every time I talked to her, she said, "Another occurrence will be fatal." But I want to. I'm a farm worker, I'm an organizer, so I didn't know what to do. I was supposed to go organize for FLOC the next summer. If you have labor contracts, you have to go into the fields to check with the farm workers about how things are going. And not only did I love my work, but those were the ways I made my living.

> Not only do I know and understand God's calling on March 3rd, 1988, but only until today do I realize (did I realize as I took a leaf off of a beautiful succulent plant and thought I shall plant it and use it for propagation—I also thought, "When I go back to the fields . . ." Oh, my God! You have taken away my most beloved obsession, working in the fields where I'm most embraced with Mother Nature) that God has made me part of Mother Nature, but I must now suffer this loss (greatest loss of my life) so that I follow his light through the darkness . . . I can not be a farmworker now, but an ambassador for Farmworker Justice and rights. (Diary, April 13, 1988)

Sometimes I'd think I understood, like when I wrote this in my diary, but then that understanding would leave me.

I went through such a terrible struggle during the next months as I tried to decide if I should go to Ohio to organize in the fields the next summer. My kids, they were really against it. And I kept having so many symptoms. My voice like really changed, and for a long, long time I couldn't sing. Even today I can't sing like I used to. I also had such terrible burning inside of me, and all those pimples, like hot sauce on my face. And I had trouble breathing. If people were smoking around me, I'd get real sick, and my family at Mom's house, they wouldn't quit smoking.

The worse part was when I was writing everything backwards, like reversing. Then I would open my purse to get something out, and I would forget what I was going after. If Eduardo or Pablo would say, "May I have the car keys?" I'd say, "Sure." Then I'd hand them my glasses. And I'd change numbers around, like when I was dialing the phone. And sometimes I'd totally forget where I was, and I'd get so frightened I couldn't breathe and I'd start crying really hard. Then Mom and her *comadres* would come and put their hands on my head and pray for my healing.

Chemicals are bad, and we don't need a nuclear bomb to destroy us. The people that are creating these chemicals, they are destroying us, and they are so powerful. I think they've got control of everything because there's so much money involved. They want to have it all, and I guess they think, well, if I'm only going to be on earth for a short period, I want to live it up. I'm going to have what everybody else has. But that is being so self-centered. With all this destruction of human beings and the earth, it's going to be too late to change it. I keep wondering how come we on the bottom can see that and they can't. These people must be super-intelligent to be able to make so much money and to be able to accomplish so much, yet there is something missing in their brains or hearts or whatever. Think what greed can do.

Finally I decided I would go. I decided I would just have to take the risk. I didn't think I would necessarily have to go into the fields, but I would have to go into the camps. And, I went for other reasons. It is still my hope, my dream, to organize in Illinois, and I still thought FLOC might send me there.

I knew it was going to be dangerous, but it seemed like it was going to be dangerous whatever I did. And going back to organize for the summer again would be like seminars or a workshop. The more I learned, the better I'd be able to organize in other places.

So I went. Most of the time, it was reading out the contracts to the people and also signing up more people, getting them to sign more union cards. My main job was to explain to the farm workers their rights and to explain the function of a labor contract between the company and the growers.

But it was a very hard summer. I came in some sort of contact with the chemicals five times. The first time I was just driving down a country road that I drove every day, a very regular routine, and, suddenly, I came in contact with the spray, and it was the worst time. I got completely lost and disoriented. I had to stop in the road, and I didn't know where I was. I think all together it took me about twenty minutes before I could move. I was real weak for about three days. But when I had my medicine, it would help.

Another time I got sick from a grapefruit I was eating and another time when I went to Illinois for a meeting. The last two times my sister Norma was with me, and we were driving down a country road. All of a sudden, I made a turn, and there was this tractor spraying. And as much as we tried to, even with speeding, we couldn't get by it because there was no way I could make a turn on that road. By the time I got to town, I was really sick, and it took me about an hour and a half before I could go on. Then I was sick for about three days, and, again, I couldn't remember. The last time, an airplane, it was spraying. And as much as I tried to get away, I still had to go through there. Sometimes you can't find an immediate place to turn around and leave. That time they were spraying so many places, and it was in the evening, with like fog with the spray. I had a lot of problems with the pain and the difficulty to breath.

Balde and Fernando saw how bad it was for me at times, and in the beginning, I told them how sick I was after the exposures, but Balde said there really wasn't anything else for me to do. What they really needed was a field worker, someone who could go out to the camps and the fields to talk with the people. He said, "You should pray, María Elena, and depend on God to heal you." Like he was saying that if I prayed hard enough it would be safe for me to go into the fields again.

When he said that I thought, gosh, I've been doing that all the time. It seemed to me he was saying, "Well, this is what we've got, and you've got to make up your mind about whether you want to be with us or not."

Like, "You either take it or leave it." I kept thinking, maybe he will say, "We know your condition, and we don't want to expose you to danger, but we can use you for fundraisers or organizing around the convention, things like that." But that never happened.

Part of the time, I had to go without my medicine. The union was supposed to give us a medical allowance of up to $200 to $250 per person, but I never got it so I couldn't pay for my medicine. One time my friend who was an organizer paid for the medication. It was seventeen dollars. My God, that's a lot of money. She also lent me ten dollars to pay a medical clinic because it takes ten dollars to be able to go in and get the doctors to see you.

Also, I kept making doctor appointments because I was so sick, and four times I had to miss it 'cause they told me, "You can't go. We need you more to be at this meeting." But we had a real good sister, a nun, working with us, she fought them for me and said, "María Elena has got to see the doctor." And they let me go.

That sister was real good and made everything different. The discipline was not so much because she made the leaders listen. They'd say something and she'd say, "No, just plain no!" Then Balde would turn red and yellow and white and sweat and start moving his chair, but she was firm.

It was an easier campaign for us than in 1985 because we came home earlier at night than we did that other summer. But there was a terrible drought that year, and many of the farm workers left early 'cause the crops were so bad. Some of the people stayed, and they suffered a lot because of even the lack of water in the camps to wash your clothes, and the water was so bad to drink. But I heard that most of the people in the camps were not as hostile as the 1985 campaign. They were more open, more supportive, understanding.

There was one camp that was very hard for me because of one guy in it. There's always bad people and good people, and most of the people are good, but I went in there several times, and there was this guy who always cut me down. He said that I should go out there in the fields so that I would know what it was like. I thought, yeah, if he only knew that's where I spent all my life.

He says, "Yeah, Baldemar and you are making all the money, huh?"

"No, you're wrong."

"Yeah, you should come in the fields and try it out. That's how we make our money."

"Yeah, you see, I've been a farm worker all my life."

"Yeah, sure." Most of the people in that camp were anti-union.

Also, the grower there is not good, he's not really sincere. I know because I personally have talked to him, and that's got a lot to do with the people's way of thinking. The people there get intimidation from the grower, so they are afraid and respond that way to organizers.

But once, we were really discussing, and it was hot and I was really thirsty, so I asked one of them for a glass of water, and they sent a kid to get a glass of water. When the kid came back with the water and I took a big drink, it was full of salt! I like threw the water forward and started coughing. They had put a lot of salt into it to get rid of me. My God, it burned my throat right away, and I felt so bad! I was risking so much to try to help them. Then they started laughing at me.

I said, "Oh, I think there's something wrong with your water. Here, thank you, I'd better go." And I just left. I turned around and wanted to cry. I tried to say to myself, that's OK. They don't know what they're doing. I'm not going to let this get me down. I went back to that camp again and again.

We women organizers also had a hard time in our living conditions. Much of the time we lived in a real poor, broken-down black section in Toledo, Ohio. At first we didn't even have a stove that worked or food to eat or fans to help with the heat. And at night we could hear a lot of fighting, especially between one man and woman. I had a tape recorder with me, and sometimes late at night and early in the morning, when I was in a lot of pain, I'd turn on the tape recorder and talk into it and sometimes even cry.

Good morning, Lord. You look beautiful today. I saw you shining through that old building over there through the broken windows. It is abandoned. It's empty. All the stores are gone from here now, in the past. It's all history now. There's a church in front of you. It's got beautiful tinted glass windows. It's painted in green, light green, and white, and it's got a steeple on top of it with a cross and lots of beautiful birds that are singing.

The neighborhood is quiet and pleasant, but last night it wasn't.

Last night it looked like hell. There were shadows in the alleys, and I kept thinking and wondering. I wanted to hide into one of them. I was kind of worried, not frightened, just worried and concerned. There were a lot of people drinking and howling at each other . . .

. . . I got up at six o'clock in the morning and started walking outside at sixty-thirty. Everything was quiet, just the birds and the squirrels and the trees. The beautiful trees. They look graciously at you, and I could talk to them. They're tired. They didn't sleep well last night, but they're happy.

As I went out walking this morning, I couldn't help looking at those broken windows. There's so many houses with broken windows, and it seems like every other house is just abandoned. It's got boards in the windows, and the windows that don't have boards are broken. It's kind of sad. It's just like they're dead or they're just waiting for something to come back to life.

I keep thinking about a man and woman who keep fighting, they keep drinking and fighting. . . . They call each other names and keep threatening to lock out the other one with the children. I've been thinking about a song one of their kids might sing.

Later in the morning, Daddy,
Shining in the windowpane,
Doves and sparrows in the steeple,
Broken glass in the City of Despair.

Gonna tell, gonna tell,
Gonna tell the world out there.
Daddy drinks, Mama cries,
We all live in the City of Despair.

Shadows in the alley, Daddy,
Raindrops falling from your eyes.
Glitter shining in the moonlight,
From the broken bottles of wine.

Gonna tell, gonna tell,
Gonna tell the world out there.
Daddy drinks, Mommy cries,
We all live in the City of Despair.

(Diary, June 17, 1988, "City of Despair," Toledo, Ohio)

A really big disappointment for me was that they wouldn't let me go to the Democratic Convention in Houston as a Jesse Jackson delegate, even though I'd made them promise before I agreed to come. They said they needed me too much. Also, another time, a group wanted to sponsor me as a farm worker ambassador to the people of South Africa. I wanted to go real bad, but that time I agreed, there was just too much important work for me to do in Ohio, so I missed that opportunity. But this time I had made them promise to let me go to the convention and they wouldn't.

We did get more people to sign for the union in 1988. I know I signed over a hundred and eighty-one workers in Ohio, but the campaign wasn't as successful as in 1985. In 1985 we signed thousands. But by 1988 a lot of people were already signed, and we just got new ones.[1]

Some things were real successful. I raised $1,000 when I went to speak to the United Auto Workers, number 900, in Wayne, Michigan. Boy, were they nice people. They donated a copier, a duplicator, and a copy machine and offered the building in there for whenever we needed to have meetings. Another place I went to speak was to the UAW Local number 22. Pete Hoover introduced me as Sister María Elena Ortega, and I said, "Thank you, Brother Pete Hoover," and I started talking. I only talked about five minutes, and we raised another $1,000, then I collected $127 at the door as a donation. So that was exciting.

Our farm worker convention that summer both was and wasn't successful. We didn't have any major keynote speakers. César was in bed with the fast.[2] Dolores Huerta couldn't make it. Jesse Jackson didn't go. The governor didn't show up, but we had more delegates in this convention than we did in the last one. And we had some people from Mexico, which I thought was very good. You see, these companies are international now, and we're preparing for that, for the future. The companies practice the international tactics of business. In Sonora, Mexico, they have a Campbell's company, a tomato processor, that is exploiting the people. They produce them over there, they process them over there, and they bring them to the United States. This way they pay real cheap labor, and they come and sell it at U.S. prices. What we're doing is we're having

1. In 1987, a new contract with Heinz U.S.A. and Heinz pickle growers had been negotiated, and in 1989 FLOC renegotiated a three-year agreement with Campbell Soup Company. The life of the Dunlop Commission was also extended for another two years.

2. Despairing about the continued use of pesticides, in July, 1988, Chávez had undertaken a water-only fast that triggered several weeks of coverage of pesticide issues by the national media.

meetings with representatives from over there. We've been saying that we should demand contracts for the employees there, too, so that the companies know that this is not just a U.S. thing—it's international, and we're going to be fighting to end the exploitation of those people too.

During the convention, I got to just talk a little when they introduced the chemical resolution to support César Chávez and Dr. Marion Moses. I got up and gave a testimony, what happened to me, but other than that I just sat with the board members up on the podium [dais]. But it's important that we show female participation, so we, the women, were very rowdy from up there, chanting and clapping. I think it's very important for the rest of the women to see us.

I think that Balde and Fernando think they're trying real hard for women and to make the union into an equal thing, but I don't really think it happens that way. I'm not sure they understand there's a great need for the female influence or input for female freedom. I think that's one difference between them and César's union. Dolores Huerta has got the same kind of power that César has, and so she reaches in that direction. I think I've tried to do that, but it really hasn't developed, it hasn't really happened, but it's very important and necessary. See, we've had other women organizers, but from what I can see in terms of real leadership, in terms of real ability to enable other women, I don't think it's happened. I think it's very important to have women that FLOC has seen as equal. I think the presence of a woman in a major decision-making staff is very important, women that have been around, that know how to communicate, to deliver a message.

And, of course, it's just harder for a woman. Like Balde and Fernando, they have all the support of their wives and families, but most of us women have to work against our husbands and all the services they expect.

There's been times as a woman with FLOC that I've felt swatted like a fly, and as a woman, I think that's wrong. It's not good organizing for that to happen. One by one I've watched the top women leaders leave, and in June, 1989, I was the only woman board member left, and I wasn't really there anymore. No one ever contacted me.

As a woman, I feel powerless, and I wonder if this is the way it is all over the world or all over America or like with the president and his government. I wonder if women like us who are trying to be part of growth and development, of a better life, I wonder if it's like this all the way through. It seems like every time a woman tries to express herself or say, "Well, that's not right," "Well, that's wrong," or, "If we do it this other way it might work," we're put down.

I'm not saying we should ignore what men say, and I'm not saying they're wrong, I'm just asking them to give us a fair chance that we may be able to operate. After all, we make things roll and work, so why do they put us down? I know that Balde is a good man and that he's trying, and I know that Fernando Cuevas, oh God, he's an angel, but women need to be allowed to be more important in final decisions.

After I got back from that summer, I heard there were big problems between Balde and the sister that I cared so much about. I know pretty much in my mind what was happening, but finally I got a letter that informed me that she was resigning for health reasons. I was so frustrated I cried, and then I called her and said, "Sister, I know what's really happening. I want to tell you I love you. When will we women ever be free to say what really happens?"

Sometimes I start doubting so many things. I think, sabrá Dios UFW cómo será. Me pongo a pensar, siempre he alabado a César Chávez. Siempre lo he visto como un Moses y no nomás a César Chávez pero a otros hombres que, como a Jesse Jackson también, que yo veo a estos hombres como un Moses también. Como unos discípulos de Cristo. [God knows how UFW must be. I begin to think, I have always praised César Chávez. I have always seen him as a Moses, and not just César Chávez but other men like Jesse Jackson too, I see these men like a Moses too. Like some disciples of Christ.] A veces me pongo a pensar que las mujeres que anduvieron con ellos, que andan con César Chávez y con Jesse Jackson, si también a veces ellas no tendrán los mismos problemas como tenemos acá con FLOC. [Sometimes I wonder if the women that were with them, the ones that are with César Chávez and Jesse Jackson also have the same problems that we have here with FLOC.]

But my feelings are so mixed. Lo que [Balde] está haciendo es bueno y lo que está haciendo es algo que yo le admiro y le respeto mucho y por eso a veces, por eso vuelvo y lo sigo y lo apoyo y por eso lo defiendo donde quiera, porque respeto lo que está haciendo y César Chávez, y Jesse Jackson, los respeto mucho. Es un gran amor él que uno le agarra a estas personas. [What he is doing is good, and for what he is doing I admire and respect him a lot, and that's why, at times, I go back and follow him and support him, and that's why I defend him anywhere, because I respect what he is doing; and César Chávez, and Jesse Jackson, I respect them very much. It's a great love that one feels for these people.]

Finally, some things happened that left me hurt so bad, that when I was supposed to report on May 1, 1989, I just didn't show up. But despite everything, I still believe in it, I still believe it gives us hope.

> Listen to my silence.
> It is soundless and empty.
> It is vast and deeply profound.
> Oh God, my silence is so loud,
> that it wakes my nights
> and it makes me break down
> without sleep.
> Listen to my silence,
> It moves like the presence
> of grief around me
> and denies me the right
> to speak.
>
> (Diary, April 8, 1990, Domingo de Angustia)

PART THREE

Contemporary Border Life, Self-Expression, and Religious and Political Action and Theory

CHAPTER TWENTY-TWO

Life among the Defeated

Most of the time since then, I've spent in Texas, but sometimes I go to Mexico to visit Pablo's relatives or north to visit my kids. Now, all together, I have twenty-one grandchildren. And both Eva and Oscar are getting pretty close to being ready to apply to law school. Isn't that wonderful? And Gloria inspired them. Sulema, Oscar's wife, got training to work with a dentist. When she came, she didn't even know English. And Gus, Eva's husband, who's also from Mexico, got some mechanical training.

I'm so proud of all of them, but people will never know what they all did to go through school. First, three of the families all lived in the same old motel in Illinois. Then, when they had to go to a new four-year college, they all moved together in this big old house. That was five adults and ten children. But HUD was helping them. HUD had rules about how many people could live together, and my kids got caught. This time they really got in trouble, but they stuck with college.

A funny thing happened with my kids not long ago, but part way through, I thought I might not survive it. Oscar and Sulema and Eva and Gus had never had a church wedding. That happens a lot with our people. They get married in a civil ceremony 'cause they can't afford a big, fancy church wedding with all the relatives and friends invited, then when they can afford it, they do it. Anyway, they all got close to a priest in Illinois who talked them into having a double church wedding with their seven kids as part of the ceremony. And, of course, Pablo and I had to go up for it.

Well, at that time, all we had to drive was Pablo's old red truck, and he never goes over about forty-five miles per hour anyway. We also had Gloria's three girls staying with us, so they had to come. It turned out to be such a wonderful wedding.

But it was a very unique wedding because the priest, when it was all over and we were having dancing and the food, he says, "There's always a first time for everything. And this is the first time I've had geese and rabbits and turkeys and chickens at a wedding, and I'm never going to forget it."

See, what happened was that by that time Pablo and I had geese, ducks, chickens, rabbits, and a pig that we were raising. Pablo would go around and gather leftover food for them. We looked and looked but we couldn't find anybody to come in to take care of them in Los Fresnos while we were gone to the Illinois wedding. So, finally, there wasn't anything to do but take them with us. Except we just left the pig lots and lots of food and water. We had a bunch of old crates, so we just packed everything in them and piled them in the back of the truck. Then we put a board up front for the three girls to sit on, and we started north. You should have seen people look at us as they drove past us.

But the trip, it was really pretty hard. We had one cage on top of the other, and the geese were running around, and two hours after we left, when we made the first stop just past the immigration checkpoint, the board was so full of goose shit, and the girls were all full of shit, everything was covered. *Pobrecitas.* Have you ever seen how wet and messy it is?

So when we finally got to Illinois, we had to put the cages in Eva's backyard, and when they started in with their "cock a doodle-doo," the whole neighborhood showed up, and it was like a zoo. 'Cause of that, we couldn't leave the cages there alone, and we had to take them with us to the church to the wedding.

So anyway, the ceremony, it gets going, and the church is crowded with kids. Then some other kids come by, and they see all the animals outside, and they open up the cages. All at once, a whole bunch of our kids look out the door of the church and go just running outside, during the ceremony. There's nothing we can do but watch them. Then one of the kids comes running back to the door and calls, "*Abuelita* [Grandma]! There's been an accident!" And another one of them comes running up, holding a dead chicken.

Through all this the ceremony keeps going on, and they're videotaping everything. All these kids and animals, they just keep going in and out, and Catholic weddings are very long. And I said to myself, oh, my God, what I live through.

After it was all over, the priest, he like interviewed everybody on the video camera, and asked our opinions on how we liked it. When he got to me, I said, "I'm very tired, but I'm very happy. My kids got married in the church. And that's what matters."

But I've been so sick for so long, especially during the seasons when there's lots of spraying, that it seems like it takes most of my energies just for our daily struggle. All of the money from selling the fruit stand was gone a long time ago, and Pablo and I've been so poor. I can't do any work in the fields for pay now.

I sometimes have to borrow from my family. The lawyers kept helping me get money for my medicine or things would have been very bad. We're trying to sue the crop duster and farmer, because they sprayed illegally, but that takes forever. And at times, Pablo was very hard on me. He'd humiliate me and tell me I was dragging him down. Also, my car was totalled when another driver hit it. So I didn't have any transportation and just had to depend on my sisters and sometimes my mom.

People tell me I should try for welfare, but it's hard to explain how it is down here. They give you such a terrible time, and they expect you to find a job and I can't go to work. They are so rough on you, sometimes it makes you sicker. I say, "No, forget it, I'd rather be hungry." I know I'd spend days and days and days *de humillación,* and then I don't think I'd get any help.

My dad and some of my relatives live in one of the nearby *colonias.* There are *colonias* all around Brownsville, outside the city limits. Lots of the people there don't even have outdoor toilets and no drinking water. The city won't expand out to them because they don't want to provide services. The people have to carry their water in barrels, and the school buses don't even go into them because there isn't enough money. The people carry their children on their backs and in their arms until they get to roads so the school buses will pick up their kids. They use little home-made outdoor toilets, just holes in the ground, and when it rains hard, the toilets flood, and kids and everybody, they just have to walk through what comes out of the toilets. Thousands of people live like this, people on this side of the border.

Some of them have been living like that for years and years. All the politicians do is make *promesas, promesas, promesas.* I think there are some politicians who want to help people out, but once they are in office, they find out there are other people in control and that it's corrupted. That's why a lot of people don't vote even if they're citizens. They don't believe in the system anymore. They say, "No, this is my own sad story, and it seems like I have to solve it in my own way. Nobody cares, it's no use."

I was involved with a bunch of these people, either through the UFW Service Center in San Juan or trying to get them to vote for Jesse Jackson, but it's so hard when people are so poor. They don't have any energy. They say, "Well, I have to just put my energy into trying to get some work and trying to keep us going." Or you invite them to a meeting or to go out to vote, and they say, "Well, I have to wash that day. I have to prepare the food, and the kids are in school." Lots of things.

Lots of these people are migrant families who stay down here during the winter, but there are so many fewer migrant jobs than when I was little. So most of these people don't have any work. And for the farmers down in this area who have work year round, they don't need them. Mexicans wade across the Rio Grande, real early, like three or four in the morning, then they work on the farms around here all day and maybe get paid two dollars in cash so nobody can trace it. Then they wade back across the river when it's dark, and they sleep in Mexico for a few hours before they start again.

And the people with jobs down here, they still look down on migrants. When my daughter Gloria was down here with her three kids, and they thought she was just another migrant, they treated her like she wasn't good for much of anything. But when they found out she had some school and was looking for a job, they changed how they talked and everything.

It hurts me to know how people live. Like with Ana, the woman who helped us so much when we were little. When you're organizing out in the camps, or, in my case, when I visit people, their lives are so hard that sometimes I have to stop myself from getting involved with every individual situation 'cause I can't do it all. That's when you begin to think in terms of the general, not trying to solve the individual problems. We have to see what we can do to try change what's causing the problem, but it's difficult. It takes years of work. And Ana is like family.

Before I got poisoned, I saw Ana at Mom's house, and she was crying and talking about how bad it was, how, now that she is old, she has to collect aluminum cans and scrub on a wash board for a living. So I told her, "When I get my trailer, Ana, you can come and live with me, and you won't have to worry about food or a place to sleep." But then I got poisoned.

Now whenever I see her, she says, "Güerita, I'm still waiting."

The last time I went to visit her, we were so happy to see each other, but it was also very sad. Her daughter was sick and losing weight real fast 'cause she needed a "D and C" but didn't have any money to pay for it. Her daughter's name is Celia. Mom delivered her about the same time she had one of her own babies, so Ana named her after Mom, and they used to wetnurse each other's kids. Now Celia has a little daughter, so Ana is a grandma. Ana came home while Celia and I were talking, and she was carrying a long stick with a nail in the bottom to collect cans.

Ana and Celia and the little girl were just waiting there, in that apartment. They were going to get evicted the next day, and there wasn't nothing I could do 'cause I didn't have a place safe enough for someone as old as Ana. So we had a good visit, but then I didn't find out where they went when they were evicted. They were supposed to tell Mom but they didn't.

Ana's still not legal, so she can't get any help even though she's been in the U.S. for thirty years. She'd have no trouble with the papers, but none of us have the three hundred dollars it would cost to do it.

I have trouble accepting what happened to another person, a teenager whose family I've known for years. Her mother left her when she was a baby, and her father was so cruel, so *bruto,* that she was on the streets doing you-know-what for men when she was only nine! Then she married this older man when she was twelve, and he was so bad for her she finally got like a divorce. Sometimes people would find her sleeping on their doorstep.

I kept taking her in and trying to help her, but sometimes it was like she didn't know any other way of living. I kept telling her that I was going to train her to be an organizer, that the world needed women who'd been through things like her, that she had a future. But she kept telling me she wanted to die, and my help didn't work. Finally, drugs took over, and I think she's back on the street. I feel terrible about it.

People here really put down women who go to bed with men for money, but for some of them, it's just about the only choice they have, either that or dealing drugs. A few years ago, I decided to see myself what was so bad about what they did. It happened before Thanksgiving.

I had gone to a tavern close by to learn what it was that so condemned the women who made their living by selling their bodies. I went at least four times and by this fourth time my mother has almost condemned me too.

Thanksgiving day everyone in my family had a turkey for their table. I asked everyone, one by one, if they would like to come to my torn-down place and feast with us, but no one wanted to come. Not even my mom. The day of Thanksgiving, my table, poorly but bestly dressed for the second most cherished Thanksgiving, was graced with Rosalva, Laura, La Huera, Cuca and three other ladies and Eduardo. All undocumented and the women all prostitutes. They all prayed, and their eyes told me stories of far-away yearnings and distant loved ones, and their eyes were those of someone I've cried for, but the pain and hurt in Jesus' eyes is very well known to me . . . (Diary, April 14 and 15, 1988)

It's just so bad down here. There's hardly any legal work for poor people without much education. If you live on welfare, you almost can't make it unless you do something against their rules, like two or three single mothers and their kids living in a place where welfare says only one mother can live. Things like that eventually get people in trouble. Some women sell their bodies, and some people sell drugs, almost like jobs, almost like people used to work in the fields.

Even some women with children deal drugs. Some of them are just bad people, but I know most of them do it because of the poverty and because there are no choices, and they get so desperate. But I say to anyone who will listen, "Please, don't do it. It's going to contribute to corruption, somebody might die, somebody might get killed over it. Stay away from it, no matter how desperate you're feeling."

The big dealers, they have ways of trapping poor mothers into it, and then they say, "You can't get out and you can't tell anybody, and if you do, we'll kill you or your kids." It's just a nightmare for so many people. It makes me sick! But I can also understand how women let it happen.

> I fell in love with God
> and he is too old and busy to care
> Then I fell in love with Christ
> and he was too young, too busy to share.

I stood alone, confused, so sad
I feel abused, cheated, forsaken.

[But the devil] seems to be there,
he's the only one.
    He offers me roses and wine
    Bread and honey
And makes the hell burning inside me
turn to heavenly paradise.

                        (Diary, November 13, 1988)

When you go into Mexico, things are even worse. Especially up here in the northern part, what they call *La Frontera*. When I was a little girl and walked along the Mexican side of the border, people lived in cardboard shacks. The only difference now is that a few more are made from wood. But they come 'cause life in Mexico is so bad. I've traveled a lot and I know.

Dear God,
    Here I is, at the town of Padilla Tamaulipas, Mexico. Pablo and I are with José Hernández in his red van . . . [They get out of the van, then she continues.] There is a little boy, dark skin, cold, dirty, covered with a sleeveless raggedy cotton jacket. I go into this narrow 2 × 8 opening he's laying on the bare floor, filthy ugly smelling floor. I woke him up, he said he's from Monterrey. He's sick, has no home. I give him a dollar, not enough, that's all I had . . .

                        —Diary, January 29, 1990

Not long ago, I met some people who are organizing over there in Matamoros with the *maquiladora* workers, the workers in the twin plants. These people took me around to teach me about the conditions. When we got to where the *maquiladora* workers live, I wanted to cry. They came from all over Mexico to live in tiny cardboard homes that are crowded together just anywhere they can put them. And their living conditions are so bad, no sewers, no plumbing, no electricity, no tables, no chairs, nothing. *¡Qué horrible!* And they work under very bad conditions.

This man, I'll call him Gene, he also used to work for César. Several times, he said to me, "If you get strong enough, I want you to come and work with us. Will you think about it?"

I'd love to do it. Even the farm workers don't have it this bad. What really gets to me is that these are U.S. companies. Miserable dogs, forgive the expression, but when will they ever have enough money? It's like they feed on money, to do this to people.

They've been organizing like this for ten years now, and I hadn't even heard about it because they try to keep it very quiet. The organizing is done different from César's and Balde's. With the farm workers, we have a lot of rallies, and sometimes it gets rowdy because you're trying to get people's attention. But this is very quiet. 'Cause in Mexico, if they think you're unbalancing power, that's a good reason to kill you. A reporter was killed because she started writing articles, and organizers also.

It's amazing to watch, it's like Sunday-school teachers going to your house and having prayer and Bible study, so nobody pays attention. But really the organizers go to the people's homes and teach about labor law, about the workers' rights. See, the *sindicato,* the unions over there, are with the companies. So what the organizers are doing is teaching the workers about their rights so that when they have meetings with the union leaders, they can bring all of these new ideas and all their complaints. That way they sort of put the union leaders in a position that they have to comply with what's written in the constitution. They force the union people to do their jobs, but really it's the people that are doing it. I think it's a marvelous way of organizing without violence.

There are quite a few women doing it. I spent a lot of time with one woman who I really admire, then I saw another woman who I already knew. She'd been with the United Farm Workers in San Juan. I said, "What are you doing here?"

She said, "María Elena, you know that my heart is with the UFW. I support them, but when you look at all this, all this terrible suffering, how can I not be here?"

I told Gene, "I'm impatient and kind of anxious, desperate, Gene. I see so much that needs to be done, and I have so little time, and it takes forever to do anything, to make any small accomplishments."

He said, "That's what I like about you. That kind of impatience. That's what we need."

I especially think of one *colonia,* though, it's called *La Esperanza,* The Hope. The *maquiladoras* there are chemical companies, and it's horrible.

You get close to them, and it chokes you. I thought, Jesus, this would kill me in twenty-four hours. These people are going to end up with all kinds of problems.

But I guess what's touched me the most in the last couple of years are all the undocumented that are flooding across the border. We have Mexicans, like always, but also thousands and thousands of Central Americans. We've got *nicaragüences* and *hondureños, salvadoreños* and *guatamaltecos.* They'd been coming for years, but they'd stop at Immigration and apply for asylum and get a seal and then move on. They'd go real quick to other cities, like Miami or Houston or Chicago or New York or even Los Angeles, then lots of them would just disappear 'cause they knew they had very little chance of being given asylum, no matter what had happened. Then, suddenly, sometime in late 1988, *la migra* changed its policy and stopped them right here in Brownsville and Harlingen, in the Texas Valley, and wouldn't let them go any farther. And they just started backing up, standing along the roads, thousands and thousands.

Right before it happened, Pablo had bought a whole field of sweet corn that hadn't been harvested on time. It had got too hard for most people to eat it, so he bought it for us real cheap, and we ate corn for quite some time. Then the first time I drove with Pablo in his old truck past Immigration and saw hundreds and hundreds of people just standing and sitting and waiting on the ground, including many children, I couldn't believe it. It was real awful. You could see men, their eyes, like crying. They didn't have a place to wash their face or go to the rest room. They were staying like wild animals in the ditch.

People started coming up to us with their hands out begging. *Ah, Dios, ¡qué horrible!* Hundreds were outside Immigration, and hundreds and hundreds were across the road from Casa Romero, the only shelter for Central Americans that was around. It had filled up beyond what it could hold right away, and thousands of people were just living on the ground in the woods across the road.

If you stopped, they came up to you, "Señora, por favor," begging. Men, women, and children. Oh, that haunted me for days and nights. I kept seeing their hands stretched out, and I kept thinking, what can I give? Oh, my God. They didn't have anything, not even a piece of cardboard.

That day I cried and I hollered to God, "Where are you? If there is a God, where are you?" Then I thought, maybe God is in prison. Maybe God can't come out of it. Maybe God is trapped some place. I believe that

God put a lot of himself into us, but there is also that evil part in us that is destroying ourselves. Whatever it is, it is some kind of very powerful evil that we have around us. It's so sad because the whole world is a beautiful paradise. But a lot of people have turned all the good powers that God gave us, and maybe that's where everything went wrong.

Then, that day, I thought, maybe I was meant to represent God. Maybe God divided himself into so many little pieces and gave each one of us a little piece of himself, so that we could carry on with something good. Maybe that's where he's at. In me, in you, in the people that he thought might be able to do something about it. 'Cause of that, maybe he can't do it without us.

So I started getting myself together, and I said, "Pablo, we've got to do something. We can take the corn, we can help them fill out applications, we can raise hell 'cause this is wrong!" Then maybe when all those particles of God come together, we can form one strong force of God and put him back together again. So Pablo and I, we started working.

At first we cooked corn in some great big tubs we had outside, and we kept taking corn to the people and handing it out. But we didn't have enough gas to keep traveling back and forth day after day. It makes my skin shiver when I think about all those people. After we'd give out corn, I'd start filling out applications because people from here were beginning to exploit them terribly. They even opened up an office and started charging them a lot to make copies, and for translating a few lines, they'd say, "Son dos dólares," or "Son cinco dólares." That'll be two dollars, or, that'll be five dollars.

Sometimes it would be real cold or raining and little kids, pregnant women, young kids traveling all by themselves, they'd just be standing in line, holding a piece of paper. Other people came to help. Women brought old clothes and food and sandwiches. Sometimes they'd give the kids enough money to eat at McDonald's.

They almost trampled the little woods across the road from Casa Romero, and they lived in the woods with no plumbing with just a few square feet for each person. They divided the woods into four camps, for *hondureños, salvadoreños, nicaragüences,* and *guatemaltecos.* They had no *baños,* no *agua.* It was heartbreaking. And the neighbors, not far from Casa Romero, they built a watchtower so they could climb up with binoculars to watch Casa Romero and report anything to Immigration. They didn't want them here. Isn't that terrible? And what kind of government do we have? How can we do this?

A few of the churches took some of them in, and one day Pablo and I picked up five guys to come to work for us because we had a little money to pay them. Then, that night, when we took them back, the church had kicked them out! So that's how I got five Central American men living with Pablo and me and Eduardo in our little camper trailer without any plumbing. The men had already applied for *asilo político,* political asylum.

I slept sitting up on Pablo's bunk where he slept, and everybody else slept on the other bunk and on the floor and in my broken car and Pablo's truck. The situation with our rest room and the water, that was our mutual problem. Pablo would take them all with him to help him in the cornfield and with selling, but then I had to cook for everyone. I had to wash their clothes and keep the place clean. Mostly I fixed potatoes and rice and vegetables and lots of beans, but we were also very cold because we didn't have heat in our trailer and it was winter. And Mom certainly didn't want us staying at her place. But they were good people and they told us such sad stories, about killings and being hungry and being forced into military activities and having to leave their families.

As time went by and the men left, we took in some women, but taking Central Americans, it was very hard for us. We didn't have space or money. A few months later the government started to put up great big detention centers, prisons, and started putting the Central Americans in there, which was even worse for everybody. The men who'd stayed with us had got away, but this was so terrible.

I got to know a Guatemalan woman who was a mother who'd come looking for her daughter. Her daughter was just eighteen. She'd left home to come here so she'd be safer, then her mother heard that she'd been caught and been put in the detention center in Los Fresnos. So she came looking for her 'cause she didn't know if she was alive or if she was being tortured. She didn't know what happens in prisons *en el norte.* Of course, when she got here, she couldn't visit her daughter 'cause she was also illegal.

So I told her mom I'd go visit her daughter and take her some things. They frisked me and went through my purse, then, after a long wait, the girl was brought out so she could sit behind a screen and talk to me. But mostly she just cried. She said, "Tell my mom I love her."

And I said, "And she loves you too." So that was all I could do. I just pressed my hand against her hand when I left. She looked so young. Then, of course, her mom cried, but she was glad she looked healthy and she was alive.

Isn't it amazing, the risk that these young kids take, crossing all these countries for a better life? In my mind, I can see her mom the day she left, her mom crying and giving her blessing and praying a lot and trying to make that *resignación* about letting her daughter go because there's nothing else. You have to do it. Like letting your son go to war. You don't know if you'll ever see her again. Now there are Panamanians and Colombians coming, and it's not going to stop until the situation down there changes.

A young woman, María, who lived with me quite a while ago, had a very bad experience. She was picked up by an immigration officer, and he offered her a job, and he took her home to where his wife and two kids lived. María said it was close to the sea somewhere, far away, and she had no idea where she was. His wife went to work during the daytime, then he worked the night shift.

But as soon as his wife left, he started going after her. He started taking out his organs and chasing after her and calling her and telling her what he wanted. And she was really scared. Even in front of the kids, he was doing it. She said in Spanish, "¡Váyase, déjeme! ¿Y su señora?" Go away, leave me alone. What about your wife? She said that the wife was really pretty and she was a real good woman.

Eventually she ran away. At nighttime, when he went to work and everybody else was in bed, she sneaked out. She had no idea where she was, but it was deserty, sandy, with lots of cactus, and eventually she got to a highway, and someone gave her a ride, then they took her to my place.

Then the same guy caught her here again one day, but this time he was in a group. He slapped her, and they treated her real bad, and she told them she was staying with me. She was a beautiful, dark-skinned woman, but when they brought her to me, she was terrified. The poor thing, she was so scared she was sick.

I keep thinking about the people who stayed with me, wondering, What happened? I drew a map with Mexico and Central America, then I wrote a poem on top of it.

Adiós Patria Adiós

Cuando des una pisada,
da otra—pero cuida tus pasos.

Pues Dios nos dio dos pies,
y así, de dos en dos es todo.

El cielo de la tierra y el techo de mi casa,
La vida, y la muerte,
La noche, y el dia,
Lo bueno, y lo malo,
La mujer, y el hombre,
El aquí, y el allá,
Lo hermoso, y lo feo.

El amor de la paz y la discordia de la guerra
Dos manos para dar
Dos manos para cosechar
Una razón tierna para decir Adiós Patria Adiós
y un compromiso humano para amarnos
Tú y yo—decirte, Bienvenido.

[Goodbye Homeland Goodbye

When you take a step,
take another—but watch your steps.
For God gave us two feet
and so, everything is two by two.

The sky for the earth and the roof to my house,
Life, and death,
Night, and day,
The good, and the bad,
The woman, and the man,
The here, and the there,
The beautiful, and the ugly.

The love of peace and the discord of war
two hands to give
two hands to harvest
One loving reason to say Goodbye Homeland Goodbye
and one human commitment to love each other
you and I—to say to you, Welcome.]

(February 8, 1990)

CHAPTER TWENTY-THREE

A Different Madre de Cristo: Changing the Roles of Males and Females

Sometimes I think about the way we do things, what things make us strong. One thing in our culture, even today, kids never get kicked out of their family. We're just so bound together. And even if you do get married, your mom's home is the family home, and your grandma comes and stays with you after she grows old. It's just something you don't even talk about, that's the way it is. I'm always thinking that eventually my home, God willing, if I ever really have one, it'll be the kids' home, and they'll be able to come here for the rest of their lives. And whoever stays here will also know that they have to accept the rest of the family in case there's a tragedy or something. Like my mom's home, even though it's just now a two-bedroom apartment in the projects, if the weather really gets bad, maybe twenty or thirty people will stay there.

And my father, he does the same. He always says, "If it gets cold, honey, you can always come home. If you want to stay here it's no problem." Of course, then I'd have to put up with his criticism. And I don't stay with Mom often 'cause it's so crowded, and with the television and the phone going all night, I can't sleep. Still, it's there for me.

Not long ago, I had a nightmare at my trailer. I'd taken baby chicks in there with me to keep them warm, and I think that was my mistake. We were gone a few days, and when we came back we had *culebras de cascabel* [rattlesnakes] in our trailer! It was so terrible. We threw pots of boiling water on the floor to try to scare them out, and Pablo and one of them men got bug bombs and set them off inside, but a couple of them wouldn't leave. So we slept outside by our cement blocks, and I made a lot of noise to try to scare them away from me whenever I went to cook in the trailer.

Well, when my mom heard that, she and my brother Martín came to get me. Martín was very upset. He said, "I don't want you to stay here."

"No, I'm staying. I'm sleeping outside."

"For God's sake, you're living *como un animal.*"

"I know, but I'm sleeping on the cement." See, Pablo and I are trying to build a house with cement blocks. We've got our floor poured and some of the walls, and I've got all my plants and animals, and if I leave I know everything will fall apart, my home will never get built. So Mom and Martín were real upset, but I stayed, and now two of my brothers and one of my sons are helping me build my house.

Mom and I fight sometimes, pretty bad, but regardless of what happens, when we need her, she's there for us, and home is home. And if I don't show up in town for awhile, she'll call my sister Mary Jane, and Mary Jane will come over and say, "Mom's all upset because you haven't showed up there, and she says to go for you now." Mom's got sixteen kids, and she still does this. So we may get real upset with each other, but the next day it's gone, disappeared, and love is back, and that's the way it's always been.

And families always share. That's how come, some of the time, none of us have nothing. With so many people, somebody's always in trouble and whatever you get is loaned out. But that's also what keeps us going. That's how it works with almost everybody in my culture. Families stick together and help each other out. Most of the families in Onarga are related to each other in one way or another, and they do that for each other. My kids helped each other through college that way, and when Héctor's wife left him with the babies, his sisters and brothers, they've been helping to raise them. We make a close unit. Even if there's eight kids sleeping in one room, no kid is ever turned away.

But how men and women act with each other, that's where I have my struggle. I don't know much about how most Anglos and rich people live. They probably have the same conflict, but I don't know 'cause I haven't seen it.

I hate to say it, but all my life, I've seen men treat women with violence, sometimes with hits and sometimes by hurting their feelings. Not all men, but a great many. I try to imagine how it got started like this, and I guess it goes back to the people who wrote the Bible. Even when you look at the story of Adam and Eve, it's a masculine thing. Eve came from a man's rib, and they blame Eve for being so seductive. They don't say it's the serpent that tempted her, 'cause the serpent is considered a male. Even with the beginning of creation, they didn't give women credit. They didn't even things out so women would have self-esteem, confidence, so men would respect the woman.

I always fight with Pablo about the Bible, I always defend the female side, how I feel it's being squashed and smeared, totally stepped on. What would have happened if Jesus had been a woman? I'll tell you. If she had been a woman, a female, she would have gotten killed right away unless the divine spirit of God would have prevented it.

When I hear men say, "You women want to conquer the world and you want to dominate men," I just get so frustrated.

I answer, "The reason we are all dying, the reason we're in the economic situation we have, the reason we have war is because of men. If we women were given a fair-square chance and equal opportunity, I don't think that things would be so bad." I think women are taught to take better care of other people and the world, to keep it clean and safe. I think we have all these chemical problems, 'cause some man's up there after power and money.

But sometimes I also think the machismo has also rubbed off on the woman in the sense that the female accepts, like my mom and other parents, when they themselves, or we ourselves, turn around and allow our sons to do the same things to our daughters-in-law, and we allow our daughters to be abused by their husbands, and we allow our sons to abuse our daughters. This is all over our culture, and we're creating the same situation, reproducing it again.

I think I've been successful in bringing up at least two of my sons who are very conscious in not participating in that double standard. Not long ago, my daughter-in-law, Sulema, she says, "You know what, *Suegra?*" That means mother-in-law. "So-and-so came over and said, 'Well, who's the boss in this family?' So I said, 'Well, I guess Oscar.'"

When Sulema said that, right away I turned around and said, "*Mi'ja*, if it ever happens again, stand up in the door and say, '*I'm* the boss.'"

Oscar started to laugh. I said, "It's not that I want to weigh one's rights over the others, but what do they take her for? Sulema's got to fight back when men say things like that."

I hate to say it, but our parents teach those kinds of attitudes. Usually our women are kind of prepared by their experience growing up that men are going to push their power. The girls go into marriage with some kind of fear that if they make the wrong move, they're going to get a whipping. I know this by listening to my younger sisters and the younger generation and watching how they talk to each other, the way men handle women.

It even happens to my sister who lives with her husband in my mother's house. Her husband can be drinking a *cerveza*, sitting in front of the television, and the baby will be on the floor in front of him, and my sister is out in the kitchen making dough for tortillas. If her husband says, "Hey, come and get this kid out of here," she'll get that look of fear on her face and wipe her hands real quick and go get the baby.

See, if she says, "Well, you're closer to the baby. Why don't you pick him up? I'm making tortillas and my hands are covered in dough," if she doesn't obey and respond to his demands real quick, he will be out there and say, "Who do you think you are?" And, slap, she'll get it. This happens right in front of my mother, and she won't do anything to correct him.

I've also seen the way my mom treats some of my sister-in-laws. I've heard one of my brothers come over to my mom's house and say, "I don't know what's wrong with this woman, Mom." I mean, he comes home and complains to Mom. Then Mom turns around and says, "My son is so good. She does not deserve him." And I think that's wrong. My poor sister-in-law, they put her down so much.

Something real bad happened to the daughter-in-law of another family I know. Her husband, one of the sons of the family, drove a stolen car into Mexico 'cause he was on drugs and needed money. That was very stupid. He got caught down there and put in prison in Matamoros, which is very bad. So his mother had to start paying bribe money, to get him good food and so they wouldn't beat him. And the prisons in Mexico, they are different from here. For a fee, the family can arrange, how do you say it, conjugal visits. Well, the son, he's married to a sweet young woman who is totally controlled by her mother-in-law. And the mother-in-law decided she wanted the girl to go down for conjugal visits because she says that otherwise her son will get diseases from the prostitutes who come to the jail. But the girl hates going. She's afraid of being locked in the jail overnight every Friday, but, even worse than that, the guy is getting drugs and using needles there in the jail. So the girl is in danger for AIDS, but still she can't go against what her mother-in-law tells her. We try to talk her out of it but it doesn't work.

And my father still mistreats one of my sisters. Even recently, he'd still hit her or pull her hair, but he'd never do that to one of my brothers. That sister married a man who beat her up real bad, and she'd come home all torn up, and they wouldn't interfere. So I say to all my family and everybody else I can talk to, "We've got to stop this kind of behavior. We can't treat women like this."

Then they say, "You have a loud mouth, you think you're very *cabrona*." That I want to dominate.

But I tell my brothers, "No, but turn things around. You've got a little girl. How would you feel as a daddy if your daughter was in this situation? If her husband starts beating her? Because it hurts parents, at least wise parents, when they see their daughters being mistreated like that."

But my brothers say, "Well, it'll be her marriage, and I shouldn't butt in."

Also, in Mom's neighborhood, the neighbors don't interfere if a man is mistreating his wife or child real bad. They usually say, "We'd better stay out." They might call the police if it gets real bad, but they'll do it with a lot of fear. And, by the time the police get there, nobody's had any problems. They'll ask the wife, "Was your husband beating you up?" And she'll say, "No, we were just arguing." Then the man will say, "Hey, nothing's happening in here, everything's alright. It was a mistake." And even the older women in the family will cover for their sons and son-in-laws 'cause they're afraid.

But I'm beginning to see some changes. Now, even in our culture, the girls are beginning to be more into family planning. All of my kids have done that. Gloria even went against her husband to do it. She'd had three baby girls real fast when she was first married, then she had a tubal, even though her husband was real unhappy 'cause she hadn't had a son. But she did it. So, in a way, the young women are more liberated, even if they're still frightened of their husbands.

Even the girls in the Sierra Madres in Mexico, the very remote areas, on almost all levels, there are at least some changes. If nothing else, they've heard that the women in the United States are less submissive. But, I tell you, the women left behind in Mexico, many of them suffer. I wrote about a woman left behind in my diary, then I wrote a song about her.

. . . María Guadalupe . . . is the second woman in my life that I see in her eyes a very deep profound hurt (the first one was Dolores Huerta, lst vice president of UFW of American Union), a kind of sorrow and sadness only Mother Mary had in her eyes and face at the time of Jesus Christ's crucifixion. I'm never going to forget this innocent woman victim of the Great Immigration Barrier.

El Bolero de María Guadalupe

Levántate Mujer
Ya deja de tristear
Aprende que de noche
también se puede ver

Si ya nunca volvió
enséñate a olvidar.
Que'l amor y la vida
siempre vienen y van

Ruleta de Maldad
la que juegan los hombres
Con el amor sagrado
de una buena mujer

Mujer abandonada
que tristeza me das
Yo también estoy sola
aprendiendo a olvidar.

[Stand up Woman
Quit being so sad
Learn that in darkness
you can also see light

If he never returns
learn to forget.
For love and life
always come and go

Roulette of Evil
is what men play
with the sacred love

of a good woman

Abandoned woman
you make me so sad
I too am alone
learning to forget.]

(Diary, February 1, 1990)

I know that sometimes I shouldn't talk about how men treat women because I've put up with a lot of bad things from Pablo, but, one thing, he's never hit me yet. He's told me, "I'm going to slap you," especially when I told him in his face or in front of his friends that he's done wrong, but it's never happened.

Sometimes I think that Pablo's afraid of me, that he thinks I'm some kind of witch or that I have some kind of powers, and that helps control him. Once something incredible happened. One time in Onarga we made a dance to earn some extra money, and I always ended up in the kitchen cooking so everybody else had fun except me. This one time, I'd taken a break and came and sat with Pablo. And while I was sitting there, a guy came by dancing with this beautiful woman who was wearing a tight, shiny dress, a satin dress. It had a slit, and her beautiful leg was showing.

And I saw Pablo make a gesture to the man, like, boy, she's good, and I got so mad. I was so hurt. I went outside and got in the pickup. He came out after me and got in the truck too, and I started fighting with him. I told him, "I'm leaving you!" And I said bad words also. I was so mad that I wanted to do something terrible, but I didn't know what.

But do you know what happened? The pickup turned on without any key! How can you explain that? And right away, Pablo started praying and saying, "*Ave María Purísima,* she's the devil!" I'll never forget that, and I think it made Pablo nervous about mistreating me. I overheard him say to one of my grandkids, "Your grandma's got powers."

We still have a long ways to go with the men. You know there's going to be opposition when women organize, and there's going to be temper. They're going to start complaining because they want their wives home, and they want their meals served. Men don't even think they can fix their own plate, let's forget about cooking the food. And Pablo's one of them.

Not long ago, we were sitting at the table at my mom's house, and Pablo looked at me with the meaning, serve me a plate of food, but I just turned and looked at him, and I didn't say anything. I just waited for him to get himself something to eat. So he got very nervous and went to the kitchen and started kind of throwing things this way and that and looking at Mom like desperate.

So Mom says, "María Elena, you better go take care of Pablo. He can't get himself served, and I don't want him to mess up my kitchen."

Well, I ended up serving him 'cause he was in my mom's kitchen, and she got upset. But we've got to have those kinds of revolts. It's amazing that women are the ones who worry about the beans on our table and the jackets on our shoulders and a roof over our head, and men just don't seem to see that. It's gotten to the point where we work, we're mothers, and we're leaders. But there's always a male around to say, "I'm the boss," and to take credit.

Sometimes it helps when a woman earns some of her own money. When I was young, at first I turned my money over to Andrés, but then I started to learn. Now, whenever I get my own money, I go buy me a bra or shoes or toothpaste. I buy something that I feel like eating, but if I ask Pablo, he chooses what *he* wants to eat.

I saw this change with my daughter Christy. She used to be real meek and dominated by her husband. But she's earned her own money in a factory for a long time now, and it's like she's changed. I think she's becoming a strong woman.

Sometimes people will say to me, "Do you mean men and women don't have different roles to play?"

And I say, "Well, that's a hard question." There are some things that women can do that men can never do, like nurse a baby or go through childbirth. And in a way, I've never wanted to be equal to a man in the sense that now I can go and get drunk in a tavern. That's not what it's about. It's the fact that we live in a male-dominated world, and that needs to be changed. Women need to play an equal role in the decision making of the family and the country. It would be better for the whole world. Women are taught to care what happens to the earth, what happens to people. And we've got to make sure that those things are taken into consideration. I think if women had more power it would be a better world.

Also, women should have rights 'cause we're individual human be-ings, not just cause we're mothers. Because we're equal human beings, nothing else. But it does seem that women think more about peace, that women don't want war, that we try to keep the family together. Sometimes I think that if we had a woman for president, she might landscape the world. And when I say landscape, I mean try in many ways to improve the whole system. It's not because I'm being biased or partial, but it seems to me like men use their strength, and we use our heads and hearts.

And there may be ways of living that I don't even know about. Once I was at a women's conference, and people were being introduced, and I was sitting there watching. Some women said, "We represent black women." Some said, "We represent welfare women." Others, "We are Indian women." Then two women came forward, and they said, "And we represent lesbian women."

My mouth just dropped open, I was so shocked. I couldn't believe it. I'd never heard anybody say something like that before. Boy, did I have a lot to think about when I left the room! But the more I watched them, the more I thought, well, these are really strong women, and they are really working hard for our cause. How can I think anything against them? It just really opened my mind. That might also be the conference where I met Angela Davis and we danced together and had a wonderful time. I was really impressed by that woman. She and Billy Jean Young King, another black woman I met.

But, anyway, things like what those two women said are never said in our daily life. That was my one-time experience. We just try to get by day by day with the men in our families. Sometimes I really wonder if it's worth all the struggle women go through trying to change their husbands. After years and years of being beaten down, I've seen women start drinking beer or just withdrawing and sitting back and letting men do every darn thing they want to, almost as if they were dead. But I also think it's possible for women to change their marriages. At least I've seen some women do it. It's a big fight and a big struggle, but Gloria Chiquita did it. Her husband was so stubborn and strict, and over the years, I saw her face him down. So I can say I've seen it.

And sometimes I wonder, is a bad father better than no father at all? And I think, yeah, usually he is. At least among the men I've known. I can say I've never known a farm worker to sexually abuse his daughter. And our culture has taught us to keep the home together, the family, and to always think about our kids. So I guess it's worth it.

Sometimes I got feeling so bad about all the conflict between men and women that I know that when a new baby boy was born, I'd look at him and think, thank God he's healthy, and thank God everything is alright, but I wonder what he will grow up like. Will he be one of our oppressors? What a terrible thing, right? Even with grandsons, I have worried. I keep thinking, we've got to change it now. And somehow we've got to change things before it gets so bad that people become violent.

That's why I wrote my play, and that's why I never stop talking about it, no matter what names people call me. See, men and women, we're caught in this together. Somehow we got to work our way out. So I keep telling everybody what I think, and sometimes when I say what I think, it comes out funny.

> . . . I refuse to believe God is a man or that there is only one God. God is not a man and if she is a man, no wonder! (Diary, March 16, 1990)

I feel real bad for some of the young undocumented women, girls really, the ones who came here and can't get asylum or papers or find any kind of work, and they don't even have a home to go back to. Many of them are working as prostitutes for old men. They're so desperate they say to the old men, "I'll work for you, I'll cook, I'll clean, I'll rub you, I'll do anything that makes you feel good, just please, Señor, give me a place to stay."

Then all the women turn against these girls. They call them *putas* and say they're breaking up the family. I tell the women that it's not the girls, they're desperate; it's the men. And the system. The immigration barriers. But lots of people just say I'm crazy.

The other danger for all of them is AIDS. They warn about AIDS on television, tell people it will kill them, but then they don't tell them exactly how it spreads. So there are lots of rumors, but people don't have information. And poor women can't afford condoms, even if the men would agree to use them. Men can get real mean about that, and the women are so desperate thinking about tomorrow. How are they supposed to think about something that might happen in a bunch of years? Like one young woman I know, she's supporting four sick kids and a mother at home by trying to work as a maid. If a man gives her a little help, how's she supposed to force him to use protection? God knows what will happen.

So all the time I talk. I try to say things but also I try not to make the men so mad they won't even listen, but I make sure that men know that there is something called wife abuse in the United States and that it is illegal. I also don't think each one of us women can just do it by ourselves, just individually, one woman after another changing her own marriage. I think we have to change things as a group. I think we women have to get organized together.

I've thought about this a lot, and I think that someday when I have my home or a better trailer, what I'd like to do is form a women's organization and say we're open for services. I'd also keep on organizing people in general, teaching them about the union, showing them the video about pesticides. But I'd especially like to have a place where I can invite women over and teach them about a different Christ, the kind of Christ that's an organizer, and a different *Madre de Cristo,* the kind that would come to us in our present times. Not the Mary from way back then, but the kind of mother that we need now and that would stand up for our rights and be with us.

I'd teach them that Christ from the past is Christ from the past, and he accomplished as much as he could. So we have to bring Christ into our present, and God's got to be one of us. The same with the Virgin of Guadalupe and Mary Magdalene and Ruth and Naomi and all those examples from the Bible.

I only hope I have enough time to do it. I look ahead sometimes and I think, oh gosh, I better work as fast as I can. But, see, I think maybe that's the whole purpose of creation. That maybe God divided himself into millions of particles, and that part of God in us is what stands up to take action when there is injustice.

> . . . Stand tall and stand together,
> hold on to hope and faith.
> with your right hand hold to justice high,
> with your left hand your [sister's] right.
>
> You've got to have the guts to fight,
> chiseled by anger, love, and right,
> for the war is just beginning,
> in the Land of Lincoln hearts.

(September 13, 1982)

CHAPTER TWENTY - FOUR

On the Wings of the Black Eagle: The Creative Impulse

My writing and my religion and my politics are all part of the same thing, they all go together. Many of my feelings come from my care and loving for Mother Earth. And I think my creativity comes from so much suffering also, so much oppression, which is where my desire to organize comes from also. Going through so much hell sensitizes you. And I think my creativity comes from God. I can be creative 'cause God was creative first.

Also, I'm profoundly touched by Mother Nature and by God. There is something super strong there. I don't just see the sky like the sky or the plants like the plants, I see beyond them. I don't just look at an apple and see an apple and eat it. I see the hands that picked it, the tree that held it. My mind goes way back to when the tree was coming out of the ground. And I do that with people also. I can look way back into people's eyes and see their hearts and minds and tell what's there. It's a different way of loving life, of seeing life.

I think that God has given each one of us an ability and a gift, individually. I also think that God has a purpose for most of us, and I think that God has used me in several ways. I didn't go to school, but, in my own way, I have a purpose to serve and a mission to carry on, and I don't feel like I've yet accomplished what God wants me to do.

I get my ideas for my songs and poems and drawings based on real life, they're true stories related to something that happened. Sometimes

289

what I write actually indicates a totally different thing. The poetry and songs have a double meaning, and in order to do it, I become different people. It's like when I approached Casa Romero and saw all the refugees standing there, longing for help. It was like suddenly Jesus Christ became them, and I had to become like Christ when He said, "I was naked and you clothed me." I don't mean that I'm comparing myself to Jesus, but it's also said that we have a duty to pick up where he left off and carry on the work.

And throughout the story of Jesus, I think that's one of the things he does. He takes the place of people and speaks for them. And in a lot of my writings, I've done that too. Like I become the beggar in the street and speak for him or a poor girl and speak for her, it's a way to try to convey a message to the people, to motivate them, to sensitize them, and to make them support a good cause.

I've written *corridos* and the traditional songs of my people, some that don't have anything to do with the farm worker life, but most of my songs are protest songs. They are songs that in some way deliver a message. "José Mendiola" is a protest song, very much.

I think you can usually judge a good song or a good poem by whether it's based on real things and touches your heart. With a song like "Forged under the Sun," not just anybody can feel it. You have to be sensitized, you have to be organized, you have to be exposed and have feelings in order to understand it. With some of my songs and poetry, when I read it or sing it, I cry. Gloria, my daughter, she is also so *concientizada,* and when I read things to her that I've written, she gets real emotional.

My song, "Forjada bajo el sol," means, "Forged under the Sun." There's a moan in the fields from a person that's very tired and is working. It's coming out of a tomato picker, a cucumber picker, whatever. I can look out over the fields and actually see the person and see what goes on and feel the same anguish.

It's late in the evening, and, all of a sudden, the person takes a deep breath, a sigh really. And the poem talks about how beautiful everybody is, all brown, because they've been forged under the sun, and especially the kids have their wonderful smiles. Then, we farm workers, we share our food and say, "Here is a bite of my rice." "This is the eucharist that we have in the fields."

Then a little later it says, "Cae el sol y llora el angelus." This is referring to a belief we have that at a certain time of the day, all the people, like all the birds and the trees, go to sleep, that everybody should quit working and go to rest because the poem says that the sun goes down, and the angel of light begins to cry and says, "It's time to quit working." But sometimes the growers keep farm workers working out there until it is so dark they can't see. Our God wants to rest and can't quit working unless we do too. Of course, I also have my stories of the beautiful dark angel of the night, the one with wings of the black eagle. See, I try to bring what really happens and poetry and how things should change altogether.

A poem or a song or something will start coming to me, like in a dream, and writing it can go on for days and nights, and I can't stop until it's done. Sometimes it will go on for most of a week, and I can't rest until it is finished. And it seems like if I get depressed or something happens, the only way I can let it out is by writing or drawing something. That's the way I get rid of my anguish or pressure. Sometimes it takes me weeks, and I will go until two or three o'clock in the morning until I really just drop and sleep. Sometimes Pablo makes fun of me because I'm writing under a blanket with a flashlight late at night. It's strange. I don't read much at all—reading is kind of hard for me, partly because of my eyes—but I can't stop writing.

I've often wondered how many other women out there, out of their depression, out of their loneliness without anybody to talk to, also have to sit down like me and write out their emotions and their feelings on paper. Sometimes it turns out in the form of a diary, and sometimes it can be in the form of poetry or like when you are appealing to God. Maybe you're writing like a *lamento*. I wonder how many other women out there do the same thing, but they never talk about it.

I know I've destroyed a lot of my stuff because I got so depressed, I didn't want a reminder anymore, but mostly I've lost a whole lot of things because I keep moving from one place to another. I haven't met any migrants, farm workers, who've been able to keep any writing, and living like this makes it hard to do a lot of creative-type work. I feel that I don't have time to sit down and do what I'd love to do because I have so many responsibilities all around me. And my financial situation makes it bad. It's hard to get pencils and paper, much less paints and a canvas.

I have another song called "El Preso Pizcador." It means "The Harvest Prisoner." It also talks about a real situation but with a larger meaning. In it I'm a little child questioning my mom, "Mother, mother, where

is God?" And she answers, "Well, God is by your side, *el preso pizcador*."
Then the next verse applies to like Central America or Mexico or wherever
the family has been separated or a parent has been killed or martyred. The
child asks, "Why did my father leave? Why did he abandon us? I want to
see his smile, I need his love."

And the mother answers, "Por nuestra causa murió." He died for our
cause. Then she says, "Allí va luchando a tu lado." There he is struggling
by your side. The harvest prisoner.

In the last verse, the child says, "¿Por qué, si Dios es tan grande y
tiene tanto poder, hay hambre y guerra en la tierra y duda de amanecer?"
Why, if God is so great and has so much power, there is war and hunger
on earth and doubt about tomorrow? Then the child says, "¿Por qué?
¿Por qué? Mamá, ¿dónde se halla Dios?" Why? Why? Mom, where is
God to be found? Then she answers, "Allá está preso en la gloria el pobre
pizcador." He's imprisoned in heaven, the poor farm worker. So what I
do in a lot of my songs is bring a God that is in our image, that resembles
our cause, to life.

God is so much a part of my life. I think the wind and the sun, the
rain and the plants have beautiful, holy spirits. And it's like they can reach
out to me. Once I was so depressed and so sad and so low, and all of a
sudden, here's this beautiful fragrance of *reseda* flowers, and it was just like
it said "María Elena," and I turned and went to it, and my depression was
left behind. I started to caress the plant, and I thought, you're beautiful,
you're precious. It was like there was no one else to help me, and she called
me and gave me this strong feeling that there is life, that life has meaning.
It was like my friend came to me in my time of need. Then I was able to
get up, go back inside, and begin to think clear again. And the same thing
can happen at night when you're lonely, when there is no one to talk to.
You can go out there and share with everything around you, the moon,
the stars, the wind, the sounds of night.

> Friend, you're like the black candle I light
> on my moonless nights.
> Angel moon, Angel moon, watch over my dreams.
> You're the moon I create when I lay me down.
> Angel night, Angel light, tell the stars tonight,
> She's the child, I'm her mom,
> lighting by her side.
>
> (Diary, February 20, 1990)

There is a very special kind of life in the plants, in the flowers, in the trees that I can communicate with. I can tell when they're happy, when they're sad, when they're praying. I can tell when they're asleep, when they sing. I think the spirits in plants and nature are different from those in people. In people, I don't see that kind of deep profound love and caring. One minute we care for others, and the next we hurt each other—there's a lot of both evil and good. But plant life is different—there's nothing evil, no bad intentions—it's just there to give. Like the sun and the birds and the crickets and the wolves, they're just there to nourish the earth and to give us life and beauty. But I see that we're here to destroy it, not everybody, but some.

These beliefs are a lot different from most of the beliefs of our people. They probably came from my grandma and the Indian background, but they're connected to other beliefs. Our Lady of Guadalupe is very important to us Mexicans because she appeared as a brown Indian to us in our world. She wasn't brought over from Spain, and she nurtures our spirit. Our mothers and grandmothers have always thought of Our Lady of Guadalupe as a very powerful woman and messenger or *intermediaria* between God and us. Sometimes I imagined that I could just lay on her chest and in her arms and be comforted.

But lately I've become so rebellious that Our Lady turned into something different for me. I imagine having a little chapel in a garden where I go to pray, but it has a remade statue of Our Lady of Guadalupe. I'd have her pregnant and in jeans and with a farm worker shirt with the sleeves rolled up. She'd have a scarf like we use when we work in the fields and a hat also, but underneath the hat, she'd have her veil with the stars. And instead of her hands together like in prayer, I'd have one hand on her chest by her heart holding a document, and her other hand would be holding a rifle that was resting against her. Her eyes would be strong and looking forward, saying something like, "You'd better behave." Or I could have her arm thrust forward with the document, like, "Here, this is the law." The rifle wouldn't be a symbol of violence but a symbol of enforcement of that law. Like, "Either you abide or you're in trouble."

The document she would be holding would say, "Justice. Power to women. No barriers between countries. Freedom in the world for all people." Then, instead of having Juan Diego holding her up, I'd have a farm worker with a basket of tomatoes and signs of the harvest. That's how she looks to me.

And now I see God more female than anything else. Mom and I fight a lot about religion and the church. I say, "Mom, what would you say if I said that I believe God is a female?" "Oh, my God, now you are saying that God is gay, that God is *joto!*" So we don't get far with our talks about religion.

Maybe God's part male and part female, but I think more female because imagine how creative she must have been. Think of our eyes, as an example. Here we are with just two tiny little eyes, but we can see the stars, and whatever is in the stars can't see us. How miraculous. And it seems to me that men just don't think about these things.

I think I turned to God as female because I never got support from males, none, and my mom was never there either. Because there was nobody else to answer my questions, I turned to God 'cause God is always there. But sometimes I want to see God as a male, times when I need the strength of a male to take care of something that deals with the power of men. Then I say, "Come on! Do your job, fight them!" But a female God can fight also.

Mostly I imagine or picture God as all sorts of different images, like with Mary Magdalene and Rachel and Esther from the Bible. I think they're a part of God coming out in different roles. Lots of the time, I try to draw these images. When I draw a portrait of Mother Nature, I go beyond just the planet Earth. I draw our galaxy with the earth on one side and light reaching out to the side that we've never seen.

If I drew God as Mary Magdalene, I'd make her very beautiful, and her eyes would tell a lot. She'd be able to speak with her eyes and would probably be a perfect organizer. I think she'd make a wonderful organizer because of all her experience and her kind heart. And if I drew Mother Mary grieving by the cross, I'd have Christ be telling her, "Mother, don't grieve. There's still work to be done."

I made a drawing of Our Lady of Guadalupe and wrote a poem and sent it to people I loved at Christmas. This time she was pregnant and dressed in jeans as a farm worker and supporting a basket of tomatoes on her head. The heavens and sun was behind her, and she stood on a globe that showed Canada, the United States, Mexico, and Central America. I called it "Un Eco Navideño" [A Christmas Echo].

>Era María, mi cara, la suya.
>En su vientre, un hijo,

en mis manos, una semilla.
Nace un amanecer,
Por primera vez, ve sus ojos,
"Ay, Madre Mía."

Mama de sus senos
la dulzura de mi miel
y la amargura de mi vida.

Pisa la tierra
y siente el sol que me quema
y el frío que me tortura.

Habla, y sale un grito que estremece al mundo
y a aquél que me lastima.

Queda su eco: soy yo,
y su grito sale del alma mía.
¡Yo soy campesina!

[It was Mary; her face was mine.
In her womb a child,
In my hands a seed.
At the birth of dawn,
He sees, for the first time, her eyes
"Oh, my Mother."

He drinks from her breast
the sweetness of my honey
and the bitterness of my life.

He walks on the land
And feels the sun that burns me
And the cold that tortures me.

He speaks, and out comes a cry
that makes the world,
and he who hurts me, tremble.

An echo remains: It is I,
And his cry leaps from my soul,
I am a farm worker!]

I feel very close to God so I can get mad at God and nag and talk back when I need to. Sometimes I'll get real frustrated and say, "Jesus Christ! Give me a break!" I nag, but eventually I give in.

One of the ways I can tell what God wants me to do is the way my heart tells me. But there have been some times when I got so upset, I almost wished I was dead. I'd think, God's got to be wrong, I can't be the person to do this. Especially since my health has been so bad, I think that I don't have the kind of intelligence it takes, the energy, it's just something impossible. But I have to do it. I also get angry at God when I see a great injustice. That's when I think that maybe heaven is also a jail, that if God's so powerful and great, why can't he come out?

I also disagree with the church a lot, like with their stand on birth control, and I don't agree with the people who wrote the Bible. I feel kind of strange contradicting the big *sabios,* the sages who wrote it, and I think that parts of creation are a beautiful story, but it can't be possible. When they tell me that women came out of a man's rib, forget it. I came out of a womb! A mother's womb. They also say God took the clay and blew and made Adam. No. It didn't happen that way. I keep thinking, here I am a farm worker, a nobody, an uneducated person, but I think things like this—how long can they fool people? If a farm worker who doesn't have an education can think these things, how long is the church going to be able to keep our eyes blindfolded? The church is going to have to change if it wants to have people stay with it.

There is another image from our culture that I think about. That is La Malinche. She's always been considered an aggressive woman who was a traitor to our people. She was supposed to have helped Cortés and slept with him, and then she gave birth to the first mestizo. And all my life I've heard women like myself who are outspoken or aggressive called Malinche or la Chingada. Pablo says it all the time. But to me, I've begun to think about La Malinche as a very intelligent, very smart woman. It seems like nobody cared what was behind what she did, nobody ever bothered to ask her motives. Maybe she was a Gloria Chiquita using her only skills. Maybe she was preparing a better road for her people. Maybe she thought she could bring about good change and set an example. God knows the condition of the woman at the time. So I have all these opinions, and when men call me that, I say, "Sure, say that. I don't call that a put-down."

God comes to me in many ways. God is in the religion of the Farm Worker Ministry and the farm worker movement, in Christ and the Virgin of Guadalupe. God is in Mother Nature and in my strange dreams. And it seems to me that God is in some way imprisoned in all of us people and waiting for us to come together.

CHAPTER TWENTY-FIVE

As the Sun Sets and the Beast Falls: The Creation of the Third Testament

Even with my criticisms of the farm worker movement, my commitment to it stays so strong. I am constantly talking about it to people and thinking about how I can explain it. I remember how I used to approach people when I was organizing in the camps, and how I explained the whole history of our struggle.

Let's say, for example, we are recruiting people in a certain area, trying to introduce them to our union. Maybe they are on a farm that is not under contract, and I want to talk to a family I've never met before. I always use my story to organize them and to make comparisons. I also always use the word of God, so I have to be careful about their religious beliefs. When they ask me what religion I am, I usually say, "I'm ecumenical."

They ask, "What is that?"

I say, "In a way, that means I am what you are."

Most of the time, most of the people that I visit sign the card. What I think takes place, really, when you organize people, truly organize them, it is a conversion. You have to somehow connect it between God and our cause. The people have to feel it, and they have to see your own sincerity.

Some people want to know about the whole history, about how everything happened. Then I need to be prepared to tell them what happened, how I see it from the beginning. Sometimes I explain it altogether, but usually the story will come out, piece by piece, over time.

I tell them how I think that it really started way back in the beginning, that Adam and Eve were the first farm workers. But then I explain how Moses was the first activist who tried to get, how do you say it, who tried to get *un descanso para la gente.* He was the first bricklayer leader, organizer, and he asked the Pharaoh for a break for the people. And I say, "This was in the First Testament, the Old Testament."

Then I explain what I believe about Jesus. I tell them I believe that at first Jesus Christ organized all the people in Galilee. He taught them a different way of life. Now this is my own theory, but what I believe is that he thought and he studied and said, "What is wrong? These people now have learned a better way of living, but the situation doesn't change. They're still poor. They're still hurting." So he got the idea that *el mal,* the problem, was coming from over there with the politicians. He thought, I've already organized these people, so now I have to go to Jerusalem and start with the politicians. Then, of course, I tell the people that Jesus went to Jerusalem and fought with the politicians and died for us in the process.

If the people aren't too tired, I keep on talking. I don't know the next story real well, but I think I understand. I talk about the time when Spain went under the control of the Moslems for about five hundred years, and they didn't allow any Bibles or any religious practices for the Catholic people. But I say that our grandmothers and our mothers maintained the belief and the teachings, that even at night they would light up a little candle and teach the kids how to do the sign of the cross and pray to the Mother of Jesus and to God. So, in spite of all the cruelty, all the persecution at that time, the Moslems couldn't take the Catholics' religion away. People held onto their faith.

Then I explain how the Spaniards came to Mexico and taught religion to the people in Mexico, and that, later on, the United States took much of Mexico for itself, and when that happened a lot of our parents, our ancestors, stayed on this side, and we were divided from each other. Then I say that I really believe that the church in the United States neglected us poor people, that the church was used to keep us under control, and that I truly believe that confession was used to control the whole community. And I say that we were also neglected in school. I tell them that when I was in school, I was just given some paper and Crayolas and told to paint and draw, but I was never even taught the basics.

Then I explain how the government did start some programs to help the poor people, but because we didn't have work and the aid wasn't enough, we started migrating north. We heard that they were giving good jobs and better opportunities up there, so we started the migration thing, and that has led us into *nuestro fracaso,* our own downfall. Because a lot of the growers and the people said, "Gosh, what a good opportunity for cheap labor." So we go up north with no rights, just shacks, to do hard labor. And these people I'm talking to certainly know what I mean.

Then I tell them about the thing that hurt me so bad when I learned about it: the law that was passed in 1935, the Labor Relations Act. I tell them how all the other people at that time got the right to organize for collective bargaining, but how, when the Department of Agriculture found this out, they paid lobbyists to go and convince the congressmen to exclude the farm workers. They did this because they thought that if the farm workers got organized, they weren't going to work so cheap. They weren't going to live under such bad conditions. I tell them how we were sold out.

After that I go into the story about the black people and all they fought for and President Kennedy. "Remember the day when we had to sit at the very back of the bus?" I say that especially to people my age or older, but I also try to be sure that their children hear it so they will understand. I say, "Remember how we couldn't go into a restaurant or a movie theater or the same rest room that white people did?" And I tell them that we should have been instructed at that time, we should have been taught about our rights, but we weren't. It seems to me that if we had known, there wouldn't have been any need for all those riots and the suffering of the black people.

But I tell them that the black people struggled and struggled and one day obtained their civil rights, and to me it seems like they opened a great big gate, and we just walked behind them. Because they did all the hard work, and we didn't even know about it. I say how it took all their sacrifice in order that we could have the liberty of going to a restaurant, to a toilet, to a movie, sitting in front of anywhere we went, and the right, also, in case anybody discriminates against us, to report it, so somebody will do something about it. I tell them that this is a very good example of what brothers and sisters are in God. In God there is no difference. It's here on earth that us people divide ourselves into different nationalities and put up barriers. Then I say how President Kennedy was the person that gave the black people their civil rights, but then he was killed, and how I've always thought that must have some connection to his death.

Finally, I say, "Have you ever heard of César Chávez? He is like Moses in the Bible. He took into his hands a whole nation of farm workers and has tried to lead us out into a better land. He has tried to take us across to the land of milk and honey. But he has to do it different than Moses did it in the past. He has to do it in the present time by dealing with the government and with politicians and by dealing with the laws."

So this all takes a very long time, but it's very important that the people get a clear understanding that our cause doesn't have to do with a hundred years or even two hundred years, it has to go way back to even before Jesus came, and then it goes on and on in the future.

I think about how the story will be continued, and it seems to me that we have two testaments that tell the story, the Old Testament and the New Testament, and that what we need is a Third Testament of life. I want to make sure that women are included this time. Sometimes I start thinking about who's going to keep records and chronicles about what's happening. I wonder if there's a way that records could be saved for future children. I keep thinking about not just my story but the stories of all the women I've known. I hope that the next testament will talk about the chemical problems and the pesticides and about how women have been excluded and what it has taken to make any gains. Sometimes I draw up lists of names for the Third Testament. I include men, but I especially include the women.

Dedicated to all the dear brothers and sisters who I love so deeply. Who've come and gone and who still remain as God's apostles on Earth truly and faithfully serving the poor and the oppressed, being their voice. For many know not even their own languages and many are just too timid to speak and all are powerless. For standing with us in the picket lines, for standing by the side of a hospital bed where many times we've prayed together for the life of a dear one dying of pesticide poisoning. For standing inside a small shack crowded with children, new friends and old friends but all brothers and sisters.

Gloria Chiquita, Don Lupito, Juan Villegas, Kathy and Román De la O., Sra. Puga, Dolores Huerta, Lucía, Father Farrell, Fran Leeper Buss, Gloria Grandota, Olgha Sierra Sandman, Gary Chapman, Glen Anderson, Bruce, Carmen, Mary Ann Poskin, Jane,

Janie, Nonie Bolinger, Mike and Kari, Sister Lolita, Mary Davis, Frank Helmes, Rich Wood, Rach Welch, Yolanda, Dessa, George and Caroline, the joyous laughter of Alice Thompson and Guy Costello, Bob Abernathy, Mark Prudowsky, Eva León, Sister Alicia, Sister Pearl, Carol Messina, Juan De la Cruz, Rufino Contreras, Benjamín Orozco, Robin Alexander, Silvestre, Chris Hartmire, Fred Ester, Benton Rhoades, Billie Jean Young King, Peggy Breslin, Susan Bauer, Jerry Jiménez, Father Charlie Kyle, Juanita Cox, María, Mine, Rebecca and Jim, Capi, Oscar and Sulema, Héctor, Gustavo and Eva, Christy, Johnny, Prieto, Francisco, Victoria, and César Chávez. (Diary, January 24, 1990)

Sometimes I think about what I would have done if I had been able to get some schooling or if I'd known about César and the movement when I was young. I think if I'd gone to school and if anybody had believed in me, I could have been a great labor leader, maybe a female César Chávez. When I was a child and for many years, I'd love to think about the theater and singing, but when I began to get involved with the movement, anything that I did with performing or singing or reading had to be linked to the movement. Nothing, in my whole life, has ever touched me like it did.

And if I'd known about the movement when I was young, oh my God, the things I would have been able to do. I had so much energy, so much strength, so much enthusiasm. But at my age, with my condition, I feel like my time is short. Every day I get up and look outside. I look at the ground and the plants and the sky, and I say, "God, you gave us a beautiful world," and then I think, and I'm running out of time.

Last night I had a dream that was so real I can still feel everything about it. I was helping some undocumenteds. It was still dark, in the very early morning, and I was supposed to pick them up in Matamoros and take them to the Mexican side of the river, out in the country. A man was supposed to be waiting for us. He was going to lead them across and then take them to a truck that was going to drive them north past *la migra*. There were six young guys and a girl . . .

It had been raining and, oh my God, it was muddy, and when we got to the river, the man who was supposed to take them wasn't there. We waited and waited and he didn't come. . . . I thought, I know the other side, maybe God is telling me that I have to do it. I'd never crossed like that before, and I was scared that I'd get picked up as a coyote, so I didn't know what to do. And the river was high, 'cause of the rain, and it didn't look the same. We walked up and down the shore, and, finally, we saw footprints where other people had gone in. So I said, "I think this is the place to cross."

The men started to take off their clothes and put them in plastic bags to carry, but the girl looked at me like she didn't know what to do. So I turned my back to the men and opened my blouse and held it out like a screen for her to change behind. It was like I covered this girl with my body. She was very scared and shaking and started to cry and said, "You're not going to leave us alone, are you?"

So I told her, "No, I'm not. I'll go with you."

Then we started into the water, but it was terrible. The current was so strong, and the water was so cold, and for a few minutes, I was so scared. Then I made a *promesa* to God to keep on helping people in any way I can, and for the first time in my life, I felt like I was being baptized, and I looked around, and it seems like angels were with us.

When we got to the other side, we had to wade through mud almost up to our knees, and we lost our shoes. We fell many times, and the Huisache thorns covered our feet and legs, and we had to walk through the woods and climb through three barbed-wire fences. We got all cut up. Finally, we reached the truck that was supposed to meet us. Then, when it was time for us to separate, the girl looked at me and said, "I never had a mother." So I hugged her and said, "Don't be scared, *mi'ja*. God is with you." And it was like I gave her my blessing. (Diary, April 12, 1990)

Epilogue

On October 29, 1990, María Elena Lucas made an out-of-court settlement on a personal injury lawsuit against the pilot of the crop-duster that sprayed her with pesticides. The settlement equaled $85,000, an amount covered by the pilot's insurance. Her son Héctor settled a similar suit for $50,000. After attorney's and other expenses, she was left with a cash settlement of $38,747, most of which went for bills she had accumulated during the previous two years. Her health is still fragile.

María Elena and Pablo separated and were formally divorced in the summer of 1991. Today María Elena lives in Brownsville where she continues to draw, paint, and write. She continues her efforts to organize poor women.

Appendix

José Mendiola (Danza de la Vida)

Campesino, pon cuidado, campesino,
Mira, busca, busca la verdad,
Si no la hallas en la tierra,
alza la cabeza, que en el cielo está.

Mira, busca al hombre, que le llaman "César Chávez,"
lo hayarás, donde cae el Sol, y Fiera,
donde vuela una Aguila Negra en mi Bandera,
y en los campos, donde canta "De Colores."

Allí pues, reinando encontrarás,
la Justica, la Paz, de Dios y—a "César Chávez—"
Vuela, vuela aguila Negra, y cuando vuelvas,
a estos campos, "De Colores" cantaras.

(Recite)
[Farm worker, Listen farm worker,
Look, search, search for the truth
If you can't find it in the Land
Lift up your head, that you shall
find it in the sky.

Look, look for the man
whom they call César Chávez.
You will find him
where the sun sets
and the beast falls.

305

There then reigning, you shall find
Justice, peace, God and César Chávez.
Fly, fly Black eagle and when you return
On this field "De Colores" you shall sing.]

Flor Campesina [The following is María Elena Lucas's English translation of her original work written in Spanish.]

ACT 1

NARRATOR: Miguel, Rosamaría, *and their children live in a small hut on a vegetable ranch. The* patrón *charges them $25 a week to use the sanitary facilities. He does not charge them rent for the hut.*

They work in the fields, picking and cleaning many kinds of vegetables. Soon they will be picking tomatoes. After they have worked Monday through Friday from 6 A.M. to dusk, and Saturday from 6 A.M. to 5 P.M., the time finally comes for them to stop working. The patrón *comes to pay them and says that they have made very good money, that they have earned $150. He takes out the $25 charge for the facilities, hands* Miguel *$125 in cash, and leaves.* Miguel *then takes* Rosamaría *and the children to the supermarket of the town, where they buy $70 worth of food and put $30 worth of gas in their old car. When they return to their hut,* Miguel *kisses* Rosamaría *and tells her he'll be back soon.*

Saturday night goes by, and it is now 4:15 A.M. on Sunday. Rosamaría *has barely slept while waiting for* Miguel. *The children are sleeping soundly. Then one hears singing:* Miguel *is arriving!*

MIGUEL: (*singing*)
 I am a happy fellow
 who loves to sing
 with a bottle in my hand,
 and playing my cards . . .

 If you want to know who I am,
 go ask Cupid [the gigolo, the Casanova],
 I am a happy fellow
 favored by Heaven . . .

[*Arriving at the hut,* Miguel *opens the door, enters, sees* Rosamaría, *smiles from ear to ear, stumbles toward her while singing. Suddenly he lets out a wild shout and struts around singing.*]

MIGUEL: (*singing and shouting*)
> Rosita de Olivo,
> White Flower of Fate,
> give me a little kiss
> when the time is right . . .
>
> Oooo-oooooo-oooaaaah!
>
> Don't ask where I was running around,
> the good thing is that I'm here!

[Miguel *approaches* Rosamaría, *tries to embrace her by throwing his right arm around her neck and shoulders, and, upon seeing her face, says . . .*]

MIGUEL:
> Whoa! What's the matter with you?

[Rosamaría *rejects his embrace with a jerk of her shoulders. She turns to him and says . . .*]

ROSAMARÍA:
> Don't touch me, Miguel! Go away!

[Miguel *shrugs his shoulders and, with a look of incomprehension on his face, goes to bed.* Rosamaría, *tired and depressed, begins to complain to herself . . .*]

ROSAMARÍA:
> What difference does it make if I leave this forsaken ranch today.
> What difference does it make if I grab my blankets and rags,
> because, after all, I own hardly nothing,
> and I go away from this forsaken ranch.
> I'm sick of this life,
> of the work and of the boss.
> Of living dead of hunger,
> but then, who forces me into this?
> Well, I really am a fool.
>
> From the time I get up at the light of dawn,
> cross myself and commend myself to God,

it's pull, pull,
like a burro, without stopping.
I work to get some money together
to get out of this misery,
and my crazy old man
to go off and get drunk.

And then there's the boss,
who gets after us and pushes us,
driving us like animals
with their horns close to the ground.

Cheapskate old boss,
he knows very well that I don't make enough
even to eat.
he knows very well that I go around barefoot,
but then, who forces me into this?
Well, I really am a fool.

NARRATOR: Rosamaría *lowers her head and begins to remember what the priest said to her when she complained to him about how inconsiderate her husband is and how unjust their boss is.*

PRIEST:

My daughter, my daughter,
It is a sin to complain.
The patrón has the right
to be rich and to enjoy.

He owns things because he's sharp
and he knows how to manage.
He is a very good man;
he is a personal friend of mine.

I know that we are going
through some hard and bad times,
but we must be patient
and live like Christians.

Go now and pray a rosary
in front of the altar.

308   Appendix

This is your penance
for complaining and blaspheming.

Serve your husband well,
and be good in your work.
Your patrón is a very good man.
He cares for you a lot, and I do too.

[Rosamaría *rests her head on the table and falls asleep crying.*]

ACT II

[Rosamaría, Miguel, *their children and many farm worker friends work in the fields picking tomatoes on the Ranch of Vipers. Some of them chat and laugh, others are singing. In the distance one can hear the sound of an airplane. It comes closer and closer . . . The plane flies over the field and the farm workers, spraying them with pesticides. Everyone complains and yells at the airplane.*]

DON LUPITO:
Damnit! They're spraying us again with their grime!

GLORIA:
Watch out, old dirtbag!

ROSAMARÍA:
Hey, we're not worms!

LUCÍA:
Hey, stop it! God, what barbarians!

MIGUEL:
Cover your face with something! Cover your face!

[*Finally the plane leaves. Everything is covered with pesticides: the tomato fields, the farm workers, the drinking water, their lunch, the ditch, everything. The farm workers rub their bodies with their hands to try to clean themselves a little, and then continue picking tomatoes.*]

GLORIA:
You know, I need to go to the bathroom, but I don't want to go in the ditch because I'm afraid of the snakes; what should I do?

ROSAMARÍA:

Gloria, let's let the men get ahead a little bit, then we'll form a circle around you near the baskets so it's not so noticeable. What do you think?

LUCÍA:

Well, we need to start staying back now, what else can we do?

[*An hour and a half later, now that the men are more or less far enough away . . .*]

LUCÍA:

Gloria, I don't think they can see from there now. Right, Rosa?

ROSAMARÍA:

No. Now you can, Gloria. Ohhhh, now look who's coming—the old man. Now you'll have to wait until he leaves.

GLORIA:

Hmmm, and now he's coming to get on us for staying behind.

[*The* patrón *approaches their circle . . .*]

PATRÓN:

Hey, this isn't good, c'mon, move it! Not a lot of tomatoes, not a lot of money, understand? C'mon, move it!

[*The boss, with an angry face, stays to watch them work. The women, serious and quiet, pick faster. After a while the boss leaves and* Lucía *rushes to* Gloria.]

LUCÍA:

Now, Gloria, because it's going to be time to eat and the men will arrive soon.

[*The women make a wall of baskets and form a circle around* Gloria *to cover her in her time of necessity.*]

WOMEN:

A human act.

[*Soon one begins to hear the men shouting that it's time to eat. Some run to the ditch to wash their hands, others break up tomatoes to wash their hands with the juice, then all of them gather at the edge of the field to eat, laughing, chatting and offering their lunch to each other.*]

NARRATOR:

And this is how, day after day, the beautiful harvest season is spent, and the many seasons of harvest, and many things happen . . . Miguel *is consumed by drunkenness and wastes away, and* Rosamaría *is left all alone.*

ACT III

NARRATOR: Rosamaría *continues living the only life she has known, dragging her burdens along the ruts in the fields, harvest after harvest, state after state; the summer harvest ends, and winter arrives, lashing at her with cold, hunger, misery, gnawing away, like a hungry rat, her mind, her energy and her youth.*

ROSAMARÍA: [*As* Rosamaría *works, she is surrounded by signs . . .*]
Texas, Ohio, Florida, California, Montana, Washington, Colorado, Arkansas, Michigan, Wisconsin, etc., etc. . . . Discrimination, pesticides, bosses. Winter, cold, hunger, misery, poverty.

NARRATOR: *One day comes the last straw.* [*Another sign appears labeled, the* National Labor Relations Act *of 1935.*]

ROSAMARÍA: (*shouting*)
Noooo! No, it can't be possible, my God! I don't want to be a slave! Why, my sweet God? Why, answer me! Why have you abandoned me, if I've never offended you? Answer me! Whose God are you, then? Answer me!

[Rosamaría *cries pitifully until her cries are silenced by a tender voice . . .*]

THE VIRGIN:
Rosamaría, Rosamaría, don't cry anymore, please, Rosamaría. Look, search for the man whom they call César Chávez.

You will find him
where the sun sets and the beast falls,
where a black eagle flies in my flag,
in the fields
where they sing "De Colores."
There, reigning you shall find
Justice, Peace, God and César Chávez.
Fly, fly, black eagle,

and when you return to these fields,
"De Colores" you shall sing.

[*By the time* Rosamaría *raises her head,* The Virgin *is gone.*]

ROSAMARÍA: (*shouting*)
Lucía! Chumba! Lola! Don Lupito! Gloria! Rosa! Trino! Chita!
I'm going to go look for César Chávez!
We'll see each other when I come back as a Chavizta!

NARRATOR: *And that is what happened* ...
*Ladies and gentlemen, the President of the AFL–CIO United Farm
Workers, Mr. César Chávez.*

[*Final scene: The stage is set as a farm worker convention, and the audience
represents farm workers.*]

CÉSAR CHÁVEZ:
Brother and sister farm workers, welcome to the first meeting of the
AFL–CIO United Farm Workers of America.

The brother farm worker at the first microphone, what is your name,
please, and what committee do you represent?

FARM WORKER: [*Resurrected martyr.*]
Mr. President, my name is Rufino Contreras. I represent the Farm
Worker Organizing Committee on the Ranch of Vipers in this town.

Given that
    in the fields there are no facilities for our most basic and
human needs, and

given that
    we are constantly sprayed with pesticides as if we were
insects, and

given that
    on many ranches they pay us miserable wages that are much
less than the minimum wage they should legally pay us, and

given that
    in this state, we farm workers are excluded from the law
governing human rights, and

given that

in this country, the United States, in 1935 congress passed a
law, the National Labor Relations Act, that was very bad for
us and that excludes all farm workers from the right to bargain
collectively, and

given that

because of all these injustices and bad laws, we live in
slavery and suffer all kinds of inhuman indignities, and

finally, given that

the woman farm worker is the most suffering, the most
oppressed, and the most enslaved of women,

we resolve that

we the farm workers of this state will fight against all of
these injustices and bad laws, in order to improve our lives and
the future of all farm workers, in a peaceful, nonviolent way,
humbly under the commandments of God, and courageously under
the rules of the AFL–CIO United Farm Workers of America, which
you direct, President César Chávez.

Finally, we resolve that

from now on, we male farm workers will respect, honor, be
considerate of, liberate, and love women farm workers,
recognizing them around the world as "The Brave Women."

Mr. President, I, Rufino Contreras, move that these resolutions
be approved and adopted on this glorious day. Thank you, Mr.
President and fellow farm workers.

CÉSAR CHÁVEZ:

Thank you, brother, you are an example for humanity.

The sister farm worker at the second microphone: your name and
whom you represent, please.

ROSAMARÍA:

My General César Chávez, my name is Rosamaría De Los Campos,
alias La Chavizta, Mr. President. I represent the AFL–CIO United
Farm Workers in this state. I second the motion to approve the resolutions made by our companion and dear brother, Rufino Contreras,

because I believe in God, peace and justice for the farm workers' struggle. Thank you, Mr. President.

[*And the great Moses of the farm workers movingly requests a general vote . . .*]

CÉSAR CHÁVEZ:

All those who are against us, let them fall on their knees and beg God to forgive them.

All those who are for us, let them sing "De Colores," and may God bless them, and long live the United Farm Workers!

END